D1204640

Buddhism, Sexuality, and Gender

Buddhism, Sexuality, and Gender

Edited by

José Ignacio Cabezón

State University of New York Press

An excerpt from *Poems of Love and War from the Eight Anthologies and Ten Long Poems of Classical Tamil* by A. K. Ramanujan reprinted by permission of Columbia University Press © 1985.

Published by
State University of New York Press, Albany

©1992 State University of New York

All rights reserved

Printed in the United States of America

No part of this work may be used or reproduced
in any manner whatsoever without written permission
except in the case of brief quotations embodied in
critical articles and reviews.

For information, address the State University of New York Press,
State University Plaza, Albany, NY 12246

Production by Christine Lynch
Marketing by Fran Keneston

Library of Congress Cataloging-in-Publication Data

Buddhism, sexuality, and gender / edited by José Ignacio Cabezón.
p. cm.
Includes bibliographical references and index.
ISBN 0-7914-0757-8 (alk. paper). — ISBN 0-7914-0758-6 (pbk. : alk. paper)
1. Sex—Religious aspects—Buddhism. 2. Woman (Buddhism)
3. Buddhism—Doctrines. I. Cabezón, José Ignacio, 1956- .
BQ4570.S48B83 1992
294.3'378344—dc20 90-46557
CIP

10 9 8 7 6 5 4 3 2 1

Contents

Introduction

José Ignacio Cabezón

Although the last decade has seen the appearance of several works that deal in part with issues concerning the place of women in the religious traditions of Asia[1] and some that deal specifically with women in Buddhism,[2] to date little scholarly work in the field of Buddhist Studies has employed gender as a variable to elucidate the dynamics of religious symbols, philosophical concepts, and social groups.[3] What is more, except for very cursory studies that include Buddhism as one among other world religious traditions,[4] there is a tremendous dearth of scholarship relating to Buddhism and sexuality in general and to homosexuality in particular. A great deal of work *has* been done concerning the issues of gender and sexuality in the context of Western religions. Only recently, however, has the Western scholarly community come to realize that much of the methodology of gender studies is as relevant to the Asian religious traditions as to the West, that the Asian traditions contain a great wealth of material deserving of analysis, and that this material is not only interesting in its own right but also a comparative springboard for more general and theoretical discussions.

The essays in this collection focus on issues related to gender and sexuality in different Buddhist traditions. They prod us to think not only of the status of women in the Buddhist tradition, something they all address to a greater or lesser extent, but on a wide range of questions related to the more general notion of gender, culturally constructed concepts of maleness and femaleness. In having gender and sexuality as their primary analytic variables, the contributors to this volume offer a perspective on Buddhism that is either frequently overlooked or else not treated with the scholarly rigor it deserves.

Gender Studies as an academic discipline maintains that the concepts of gender and sexuality are crucial variables in the understanding of the world in which human beings live and interact.[5] In its most general form the claim is that the myriad expressions of human creativity — artistic, intellectual, social, and so forth — are both *created and experienced* by gendered and (at least potentially) sexual beings.[6] Neither human creativity within these areas nor the human experience of them is gender neutral. Our nature as sexual and gendered beings is a crucial factor that must be taken into account in the analysis of all areas of human concern. This is the most fundamental premise of the essays in this book.

We find that the papers collected here fall naturally into five groups: two that deal with gender principally in the context of institutional history (in classical India and in Srī Laṅkā), two that discuss gender and sexuality in contemporary Buddhist cultures (in Japan and India), two that explore the rhetoric of gender in Buddhist texts (in India and China), two that concern gender and symbolism (in India-Tibet and China), and two that deal with Buddhism and homosexuality[7] (in India and Japan).

The first essay, the longest, sets forth the groundwork for much that follows in the volume. Although providing an introductory overview of many of the pivotal issues, Sponberg's principal goal is to identify four distinct attitudes toward women and the feminine during different periods in Indian Buddhist history. Is it possible to identify a single Buddhist attitude concerning the status of women? Sponberg suggests that these attitudes did not constitute a monolithic unchanging world-view. Instead, at least four distinct attitudes can be identitifed: (1) soteriological inclusiveness, (2) institutional androcentrism, (3) ascetic misogyny, and (4) soteriological androgyny. His major contribution is to provide us with a framework from which to analyze Indian Buddhist perceptions of women in a historical perspective.

Tessa Bartholomeusz in a sense takes up where Sponberg leaves off. Her case study of the history of the female mendicant in Srī Laṅkā spans the entire history of the nuns' order in a Theravāda Buddhist society. Relying on texts of the classical period, on archival material from the nineteenth and early twentieth century, and on interviews with contemporary Srī Laṅkān women, she weaves for us the fascinating picture of the evolution of the movement of women religious, from its founding on the island until modern times. In so doing she demonstrates the extent to which movements to reestablish the order have looked back to (and drew considerable inspiration from) its "mythical" founding. Perhaps more important still, she shows us how contemporary revitalization movements are not the mere descendants of similar Burmese movements but instead are traceable to a complex series of events that led to the separation of *saṃgha* and

State in Srī Laṅkā, a phenomenon referred to as the "disestablishment" of Buddhism.

Of the two essays that focus on gender and sexuality in contemporary Buddhist cultures, Bardwell Smith's essay deals with a Buddhist memorial rite for aborted fetuses extremely popular in Japan today. In his study Smith demonstrates how, at the institutional level, Buddhist temples serve the very important function of consoling women who have had abortions or miscarriages. He argues, however, that the high incidence of abortion in Japan is due in large part to women's place in the society, in turn a symptom of a greater cultural malaise, to their relationship to men (their husbands, their doctors, and so on), and to an insufficient range of procreative choice, making abortion the most commonly used means of birth control. Hence, although Buddhist institutions assuage the feelings of women during this moment of crisis, the crisis itself is to a great extent the result of women's position in Japanese society, a position that Buddhist institutions themselves have a part in creating and from which they stand to profit, the income derived from such rituals being significant in the budget of many temples.

From a woman's perspective, what does it mean to be Buddhist? Eleanor Zelliot uses interviews and written material solicited from ex-untouchable women converts to Buddhism in Maharashtra (India) to examine women's perception of themselves as Buddhists. Her goal is to characterize ex-untouchable women's unique religious self-identity. What makes her own essay unique is that built into the very nature of her subject matter is the question of race-caste, another crucial variable often overlooked by those who analyze religious cultures, symbols, and institutions. Moreover, because she presents us with information concerning women of different socioeconomic and educational backgrounds, she fully takes into account a third major variable in her analysis, that of socioeconomic class. In this way Zelliot demonstrates how the variables of gender, race-caste, and class are all factors in the religious self-identity of ex-untouchable women.

Although all of the essays in the volume rely on Buddhist texts of one form or another, in these first four essays we find that the analysis of texts, both oral and written, is more a means than an end. Though Sponberg makes extensive use of Pali and Sanskrit canonical material and though Bartholomeusz relies on Pali historical-religious works and on Siṅhala materials in her study, both utilize them as historical source material. Smith's and Zelliot's essays fall under the rubric of what might be called *contemporary cultural criticism*. Relying more on the methodologies of sociology and folklore studies, their use of oral texts is essential. However, as in the case of Sponberg's and Bartholomeusz's essays, where the focus is clearly historical, texts are used in the service of a methodology and goal that is not explicitly textual.

By contrast, the third group of essays are concerned more overtly with texts qua texts. The principal methodology here is literary criticism and the primary focus of both Richman's and Levering's essays is the persuasive power of words, rhetoric. Paula Richman looks at the sixth century Tamil Buddhist epic *Maṇimēkalai,* a tale of a courtesan's daughter who becomes a Buddhist nun. She shows how the author, Cāttaṉār, employs a "rhetoric of persuasion" that has at its core a sophisticated understanding of gender. Cāttaṉār seems to have taken upon himself the task of making more palatable to the Tamil society of his day the role of the celibate Buddhist monastic life for women. Richman shows how, to that end, Cāttaṉār draws upon culturally constructed notions of gender to enhance the status of the woman renunciant, contrasting it to that of the beautiful and sexually active courtesan.

Also focusing on the analysis of rhetoric related to gender in Buddhist texts, Miriam Levering's essay on the Lin-chi (Rinzai) tradition of Chinese Ch'an (Zen) Buddhism, shows the tension that exists between a "rhetoric of equality," which stresses how the distinction between men and women is irrelevant to the project of enlightenment, and a "rhetoric of heroism," which characterizes such an accomplishment as heroic qua male attribute. Though the epithets of the *hero* are also applied to women, Levering suggests that "in associating a 'masculine' ideal through gender-linked qualifiers to a feminine subject...one is leaning over backward in making the application for the sake of flattery or an insincere rhetorical effect." She also demonstrates that despite the Ch'an masters' repudiation of the gender distinction at the ultimate level, they are only too aware of its effectiveness as a rhetorical device on the phenomenal level (that is, at the level of words and conventions). What is more, the metaphors that are at the core of such rhetorical devices, she concludes, are clearly informed by the conceptions of gender that exist within the culture, conceptions not always favorable to women.

Much of the background essential to the understanding of the essays of Bartholomeusz, Richman, and Levering will be found in Sponberg's historical piece. The diverse attitudes toward women in the different periods of the history of women mendicants in Srī Laṅkā, as well as the diverse voices of both the Buddhist epic with which Richman deals and the Ch'an texts that are the focus of Levering's piece, are echoes of the multifarious voices that Sponberg identifies in his essay. For example, though the latter discusses the idea of "inclusiveness" principally from a historical perspective and the other more from the viewpoint of literary criticism, it is no accident that both Sponberg and Levering focus on this notion as a concept essential to the understanding of Buddhist history and texts, respectively.

With the next two essays we pass from the use of texts as sources for the study of rhetoric to the use of texts as the sources of symbols. How do symbols of the feminine function in Buddhism? Do they always serve to elevate the status of women and console them? In contrast to the double entendres that seem to characterize the rhetoric and symbolism of heroism in Ch'an texts, Barbara Reed's essay investigates how the female imagery associated with the bodhisattva of compassion, Kuan-yin, has been predominantly positive for women. Relying on both textual and art historical data, Reed traces the evolution of the gender symbolism of Kuan-yin from shortly after the introduction of Buddhism to China until modern times. She shows how Kuan-yin has been a symbol of liberation for women, especially since Sung times, and, in turn, how women have been the disseminators *of* this symbolism. In the texts that Reed examines we see Kuan-yin portrayed as liberating women from marriage, sexuality, and the perceived impurity of menstruation and childbirth. Here there are resonances with Richman's essay, in which the courtesan is liberated from a sexual encounter with the prince through the intercession of a goddess.[8] Thus, Reed shows how in both premodern and modern times the female symbolism of Kuan-yin has helped women to cope. Whereas the premodern accounts of Kuan-yin emphasize independence (from marriage, family, sexuality, childbearing) as a possibility for women, we find that contemporary works stress women's coping within male-dominated families.

In my own essay I also explore the ambiguous value of gender-related symbolism by examining how Mahāyāna Buddhist philosophical literature depicts wisdom as feminine and affective states, such as love and compassion, as masculine. Contextualizing the use of this gender imagery reveals the extent to which those who wield symbols rely on social conceptions of gender that are not always liberating for women; at the root of an apparently positive symbol there abides a patriarchal presupposition concerning the nature of the feminine. Relying primarily on the scriptural and postcanonical material of the Indo-Tibetan tradition, I examine the nature of the perceived tension between "analytical states," such as wisdom, and "affective states," such as love; and I show how gender polarity is used to express it.

Yet the association of analytical mental states with the feminine contrasts not only with the Western model, where love and compassion are considered feminine in tone, but with Indo-Tibetan social conceptions of gender as well.

If for a moment we change our focus and view the last four essays not from the perspective of subject matter (rhetoric and symbolism) but from the way in which that subject matter is or was used in Buddhist cultures, a number of common features emerge that transcend both geographical and temporal barriers. In widely disparate times and places we seem to find gender-based imagery used in liberating ways — in a sixth century Tamil epic to enhance the status of the female renunciant and in post-Sung China to give women a positive and liberating role model. At the same time we find that in both India and China an ambiguity to gender-related symbols can exist; for example, the conception of the "hero" applied to women in Ch'an texts or the symbol of wisdom as mother in the texts of Buddhist scholasticism in India and Tibet. Moreover, this ambiguity casts aspersions both on the sincerity with which words and symbols are used and on the presuppositions from which the corresponding imagery develops. Perhaps the lesson to be learned here is this. Although symbols liberating to women are an important part of the Buddhist tradition throughout its history, no symbol can be accepted as a positive one prima facie. Only after it is analyzed and properly contextualized, taking into account the social conceptions of gender from which a symbol derives and to which it refers, can its true character be assessed.

Sexuality, at the very least, is a secondary theme of almost all of the essays in this volume. Consideration of the nature of sexual relations between men and women in Japan, both inter- and extra-maritally, is pivotal to Smith's study of abortion. The theme of woman as sex object and the transcendance of such a role in the monastic life, though perhaps most clear in Richman's essay, is also central to Sponberg's and Reed's. Even the poems of the women converts to Buddhism in Maharashtra speak of the "heart-melting fire and the fearful awakening power" behind Siddhārtha's farewell kiss to "Yashu," his wife, the memory of which has managed to keep only *her* "between the closed eyelids of Siddhārtha." Where sexuality becomes *the principal* variable of analysis, however, is in the essays of Zwilling and Schalow. Given the dearth of scholarly research devoted to homosexuality in Asian cultures in general and in Buddhist cultures in particular,[9] these two essays are a particularly important contribution to this volume.

Basing his analysis on the monastic and metaphysical literature of both the Pali and Sanskrit traditions, together with their commentarial literature, Leonard Zwilling examines homosexuality in light of Buddhist sexual morality as a whole. He analyzes how Indian Buddhists understood homosexuality, its psychological and ethical implications, and the status of sexual nonconformists as religious or lay followers of Buddhism. He concludes that the Buddhist view of homosexuality in the sources he surveys is "at least consonant with a contemporary view of homosexuality as a probably organically or genetically based orientation, with the same moral significance (or insignificance) as heterosexuality."

Understanding the essential neutrality of Indian Buddhism on the question of homosexuality, I believe, is pivotal for understanding how sexual diversity was tolerated in other Buddhist cultures and how in Japan male love actually came to be extolled. This is the subject of Paul Schalow's essay, a study of homosexual love as practiced by the Buddhist clergy of Japan. We find as a paradigm of this relationship the older monk's taking the young temple acoltye as lover; and Schalow gives us examples of the way in which this love is encouraged in a wide variety of texts. He also examines the popular tradition that homosexuality was introduced into Japan from China by Kōbō Daishi (774–835), or as he was more commonly known, Kūkai. In his study Schalow concludes that, far from detracting from his image and status, linking the importation of male homosexuality into Japan to this important figure in Japanese Buddhist history reciprocally enhances the status of both Kūkai and of male love. Ultimately, the legend of Kūkai's inroduction of male love into Japan was considered one of his many accomplishments.

Just as concepts such as time, society, and culture are used as principal variables in other disciplines (history, sociology, anthropology), gender is the principal variable of analysis in the field that has come to be known as Gender Studies. To say that gender is an important variable in the analysis of religious concepts, symbols, rituals and institutions is to say that these are religious phenomena created and experienced by human beings as gendered individuals—that is, by men and women who are part of a culture that constructs ideas of male and female in particular and culturally specific ways—and that this cannot be overlooked in any enterprise that seeks to characterize them.[10]

What does it mean, then, to use gender as a variable? How does gender function as a category when we examine religious phenomena? In reading the essays in this volume it will become clear that at play are four major modes of analysis using gender as a variable. These are neither completely distinct nor unrelated, but insight is to be had from discussing them separately. The first mode explores the role that religion, itself a social phenomenon, plays in the creation of social conceptions of gender. The second examines the way in which religious texts, institutions, and symbols take up the norms that in any given society determine what it means to be male or female. Hence, the former mode explores religion's role in the construction of gender whereas the latter explores the obverse, how religious institutions and symbols incorporate those preexistent conceptions of gender.

The last two modes of analysis assume these social conceptions of gender and go on to explore their relationship to distinct religious phenomena. Taking these socially constructed notions of maleness and femaleness as a given[11] it is possible to then inquire as to how gender influences the creation of different religious elements, be they texts, symbols, rituals, or institutions. The third form of analysis, then, generates questions distinct from the first two. For example, under this rubric one might explore how the religious institutions created by men and women differ, or one might ask what role the gender of an individual plays in the way she or he writes religious poetry. We can also set aside the question of the gender-related origins of, say, a religious text, however, taking *it* as a given, and then ask, in a way typical of the fourth mode of analysis, whether from the perspective of its reception, that is, from the viewpoint of the reader, gender plays a role. Do men and women read religious texts or interpret religious symbols in the same way? Do they perform rituals in the same way? Hence, gender is not only a factor in the *creation* of everything religious, it is also a factor in its *experience*. Let us examine these four modes of analysis in more detail, paying attention to the way they manifest themselves within the essays in this book.

The first form of analysis is dedicated to determining how religion *conditions* the social conceptions of gender; for example, how the claims about women and men or the use of male and female symbols in a religious-philosophical text affects a society's perception of what it means to be a woman or man. Of course, one of the major preoccupations of scholars involved in the feminist critique of religion is to determine how the patriarchal symbols of religious texts and traditions have affected and continue to affect a society's conception of women, oftentimes, with a view to change.[12] In this collection, Bardwell Smith's examination of how Buddhist theological-institutional attitudes toward the fetus and abortion have affected Japanese women, their mental health, and their status in society is a prime example of such analysis. Paula Richman asks a related question. In her essay she examines not how the gender-based rhetoric in the Tamil Buddhist epic *Maṇimēkalai* affected the society's conceptions of women (and specifically of celibacy as an option for women), which is a historical question. Instead, by determining the presuppositions of Tamil society as it existed at the time the epic was written, she shows how the gender-laden rhetoric had the *capacity* to change these conceptions, which of course is one of the author's goals as a Buddhist apologist. In a similar vein, Miriam Levering explores how the gender-based, and specifically masculine, rhetoric of Chinese Zen texts during the Sung dynasty might have affected women's spiritual self-identity.

Typical of the questions that emerge within the second mode of analysis is one of how gender, as the construct of a particular society or time, influences religion. Put in another way, what kinds of cues do religious institutions take from societal norms concerning gender? In this book, for example, Bartholomeusz shows the impact that Anglo-American attitudes toward women prevalent among the Theosophists and other Western expatriots living in Srī Lankā — attitudes that, by comparison to traditional views, were quite liberal — had on the movements to reestablish the nuns' order in that country. Zwilling asks how a society's notions of manhood or womanhood, and the attitudes toward homosexuality that derive from this, affect the status of gay men and lesbian women in Buddhist institutions. From the essays of Zwilling, who treats classical India, and Schalow, who focuses on medieval Japan, it is possible to glean how two distinct attitudes toward same-sex relations led to radically different situations for gay people in Buddhist institutions. In my own essay I show how, when we take into account certain societal presuppositions concerning gender, religious symbols that seem unconditionally liberating on first inspection may turn out to be only partially so.

Questions that might fall under the rubric of the third form of analysis have in common their preoccupation with how gender influences distinct religious elements: literary, philosophical, institutional, and so forth. We might cite as a specific example the analysis of how the gender of the writers of religious texts influences the theological symbols and styles that emerge from their writings.[13] In this book, Barbara Reed discusses women's use of the symbolism of Kuan-yin, and Eleanor Zelliot cites several examples of Buddhist women's unique expression of Buddhist truths, including the beautiful poem with which she concludes her essay. Both Reed's and Zelliot's work, at least in part, are exemplary of this form of analysis.

Finally, the fourth mode might be characterized as an analysis of the way in which gender differentiation leads to a divergence in the experience of religion. The issues of men's unique mode of textual interpretation and philosophical discourse or women's understanding of doctrine or their unique use of ritual would all fall under this heading.[14] Eleanor Zelliot's study of the way in which ex-untouchable women understand Buddhist doctrine (and their relationship to it) is the clearest example of this mode of analysis among the essays here.

There is one final form of analysis that, strictly speaking, does not involve the use of gender as an analytical variable. Nonetheless, it is probably the most common preoccupation of the essays in this volume. I am referring to the elucidation of Buddhist conceptions of maleness and femaleness. The determination of the way in which a particular religious literary-philosophical genre conceives of the feminine, the masculine or distinct sexual orientations is exemplary of this analytical approach.[15] Although all of the essays in this volume are preoccupied to a greater or lesser extent with this type of question, Alan Sponberg's and Tessa Bartholomeusz's essays, that trace attitudes toward women-nuns historically in early Indian and Srī Laṅkān Buddhism, respectively, and Leonard Zwilling's (that engages in the equivalent task with attitudes toward homosexuality) are perhaps the clearest example of studies that take this as their central theme.

Although all the essays in this collection focus on a single religious tradition and use gender and sexuality as their primary variables of analysis, we can see how these variables function differently in each of them. This diversity in functional approaches allows the reader to glean answers to the variety of questions that can be posed of various Buddhist traditions at different points in time. This functional diversity, moreover, is concommitant with diversity in other areas: methodological, temporal, and geographical. The contributors to this volume approach their common subject matter through a variety of disciplines and methodologies that include the textual-philological, historical, philosophical, sociological, and literary critical. The periods studied span all of Buddhist history, from early Buddhism to modern times. The geographical diversity is equally great: from Srī Laṅkā in the South to Tibet in the North, from the Western coast of India to Japan. Yet despite functional, methodological, historical, and geographical diversity, the essays all focus on a single religious tradition, Buddhism, and they are all committed to the use of gender and sexuality as primary variables.

If one principal insight is to be gained from the papers in this volume as a whole, it is the realization that the Buddhist tradition is permeated with a complex and sophisticated understanding of gender. As these essays illustrate, from very early times gender has been either consciously perceived or implicitly utilized by Buddhists—philosophers, artists, literary figures, and ordinary women and men—for various ends. The realization that gender is a cultural construct of course is a unique insight of modernity, as is the explicit use of gender as an analytical variable. Nonetheless, the essays of this volume demonstrate that, even without a self-conscious theory of gender as cultural construct or analytical variable, from the earliest times, Buddhists have been cognizant of issues of gender. Though certainly not the rule, a few isolated cases even exist in which we find some notion of gender different from biological sex.[16] This is not to imply that Gender Studies as a discipline existed as part of the Buddhist tradition. The occasional and often only implicit presence of a conception of gender different from sex in a tradition does not imply that tradition's ability to utilize that conception as a variable of analysis. That very analysis is the function (and a unique insight) of the modern. Engaging in this form of analysis with the end of deepening insight into Buddhism is the purpose of this volume.

Notes

This volume has its origins in a panel of the Buddhism Section of the 1987 meeting of the American Academy of Religion in Boston. Three of the contributors to this volume (Zwilling, Schalow, and Cabezón) read papers on that occasion. Thanks must go to a number of individuals who have contributed to this project in a variety of ways. Anne Klein (Rice University) was the fourth member of the original panel and Elizabeth Napper (Stanford University) was the respondent. Their comments and interest in this project are greatly appreciated. Jamie Hubbard (Smith College) was instrumental in facilitating the meeting of several members of the panel at a very early date; without his help neither the panel nor the ensuing volume would have come about. Several colleagues have also been kind enough to read this introduction and have been generous with comments: William Silva and Barbara Sicherman (Trinity College), Paula Richman, whose very detailed comments were especially valuable, and Sally Davenport. Though this introductory essay benefits greatly from their remarks, needless to say, the final product ultimately is my own.

1. For example, J. Plaskow and J. A. Romero, eds., *Women and Religion* (Chico, Calif.: Scholars Press, 1974); N. Falk and R. Gross, eds., *Unspoken Worlds: Women's Religious Lives in Non-Western Cultures* (San Francisco: Harper and Row, 1980); a new revised edition of this important work is now available (Belmont, Calif.: Wadsworth Publishing, 1989); R. M. Gross, ed., *Beyond*

Androcentrism: New Essays on Women and Religion (Atlanta: Scholars Press, 1981); C. W. Atkinson, C. H. Buchanan, and M. R. Miles, eds., *Immaculate and Powerful: The Female in Sacred Image and Social Reality* (Boston: Beacon Press, 1985); Y. Y. Haddad and E. B. Findly, eds., *Women, Religion and Social Change* (Albany: SUNY Press, 1985); P. M. Cooey, S. A. Farmer, and M. E. Ross, eds., *Embodied Love: Sensuality and Relationships as Feminist Values* (San Francisco: Harper and Row, 1987); and A. Sharma, ed., *Women in World Religions* (Albany: SUNY Press, 1987).

2. Apart from I. B. Horner's classic study, *Women under Primitive Buddhism: Laywomen and Almswomen* (New York: E. P. Dutton and Co., 1930), there have appeared in recent years a number of other studies: D. Paul, *Women in Buddhism: Images of the Feminine in Mahāyāna Tradition* (Berkeley, Calif.: Asian Humanities Press, 1979); D. Hopkinson et al., eds., *Not Mixing up Buddhism: Essays on Women and Buddhist Practice* (New York: White Pine Press, 1986); J. Willis, ed., *Women and Tibet* [Dharmasala] *Tibet Journal* (special issue, 1988), recently republished as *Feminine Ground: Essays on Women and Tibet* (Ithaca, N.Y.: Snow Lion, 1989).

3. The essays of Keyes, Harrell, Richman, Black, and Hawley in C. W. Bynum, S. Harrell, and P. Richman, eds., *Gender and Religion: On the Complexity of Symbols* (Boston: Beacon Press, 1986) are exceptions.

4. For example, G. Parrinder, *Sexuality in the World's Religions* (New York: Oxford University Press, 1967).

5. For a brief summary and bibliography of the impact of Women's Studies on Religious Studies see the entry "Women's Studies" in the *Encyclopedia of Religion*, ed. M. Eliade (New York: Macmillan, 1983).

6. Though obviously related, the status of human beings as gendered and their status as potentially sexual are two issues that should not be conflated. The types of analysis that involve gender as the primary variable and those that involve sexuality or sexual preference as primary variables, as the essays in this volume demonstrate, can yield radically different sets of questions and answers. I focus on the differences in the two approaches where the differences between the analyses that take gender as the principal variable and those that take sexuality or sexual preference as the principal variable arise (for example, in the discussion of the essays on homosexuality).

7. I am aware that their treatment of homosexuality does not preclude Zwilling and Schalow's essays from being subsumed within any of the preceding categories. I find that their common and unique subject matter, however, far outweighs their methodological affinity to either of the other groups as regards criteria for their categorization.

8. I am not being completely facetious when I say that if the courtesan had been Chinese her saving goddess would undoubtedly have been Kuan-yin. Put another way, if Avalokiteśvara, a male deity who is the Indian

counterpart to Kuan-yin, had changed sex before he went to China perhaps he—or rather she—would have been cast in the part of the saving goddess.

9. For bibliographical references on works related to Buddhism and homosexuality, see my essay by the same name in a forthcoming volume from SUNY Press on homosexuality in the worlds' religions, ed. I. Swidler.

10. See Carolyn Walker Bynum's comments in the Introduction to Bynum et al., *Gender and Religion,* pp. 7 passim.

11. Accepting their existence without necessarily agreeing to their validity as determinant of what it means to be male or female, of course.

12. A prime example of this is the volume edited by Atkinson et al., *Immaculate and Powerful.* Anne Klein's essay in that volume, showing as it does the partial failure of doctrinal egalitarianism to translate into social equality in Tibetan society, is particularly relevant.

13. Though Mary Daly deals as well with the social implications of male symbols of perfection, this is certainly part of her task; see *Beyond God the Father* (Boston: Beacon Press, 1974). This same theme—namely, how the gender of religious writers affects the nature of symbols and style utilized in their work—is the subject of several essays in Bynum et al., *Gender and Religion* (Hawley's essay, comparing the poetry of Sur Das and Mira Bai, is perhaps the most notable in this regard).

14. As regards the first example, much of the work of the contributors to the volume edited by Sandra Harding and Merill B. Hintika, *Discovering Reality* (Dordrecht: R. Reidel, 1983) comes to mind, even though it does not deal directly with themes in Religious Studies. In the second case, the collection of essays edited by Nancy Falk and Rita Gross, *Unspoken Worlds,* provides a clear example of this approach.

15. Several examples of this approach in scholarly articles are to be found in Bynum et al., *Gender and Religion.* The essays of Black, "Gender and Cosmology in Chinese Correlative Thinking"; Williams, "Uses of Gender Imagery in Ancient Gnostic Texts"; and Bynum herself, " '. . . And Woman His Humanity': Female Imagery in the Religious Writings of the Later Middle Ages," are the clearest examples of studies that ask this type of question.

16. Zwilling's treatment of the "powers" (*indriya*) of masculinity and femininity are perhaps most illuminating in this regard. See p. 206. It is clear from his comments that these "powers" come very close to what we consider *gender.*

I

Gender and Buddhist History

1

Attitudes toward Women and the Feminine in Early Buddhism

Alan Sponberg

reiteration of first point

Observers of Buddhism, both sympathetic and critical, often are struck by the apparent ambivalence toward women and the feminine that one finds in Buddhist literatue. Various antifeminine attitudes certainly are evident in many early Buddhist texts, a characteristic Buddhism shares with probably all institutionalized religious traditions. The voice one hears in reading these Buddhist texts, however, is neither consistent nor univocal. Many scholars have noted an underlying tension within the Buddhist literature, a tension between certain attitudes that seem unusually positive in their assessment of women and the feminine, on the one hand, and attitudes that are much more blatantly negative, on the other. Occasionally this tension turns up even within a single text, as in the well-known Pali account of the founding of the order of nuns, a story in which we find Gautama, the Buddha, conceding that women indeed are quite capable of attaining the highest Buddhist goal of liberation, but going on to add that the creation of an order of nuns will dramatically hasten the decline of his teachings in the world.

We shall look more closely at this oft-cited story later; for now it is important to note that just this juxtaposition of apparently divergent and contradictory views has led many writers to characterize the early Buddhist attitude toward women as profoundly ambivalent.[1] But, is this really the most helpful way of understanding the disparity of views expressed in such texts? Although not inaccurate, strictly speaking, the characterization of ambivalence is misleading at the least, often carrying a connotation of uncertainty, or even confusion. The view I wish to explore here is that what we find in the early Buddhist texts is not a single, uncertain voice, but rather a multiplicity of voices, eac xpressing a different set of concerns current among the members of the early community. What we have, I would submit, is a rich multivocality—not a simple inconsistent ambivalence. In itself, the observation may seem rather obvious, yet what it means is that rather than seeking a doctrinal reconciliation or justification for this inconsistency of views in the literature, instead we must seek to understand the social and intellectual dynamics of the early community of Buddhists that led to such a discordant juxtaposition of views.

An important step in such an understanding is to distingusish more carefully the different attitudes we find represented within this multivocality: we must separate the voices, and we also need to recognize the specific institutional or intellectual context out of which each voice arose. My goal in this study, then, is to provide a survey of the various attitudes present in early Buddhist literature, one that should help us become more sensitive to the internal tensions and disputes within the early Buddhist community reflected in this diversity of views. Given the dearth of sources for early Buddhist social history, such an analysis of the scriptural texts remains the most accessible window to the development of this influential religious tradition. It can tell us something about the world-view of the early Buddhists and, even more interestingly, it can tell us also about their efforts to reconcile the tension that arose when those Buddhists sought to accommodate the radically critical social doctrines of the Buddha with the more mundane demands of conventional social values.

Before looking at the various attitudes toward women one finds expressed in Buddhist literary sources, we should briefly consider the social context within which Buddhism arose and developed. Contemporary sources for this period of Indian history are limited, yet we know enough to see that, like other important aspects of the tradition, Buddhist attitudes toward women were shaped, in part at least, in response to the social circumstances of the day. Especially relevant to our concern are two key developments, the relatively rapid urbanization of the eastern Gangetic valley and the emergence of a new sense of self-consciousness or individuality, especially among those who were on the margins, socially or spiritually, of the prevailing Brahmanic culture. Interrelated at several levels, both these social developments were in large part responses to the technological
gurated at the beginning of the Iron Age in Northern
hth century BCE, the old agrarian social order was
amatic transformation. The new technology of iron
ed more efficient tools for both agriculture and

organized warfare, and both innovations fostered the growth of a new urban culture based in a dozen or so city-states not unlike those of classical Greece.

The effect of such social transformation was at once both traumatizing and liberating. The old social and religious order with its ideological foundation in Brahmanic ritualism had never been firmly established on the eastern edges of Vedic culture, and the new social structures of urbanization further exacerbated this ideological vacuum, giving rise to a whole new range of religious and philosophical speculation. What was the place of the individual in this new, rapidly changing world of intercity trade, specialization of labor, and organized military expansionism? It was a time that demanded not just new answers, but a new ethos. Later known as the Age of the Wanderers, this time saw the emergence of a class of professional seekers or strivers who sought to formulate the structures of that new ethos, exploring a new set of questions as well as answers.

What role did women play in these new social and religious movements? Certainly they played a much greater and more significant role than allowed by the strictures of the Brahmanic social order. Urbanization along the eastern Ganges during the Age of the Wanderers fostered the creation of new mercantile and artisan classes, undermining the traditional social order prescribed by the *varṇa* system of four classes dominated by the Brahmanic ritual technocrats. There is evidence, moreover, to suggest that this same social transformation opened new roles for women, creating, for a brief period at least, opportunities unprecedented in the early or subsequent history of South Asia. Seen in that light, the prominence of women among Gautama's early followers is less surprising, though no less revolutionary. The newly emerging social order had much less invested in defending prevailing social values, and in such a climate both women and those of lower social standing generally were freer to explore and express their religious vocations. According to historical accounts recorded in the later canon, women were quick to take advantage of the opportunity, encouraged more by Gautama, it appears, than by any of the other mendicant teachers of the day, except perhaps Mahāvīra, leader of the Jains. Canonical sources, even with their androcentric bias, note that some of Gautama's most prominent patrons were women, indicating both that there were a significant number of women of independent means during this period and that their support was instrumental in fostering the early community.

Among the women followers of the Buddha, moreover, we know that some remained lay followers and others gave up worldly pursuits full-time followers. Women "wanderers" were not n this period, yet only among the Jains and the Buddhists do we find record of a sizeable, organized group of mendicant female seekers of liberation. But were these women deemed truly capable of spiritual pursuits? Clearly not, according to traditional Brahmanism; and even the Jains soon divided into two antagonistic groups split over the question of whether Jain nuns could become liberated directly or only after rebirth as monks. This same issue was to be debated later by the Buddhists though less schismatically, in part no doubt because there clearly were women among Gautama's followers who were accepted as fully and equally enlightened. This is the most significant point regarding the place of women in early Buddhism: traditional sources agree that women could and did become arhats, fully liberated individuals living free from the psychophysiological suffering that characterizes human existence according to the Buddha's teaching.

Sources within the canon cite numerous instances of arhats among the women who had renounced worldly life and even a few cases of women like Khemā, who, as chief consort to the king of Magadha, became fully enlightened even before leaving lay life (and well before Bimbisāra the king, who became only a "stream-winner" in spite of his ardent support of Gautama). These prominent women followers seem to have held positions of great respect: many, like Pātācārā and Soṇā, were known for their ability to teach the Dharma; others like Khemā were specifically praised by the Buddha for the depth of their understanding.[2] Some of these women teachers apparently had their own followings, moreover, and were capable not just of introducing the Dharma, but of bringing new aspirants to full liberation without the intercession of the Buddha or some other senior male teacher. In the canonical sources, women most often are presented as teachers to other women, yet even the conservative editors of those texts preserved a few stories of women like Dhammadinnā, who had occasion, after becoming a nun, to instruct her former husband, Visākha. In the *Cūḷavedallasutta,* Dhammadinnā answers a long series of questions regarding aspects of the doctrine and practice put to her by Visākha, a prominent merchant and lay Buddhist teacher who, the commentaries say, had a substantial following of his own. Visākha later reports her answers to the Buddha, who is greatly pleased, proclaiming that he would have answered in precisely the same way.[3]

Unfortunately, we lack sufficient contemporary records to assess fully the role of women among Gautama's followers. Nonetheless, even the brief survey I have provided here of the surviving accounts is enough to suggest that women not only were conspicuously present in the earliest community, but also seem to have held prominent and honored places both as practitioners and teachers. The later history of women in Buddhism is much more mixed. Whereas women patrons and donors remain quite visible, the order of nuns does not appear to have enjoyed the prestige or creativity one might have expected of the succesors to Khemā, Dhammadinnā, and the early arhat nuns. Even their historical continuity as an order becomes obscure within a few hundred years and dies out entirely in South and Southeast Asia. To put these surprising developments into perspective we must now examine the variety of attitudes toward women and the feminine that emerged in Buddhist literature as the tradition became established as one of the major religions of early India.

Four Distinct Attitudes toward Women and the Feminine

Much more could be said about the social and religious climate in which Gautama, the Buddha, lived, but my concern here is more with what later Buddhists made of his teachings—with how they reconciled the religious guidance he had given them with the social contingencies within which the Buddhist community subsequently grew. The focus of this study thus is on attitudes toward women expressed within the early community. With a concern to identify those themes that were formative for the subsequent historical phases of the tradition, I shall focus here on Buddhism in India, primarily the early period up to the beginning of the Common Era, but with some reference to later Indo-Tibetan developments.[4]

The attitudes I wish to examine and distinguish are those current among members of the early Buddhist community during the period that saw the rise of Buddhist monasticism, or rather we should say that they are a selection of those views, because our primary source is the textual canon redacted by one group within the tradition, the senior monks. Gautama's personal views on these issues no doubt played a decisive role, yet we are rather limited with regard to what we can ascribe with certainty to him, especially as he appears to have eschewed discussion of many topics he considered nonconducive to the soteriological task immediately at hand, namely liberation from suffering.[5] Although the earliest canonical literature certainly reflects something of Gautama's views on the place of women, we must remind ourselves that those texts also inevitably contain much later material as well, material in which one may discern not only doctrinal and institutional development and change, but also inconsistencies that reflect the varied concerns of different subgroups within the broader community. When the later tradition turned to the canon for guidance on issues regarding the place of women, it found a diversity of views, not just those of the historical founder. Among those various voices recorded in the literature, we can differentiate at least four distinct attitudes, three occurring in the early canon and a fourth representing, in part, a later attempt to resolve the inconsistency and tension among the first three. The first three I refer to as *soteriological inclusiveness, institutional androcentrism,* and *ascetic misogny,* and the fourth I call *soteriological androgyny,* to emphasize both its innovative quality and its historical relationship to the first attitude of inclusivity.

Soteriological Inclusiveness

Buddhism, in its origins, above all else was a pragmatic soteriology, a theory of liberation that sought to free humanity from suffering, first by thoroughly analyzing the fundamental human predicament and then by offering a practical method or path for eliminating the afflictions, cognitive and dispositional, that are perpetuated as greed, hatred, and delusion. In his reflections on human suffering and liberation, the Buddha was frequently critical of conventional views, including those carrying the authority of the Brahmanic tradition. In marked contrast to the sacerdotal ritualism of the Brahmins, he offered a path that was open to all. The first canonical attitude I wish to consider, soteriological inclusiveness, thus arguably is the most basic and also the most distinctively Buddhist attitude regarding the status of women that one can find in the vast literature of the 2500-year-old tradition. The earliest Buddhists clearly held that one's sex, like one's caste or class (*varṇa*), presents no barrier to attaining the Buddhist goal of liberation from suffering. Women can, we are told by the tradition, pursue the path. Moreover, they can (and did) become arhats, Buddhist saints who had broken completely the suffering of the cycle of death and rebirth (*saṃsāra*).

A revolutionary soteriological assertion in its day, this view is found directly expressed at a number of points in the early literature. Consider, for example, the occasion when the harem of King Udena was devastated by a fire that killed some 500 of the king's consorts, including Sāmāvatī and other committed followers of the Buddha. Asked to comment on this tragedy, the Buddha replied: "Monks, among these [victims], some women disciples are stream-winners, some once-returners, some nonreturners. Not fruitless, monks, are all these women disciples who have met their end'' (*Udāna;* VII.x[6]). This passage clearly implies that there were serious women practitioners (and not just patrons) among the Buddha's early followers and, moreover, that women were deemed quite capable of achieving the standard stages of the path to liberation by which one becomes an arhat. The same sentiment is reiterated in more categorical terms and taken a step further in another passage, where we find the Buddha using the parts of a chariot to illustrate the components of the Buddhist path.

> 'Straight' is the name that Road is called, and 'Free
> From Fear' the Quarter whither thou art bound.
> Thy Chariot is the 'Silent Runner' named,
> With Wheels of Righteous Effort fitted well.
> Conscience the Leaning-board; the Drapery
> Is Heedfulness; the Driver is the Dharma,
> I say, and Right Views, they that run before.
> And be it woman, or be it man for whom
> Such chariot doth wait, by that same car
> Into Nirvāṇa's presence shall they come. (*Saṃyutta Nikāya;* I.5.6)

Not only is the path open to women, in other words, it indeed is the same path for both women and men. We must not overlook the fact that the crucial point in such passages is not that sex and gender differences do not exist, but rather that they are soteriologically insignificant, that they constitute at most a distraction from the true goal of liberation. Consider the story of Somā, the daughter of the chaplain of King Bimbisāra who became a follower of the Buddha and eventually one of the most famous women arhats. One day Māra, the Buddhist personification of doubt and temptation, appeared to her as she was resting under a tree, taunting her with the conventional belief of women's limited intelligence and spiritual capacity.

> Māra the evil one, desirous of arousing fear, wavering, and dread in her, desirous of making her desist from concentrated thought, went up to her and addressed her in verse:
>
> That vantage point the sages may attain
> Is hard to win. With her two-finger wit,[7]
> That may no woman ever hope to achieve.

Recognizing the trap, Somā banishes Māra with a confident affirmation of the strength of her meditative concentration and wisdom:

> What should the woman's nature signify
> When consciousness is taut and firmly set,

When knowledge rolleth ever on, when she
By insight rightly comprehends the Dharma?

To one for whom the question doth arise:
Am I a woman, or
Am I a man, or what not am I then?
To such a one is Māra fit to talk.[8]

Taken together these passages indicate that whatever limitations women might conventionally be held to have had, they were not to be excluded from any of the forms of Buddhist practice nor from the ultimate goal of those practices, liberation from all the forms of human suffering. Radical as this position was socially, it was quite consistent with the basic philosophical principles of the Buddha's teaching, indeed one can understand it as a corollary of the doctrine of "no-self" (*anātman*), understood to mean that the individual has no ultimately fixed or determinant nature—a theme we shall see developed more explicitly in later Buddhist thought. But how consistently was this implication of *anātman* recognized among the early Buddhists? The passages we shall consider in the following sections suggest that many early Buddhists found reason to limit women's access to Buddhist practice. Indeed Somā herself still speaks in the preceding passages of a "women's nature" even while asserting that its limitations are irrelevant.

To understand better the complexity of this inclusive spirit with regard to women in early Buddhism, we should consider further its relation to the Buddha's rejection of caste or class distinctions. Both of these social views are derived from the same philosophical principles. Just as the Buddhist goal was not limited to those born in a certain social group, so it was not limited to those born as males. Both positions were unusual for the time, indeed both were perceived as radical and dangerous by more orthodox critics of the Buddha's Dharma. Both assertions reflect an attempt to locate virtue and spiritual potential beyond conventional social and gender distinctions. Both can be seen as evidence of a newly emerging sense of individuality that began to take precedence over narrower biological and social constraints during the Age of the Wanderers. There is a difference, however.

Although unquestionably related, the distinctive Buddhist positions on caste and the spiritual capacity of women do differ significantly. The question of caste arises far more frequently in canonical literature, and the argument usually centers on the idea that the virtues (or vices) attributed to a particular caste are a matter of individual cultivation or lack thereof, not a matter of innate qualities acquired by birth in a particular social class. At least one early *sutta*, the *Kūṭadanta* (*DN*, 5) theorizes quite explicitly on the socioeconomic origins of caste distinctions.[9] Much harder to find, however, is any clear distinction between socially conditioned gender roles as opposed to biologically innate sexual differences.[10] Although parallel to the position on caste, the willingness to include women appears to have remained imbedded in a set of cultural assumptions about gender, assumptions that were never completely rejected. Though they adamantly repudiated the prevailing view that caste was genetic, the early Buddhists nonetheless felt that sexuality did entail a set of biologically given characteristics that shaped one's abilities and capacities, even if it did not inexorably determine them. They could see quite clearly that sex is biologically differentiated in a way that caste was not; what they were prone to overlook, however, was that sexual identity is as much socially constructed as it is biologically given. The lack of a clear conceptual distinction between biological sex and social gender may indeed have been one factor that allowed the discrepancy between the doctrine of soteriological inclusiveness and the attitudes of androcentrism and misogyny I shall take up later.

It is hardly surprising that the early Buddhists, including the women themselves, would have seen the woman's lot as a difficult one, that they would have considered it an unfortunate birth and certainly one to be avoided if possible. By any objective standard it was a more restrictive life, compared to the social freedom allowed men. And it almost certainly became more so as the new urban culture developed its own more rigid structure in the centuries following the Buddha's death. The constraints of childbearing are very real in any traditional culture, and certainly those constraints do arise from biological differentiation, though this need not imply that women are burdened by an irrevocably fixed nature. The inconsistency that subsequently emerged, in some Buddhist circles at least, then lay not in recognizing the realities of sexual differentiation, but rather in the additional assumption that this differentiation relegated women to a lower capacity for pursuing the spiritual path. In more contemporary terms, it arose from the failure to distinguish the limitations of social gender roles from the assumption of inherent sexual limitations with regard to the pursuit of liberation.

In the sections of this chapter that follow, we shall see that among some factions of the Buddhist community were powerful social concerns that reinforced this lack of consistency, and we also shall see that other factions struggled to realize both the soteriological and even the social promise of the early teaching. For now, however, we must be careful not to read an overt assertion of sexual egalitarianism or even equivalence into this early attitude of soteriologicial inclusiveness, while at the same time we must be careful not to underestimate the revolutionary breakthrough that even this more limited notion of inclusiveness represented at the time. There is no question that women are explicitly included in the Buddhist quest for liberation, yet it is also important to note that the question of equality, and especially of social equality, for some time at least remained a moot point.

The notion that early Buddhism was doctrinally egalitarian is potentially quite misleading, however popular it has come to be.[11] It is possible, though historically unverifiable, that the Buddha's personal view was more sexually (if not spiritually) egalitarian, but the doctrinal pronouncements that survive in the edited canon present a more restricted position, one that appears intentionally limited to an assessment of women's ability to achieve liberation; nothing is asserted about their social rights within society at large.[12] Kari Børreson provides a useful conceptual distinction that helps the issues here. With regard to early Christianity, she prefers to speak of an attitude of equivalence rather than equality, because equality implies a sense of sameness, whereas equivalence allows for physiological and psychological differences without implying any hierarchy of difference.[13] The early Buddhist texts, however, are less than explicit regarding the question of hierarchial differentiation. Hence I feel that we should distinguish further, in the case of early Buddhism at least, between an attitude of equivalence and one of inclusiveness. Inclusiveness asserts neither sameness nor a lack of hierarchical differentiation. The ambiguity latent in this attitude of inclusiveness becomes quite apparent if we consider how it is interpreted by most contemporary Asian Buddhists, who feel that women have equal access to the Dharma, but insist nonetheless that sexual differences are real and that the male sex is by nature superior to the female sex, both socially and spiritually. There is little in the early canonical literature to conclusively refute that interpretation of inclusiveness, and indeed much to reinforce it, as we shall soon see.

To avoid this ambiguity by asserting more explicitly a direct parallel between caste differences and sexual (or rather gender) differences would have been logically possible and would have been quite consistent with the sentiments of the broader teachings of Gautama. In the early Buddhist canon as it has come down to us, however, such an explicitly drawn conclusion is conspicuously absent. Whereas women were initially granted a religious role that remained virtually without parallel in the Indian tradition for some time, the door was still left open to speculation about the limitations of the "female nature," a theme prominent in the androcentric and misogynist views that were to become increasingly characteristic of the tradition as the monastic order became more institutionalized and male dominated in the first several centuries following Śākyamuni's death.

Institutional Androcentrism

The second attitude we must consider appears to have developed somewhat later, though it finds expression especially in the Vinaya, texts concerned with regulation of the monastic order and containing some of the oldest material in the Buddhist canon. Here we find a new theme, one emerging from a different set of concerns than the philosophical reflection and empirical observation that led to the view of soteriological inclusiveness. Although this attitude does appear early in the literature, it represents, in my opinion, a concern that could have become important only once the early community had become established within the broader social milieu.

Having once noted that women were quite capable of pursuing the religious life, the early Buddhist community had to determine what to do with the interest that view generated. Initially this was probably not a problem because the charisma of a venerated and widely respected teacher was sufficient to forestall most worries about internal authority and external social acceptability. After Gautama's death, however, the community continued to grow and its organization shifted more toward a pattern of established cenobitic monastic residence. With this shift we find increasing evidence of an attitude I shall call *institutional androcentrism:* the view that women indeed may pursue a full-time religious career, but only within a carefully regulated institutional structure that preserves and reinforces the conventionally accepted social standards of male authority and female subordination.

This attitude is reflected in a number of texts, but I shall focus most of my discussion in this section on one extended passage, the oft-cited story of the ordination of Mahāpajāpatī, the woman who was both the Buddha's aunt and his foster mother. Though frequently mentioned in discussions of the place of women in Buddhism, this passage warrants more careful and critical consideration than it customarily has received. Too often glossed over, for example, are the multitude of problems with the historicity of the story; and also some significant differences between the Pali and the Sanskrit versions have been entirely overlooked or disregarded in the recent literature.[14] I shall argue that what we have here is not a literal historical account of the founding of the order, but rather a more complex document, one that reports symbolically or mythically the process of mediation that finally resolved—only centuries after Śākyamuni's death—the problem posed by the existence of an order of nuns.[15] Although this lack of historicity might make our text initially seem less interesting, the mythic account it offers in fact is all the more intriguing and useful because of what it suggests about tensions within the early community and what it tells us about how those tensions eventually were reconciled.

The story of Mahāpajāpatī's ordination as the first nun survives in several different versions, which relate the same basic story except for a few significant details. The most developed version appears to be that found in the *Cullavagga* (Chapter X), second of the two *Khandhakas* of the Theravāda Vinaya.[16] I shall summarize the story from that Pali text, noting differences in the Sanskrit version where necessary. Temporally the Pali text divides into six well-delineated episodes, each marked with a shift of scene and characters.[17]

Scene 1. Mahāpajāpatī Beseeches Śākyamuni. While staying among his kinsmen, the Sakyans in Kapilavatthu, the Buddha is approached by his aunt Pajāpatī, who raised him as a child after his mother's death. She suggests that it would be good if women were allowed to become nuns, taking up the homeless life as full-time disciples rather than lay followers. The Buddha tells her to be wary of this idea, without specifying precisely what danger he has in mind.[18] Pajāpatī repeats her request three times, without avail, and then retires unhappy and distraught.

Scene 2. Mahāpajāpatī Meets with Ānanda in Vesālī. Having shaved their heads and put on monastic robes, Pajāpatī and a large group of Sakyan women follow the Buddha to Vesālī, where Pajāpatī waits outside the Buddha's door with "her feet swollen... sobbing and in tears."[19] Disturbed at their appearance, the Buddha's personal attendant Ānanda inquires about her distress and offers to take up their cause.

Scene 3. Ānanda Intercedes on Mahāpajāpatī's Behalf. Telling Pajāpatī to wait outside, Ānanda leaves to seek out the Buddha. Making the same request, he gets the same answer. But then Ānanda tries a different approach, asking, "Lord, are women, having gone forth from home into homelessness in the Dharma and Discipline proclaimed by the Truthfinder, able to realize the fruit of stream winning, the fruit of once returning, the fruit of nonreturning, or perfection (that is, arhatship)?" The Buddha replies that indeed they are. Thereupon Ānanda points out that the women should then be allowed to become nuns, both because the Buddha acknowledges that they are capable of arhatship and because he owes a great debt to Pajāpatī, "foster-mother, nurse, giver of milk, who suckled him as a child."[20]

Scene 4. The Buddha Assents, Conditionally. Conceding Ānanda's point, the Buddha agrees to Pajāpatī's ordination if she will accept eight rules (in addition to the normal monastic rules): (1) Nuns, no matter how senior, must always defer to monks, no matter how junior. (2) Nuns must not spend the rainy season retreat in a residence where there is no monk. (3) Nuns must observe the fortnightly monastic observances under the direction of monks. (4) After the rainy season retreat nuns must formally report to a convocation of monks as well as to the other nuns. (5) A nun who has broken a monastic rule must be disciplined by both the order of monks and by that of the nuns. (6) Both monks and nuns are necessary for the ordination of new nuns. (7) Monks must never be abused or reviled in any way by a nun. (8) Nuns may be formally admonished by monks, but not monks by nuns.

Scene 5. Ānanda Communicates the Decision. Ānanda then returns to Pajāpatī and reports the Buddha's decision. Honored, Pajāpatī accepts the eight conditions as readily "as a youth fond of ornaments would accept a garland of lotus or jasmine flowers," vowing she will never transgress them.

Scene 6. Ānanda Communicates Pajāpatī's Acceptance. On hearing Pajāpatī's reply, the Buddha then declares the prophecy that this compromise will result in the Dharma enduring for only 500 years rather than 1000, adding several somewhat obscure analogies of robbers attacking households, mildew attacking rice, and rust attacking sugar cane. Finally he says that establishing the eight rules is like prophylactically building a dam so that water will not overflow a reservoir.[21]

The spiritual capacity of women is acknowledged here, yet the prevailing tone of the text reflects a concern for regularizing the order even at the expense of the women practitioners. Why this apparent shift in attitude? Why this new concern for androcentric control? The two attitudes are not completely incompatible, it is true; indeed both are presented side by side, at least in the Pali version of the story, yet one is struck by the incongruity of their juxtaposition. The first point to note is that the two do arise out of very different sets of concerns, and that the latter attitude of androcentrism represents a response to a problem that became increasingly more an issue after the community had reached a certain degree of success in establishing a place for itself within the broader society. In contrast to the attitude of inclusiveness, which focused on the capability of women to pursue the path, the focus here is not on women themselves, but rather on a perceived threat to the integrity of the monastic institution as it existed within the broader social community.

This is why I prefer to read this story as a document of reconciliation, as a symbolic, mythologized expression of a compromise negotiated between several factions of the order, including the nuns and their male supporters. The issue was resolved only over a period of time, I suspect, and the document we have here is probably a still later attempt to rationalize and legitimize post facto what had already become the status quo. Beyond simple rationalization, however, I also see a theme of reconciliation and compromise, one that seeks to recognize and to validate each of the different positions represented.

In the story, each of the contending factions or interest groups is given a traditionally respected voice, with Śākyamuni expressing both the concern of the conservative and socially sensitive majority and also the spirit of wary (even reluctant) compromise and reconciliation that eventually emerged. The traditional figures chosen to voice the other positions suggest that it was necessary to take the contending factions quite seriously. As I have already noted, Pajāpatī commanded great respect as the woman to whom the Buddha owed the greatest debt. Ānanda is a more complex character: on the one hand, he was considered spiritually slow, being the last of the traditional 500 senior disciples to achieve arhatship; but on the other hand, tradition also holds that it was he who was asked to recite the Buddha's teachings at the first council, being seen as the most reliable source, because of his long association with the Buddha as his personal attendant and the reliability of his memory. In contrast to some of the other arhat-disciples, Ānanda is frequently depicted in very human terms and also as the male disciple most respected by the women followers. Even the shifts in scene, all of Ānanda's coming and going, may be narrative elements added to the more developed Pali version of the story to represent the complex process of mediation that had go on between the various factions.[22]

To understand better the social dynamics reflected in this document of reconciliation, we must recognize more clearly the concerns it addresses. One aspect of the problem becomes more evident later in the same text when reasons are given for further special rules regarding the nuns.

> Now at [one] time the entire Order of nuns went [to the monks] for [the Vinaya rite of] exhortation. People looked down upon, criticised, spread it about, saying: "These are their wives, these are

> their mistresses, now they will take their pleasure together." They told this matter to the Lord. He said: "Monks, the entire Order of nuns should not go for exhortation [at the same time]. If they should go thus, there is an offence of wrong-doing. I allow, monks, four or five nuns to go for exhortation.[23]

Although one might question whether this solution would in fact resolve the alleged problem, it is clear that the focus of the concern for the monks is public opinion. The issue is not soteriological theory as much as preserving the social acceptability necessary to financial support. The problem faced by the community at this stage of development in fact was a true dilemma, one born of the shift toward cenobitic monasticism, an institutional structure that had no precedent in the history of Indian religions. On the one hand, the two subcommunities of monks and nuns had to maintain sufficient distance from each other to avoid the question of impropriety, and on the other hand, they had to deal with the social unacceptability (indeed unimaginability) of an autonomous group of women not under the direct regulation and control of some male authority.

The latter half of the dilemma is seen more distinctly in one of the analogies ascribed to Śākyamuni above in Scene 6. To allow women to become nuns would create a situation, we are told, similar to a household that had many women but few men, one that easily falls prey to robbers and thieves. In other words, women must be protected by some androcentric social structure like the family. But the order of monks is ill-suited to that task because monks, by definition, have given up just such social responsibilities. For women to regulate and protect themselves, even if consistent with the notion of soteriological inclusiveness, was nonetheless socially unthinkable.[24] The irony is that some more or less formally organized order of nuns certainly existed by the time this dilemma became a social issue. The nuns, no doubt, had regulated themselves quite successfully for some time and probably continued to do so after the resolution, albeit now officially under the control (and protection) of the monks.

It was an uneasy compromise, most likely, but one that got the monks off the hook, while also legitimizing as much as possible the existence of the anomalous group of quasi-autonomous women. Whether the nuns of that time assented to the compromise as readily as Pajāpatī does in the story of course is impossible to determine historically. By accepting the authority of the monks, at least nominally, the nuns did gain a more acceptable place in the eyes of the broader society, even though in the long run that was to prove to be a heavy price to pay, for the order of nuns was subsequently relegated to a second-class status, a constraint that was certain to be reflected in diminished prestige, educational opportunity, and financial support. Historically it is clear that the order of nuns went into a steady decline in spite of having secured some degree of acceptability. Given the earlier precedent of accomplished women practitioners among the Buddhists and also the better documented enthusiasm demonstrated by the parallel order of Jain nuns, one might reasonably expect that Buddhist nuns would have maintained a creative religious life in the convents in spite of increasing androcentric restriction. Although that may have been, for some centuries at least, once the androcentric structure was established, life in the convents became gradually more marginalized and eventually ceased to play any role in the official accounts of the tradition. As Nancy Falk points out, by the third century CE, the order of nuns in India had already virtually disappeared from the official record.[25] We know, from the report of Chinese pilgrims in India for example, that convents continued to exist well into seventh century CE and beyond, yet there is no record of what these women achieved in their practice or what they contributed to the broader Buddhist community.

Could it have been any different? Probably not under those social conditions, certainly not without more overt support from the order of monks, who had much to lose and little to gain from asserting a place of equivalence for the nuns. For all its commitment to inclusiveness at the doctrinal level, institutional Buddhism was not able to (or saw no reason to) challenge prevailing attitudes about gender roles in society. The greatest surprise is that the order of nuns managed to survive for as long as it did, however marginally.

Ascetic Misogyny

Alongside the institutional androcentrism we have just considered, we must recognize another, even more negative attitude toward women and the feminine in Buddhist literature, an attitude that often was much more aggressively hostile in its expression. In some cases what we find what appears to be simply a Buddhist appropriation of prevailing social views regarding gender, as in the passage from the *Aṅguttara Nikāya,* where Ānanda asks the Buddha, "Pray, lord, what is the reason, what is the cause why womenfolk neither sit in a court [of justice], nor embark on business, nor reach the essence of [any] deed?" To which, we are told, Gautama replies: "Womenfolk are uncontrolled, Ānanda.

Womenfolk are envious, Ānanda. Womenfolk are greedy, Ānanda. Womenfolk are weak in wisdom, Ānanda. That is the reason, that is the cause why womenfolk do not sit in a court of justice, do not embark on business, do not reach the essence of the deed'' (*AN,* II.82–83). The distinction between androcentric and misogynist texts is not always clear-cut, and passages like this one were undoubtedly employed in support of the institutional concerns we saw in the previous section. Even so, I think we are dealing with a different attitude here, one that has its own historical development in the literature and one that voices its own distinctive set of concerns. Part of the difference already can be seen in the fact that this passage more clearly precludes (or at least contradicts) a position of soteriological inclusiveness in its suggestion that women could never accomplish a deed as demanding as liberation. Other passages go much further, moreover, portraying women not just passively as weaker human beings, but seeing them rather as active agents of distraction and ruin. The *Saddharmasmṛtyupasthāna* tells us that: ''Women are ever the root of ruin, and of loss of substance; when men are to be controlled by women how can they gain happiness?. . . A woman is the destruction of destructions in this world and the next; hence one must ever avoid women if he desires happiness for himself.''[26]

Such aggressively misogynist sentiments go well beyond the attitude of institutional androcentrism: they are more defensively hostile in tone, and they arose in response to a different set of problems. To understand the place of these antifeminine depictions in the Buddhist tradition we must first look to the cosmogonic myths that the early Buddhists inherited from the older Indian culture. Details vary somewhat, but early Buddhists, along with most of their non-Buddhist contemporaries, felt that this world had evolved (or devolved, rather) from a pure realm of formless, asexual beings. Embodiment and sexual differentiation were seen as the manifestation of a lower state of existence, one bound by attachment to the earth and brought on by eating and sexual activity.[27] There are striking parallels between this world-view and that of the slightly later Gnostic traditions in the West, an observation explored by Karen Lang, who points out:

> Both the Buddhist and Gnostic accounts of the fall have in common the following sequence of events: a deliberate act of eating brings about the transformation of originally luminous, incorporeal, and asexual nature into one that is now dark, material, and sexual. This transformation, in turn, brings about an awakening of sexual desire and the subsequent satisfaction of this desire through sexual intercourse. These scriptures imply that, since sexuality was involved

> in the fall, abstention from sexual pleasures will weaken the ties that bind humanity to the lower material world and thus enable seekers after enlightenment to ascend to the luminous state of perfection forfeited by their ancestors.[28]

Given that world-view, it is not surprising that both Gnostics and Buddhists would come to associate impurity with the natural realm and female fecundity, while seeing transcendent purity to be expressed in masculine celibacy. But are misogynist views in the Buddhist literature the result of such myths? Is it not more likely that the myths simply provide a socially acceptable rationalization for an attitude that arises from some more specific practical problems? In the Buddhist literature such sentiments most often are expressed in discussions of male religious practice, and especially in texts that present the spiritual ideal primarily in terms of ascetic purity. This suggests that the psychological demands of ascetic celibacy are more central to understanding this attitude than the legacy of cosmogonic assumptions. Consider the shift in perspective reflected in the following two paragraphs:

> Monks, I see no other single form so enticing, so desirable, so intoxicating, so binding, so distracting, such a hindrance to winning the unsurpassed peace from effort. . . as a woman's form. Monks, whosoever clings to a woman's form—infatuated, greedy, fettered, enslaved, enthralled—for many a long day shall grieve, snared by the charms of a woman's form. . . .
>
> Monks, a woman, even when going along, will stop to ensnare the heart of a man; whether standing, sitting or lying down, laughing, talking or singing, weeping, stricken or dying, a woman will stop to ensnare the heart of a man. . . . Verily, one may say of womanhood: it is wholly a snare of [the Tempter,] Māra. (*Aṅguttara Nikāya* III; 67–68)

Here the concern is not directly institutional, it is much more personal and individual. Where the androcentric attitude is more sociological in its intention, what we find here is more psychological, a fear of the feminine, and a fear specifically of its power to undermine male celibacy. What is being censured here? The first paragraph focuses on the male tendency to be misled by craving and clinging to a feminine form. Standing alone it might be read as an astute psychological assessment of the problems of celibacy; that is, the male problem of pursuing an ascetically celibate path. The second paragraph seems however to move from psychological astuteness to psychopathological misogyny. Here we find the feminine and women categorically condemned as a threat to male celibacy. The problem lies no longer within the male ascetic, now it is effectively projected onto the external object of craving and desire, in this case womankind as a whole. In fact, the juxtaposition of perspective in this same text suggests the possibility that the second paragraph is a later interpolation, one that drew on long-standing and socially accepted gender biases to shift the burden of responsibility off of the male ascetic and onto the female object of desire. As such, the emergence of conventional misogyny into Buddhist literature would represent a shift in perspective away from the psychological soteriology of the earliest tradition back toward the purification soteriology of the ascetics who had been criticized for their excesses by Śākyamuni.

Whereas such virulent passages in fact are relatively infrequent, they seem to turn up even more often in certain genres of the later Mahāyāna literature than in the earlier *suttas* of the Pali Canon.[29] Indeed, this is one reason why I feel it is necessary to distinguish this attitude from the institutional androcentrism considered earlier. Although the early Mahāyāna reaffirmed the basic principle of soteriological inclusiveness with its universalization of the bodhisattva path, a religious ideal it held open to all—men and women, monastic and lay—this rejection of institutional androcentrism did not entail a corresponding rejection of ascetic misogyny. Consider these excerpts from the "Tale of King Udayana of Vatsa," a *sūtra* from the important Mahāyāna collection, the *Mahāratnakūṭa.*

> All desires are suffering, the vilest of evils,
> The impurity of pus, extremely despicable. . . .
>
> Like the overflow from a toilet or the corpse of a dog or a fox,
> In the Ṣitavana cemetery pollution flows everywhere.
> The evils of desire are contemptible like these.
>
> Fools lust for women, like dogs in heat.
> They do not know abstinence.
>
> They are also like flies who see vomited food.
> Like a herd of hogs, they greedily seek manure.
>
> Women can ruin the precepts of purity.
> They can also ignore honor and virtue. . . .
>
> As the filth and decay of a dead dog or dead snake are burned away,
> So all men should burn filth and detest evil.
>
> The dead snake and dog are detestable,
> But women are even more detestable than they are. . . .
>
> Women are like fishermen; their flattery is a net.
> Men are like fish caught by the net.

> The sharp knife of the killer is to be feared.
> The woman's knife is to be feared even more so....
>
> Confused by women one is burnt by passion.
> Because of them one falls into evil ways. There is no refuge....
>
> Relationships with women are extremely base.
> Evil among evil—What satisfaction is there in lust?...[30]

The clear association here of misogyny with concerns for pollution and purification suggests further that this attitude evolved quite independent of the concerns that gave rise to institutional androcentrism. The prominence of the purification theme suggests, moreover, that what we find here is related to a pan-Indian tradition of asceticism, one that also may have had at least an indirect influence on Gnosticism and early Christian monasticism as well. Although the earliest Buddhists were critical of the extreme manifestations of this older tradition of śramaṇic asceticism, both on practical and philosophical grounds, outbursts like these in even the later Mahāyāna literature indicate the presence of a strong and persistent ascetic wing within the *saṃgha*. Even so, we must be careful to note the relative weight given such sentiments within the tradition. Both Schuster and Kajiyama have correctly criticized the tendency to overestimate the frequency and the centrality of this misogynist theme.[31] Even in this same *sūtra* we find mitigating statements; for example, King Udayana addresses the Buddha:

> "Lord, because of woman's deception, I am perplexed and ignorant. For this reason I have intense hate. Lord, because you bring peace and benefits to living beings, I want you to explain, out of compassion, the flattery and deceit of women...."
>
> [The Buddha] answered: "Put aside these actions. Why don't you ask about what is important and not about extraneous matters?...Your majesty should first know a man's faults. Then he'll have insight into those of a woman....Because all men engage in four kinds of wrong and excessive actions, they are perplexed by women...."[32]

Although the insidiously pernicious effect of misogyny must not be minimized, it must also be evaluated in the broader context of the underlying principle of inclusiveness. Similarly we must not minimize the inconsistency within the tradition here: misogyny is even more basically in conflict with the spirit of soteriological inclusiveness than is institutional androcentrism. The point is not to play down either the presence or the incongruity of misogynist sentiment in Buddhist literature; rather we should see the expression of this discordant attitude as an indication of conflicting interests within the early community, just as we did with expressions of institutional androcentrism.

Whereas the attitude of ascetic misogyny led to some of the most vituperative attacks on women and the feminine in Buddhist literature, we must also note that it was more effectively challenged and counterbalanced within the tradition than the attitude of institutional androcentrism. Perhaps this was because misogyny is more obviously deleterious to both its perpetrator and its object, especially in terms of Buddhist psychology. Some Buddhists, even if not all, were quick to recognize that fear of the feminine, and misogyny, generally, is itself a form of clinging and bondage. Candrakīrti and other Mādhyamikas were fond of citing a passage from the *Dṛdhādhyāśayaparipṛccha Sūtra* that illustrates this response quite well:

> ''Suppose a certain man goes to a magic show. The magician creates a magical woman, and, seeing her, desire arises in the man. Due to the mind of desire he becomes anxious and fretful, and, rising from his seat, he leaves. He leaves and contemplates the impurity of that woman. . . .Now what do you think, O Son of Good Family, has that man done the right thing, or has he done the wrong thing?''
>
> ''Lord, anyone who contemplates the impurity of a nonexistent woman. . .has done the wrong thing.''
>
> The Lord spoke, ''O Son of Good Family, in this [same way] whatever monk or nun, or layman or lay woman contemplates the impurity of an entity that has never arisen and never existed. . .has made a similar [mistake]. I would not say that such a foolish person is practicing the path.''[33]

All Buddhist soteriologists agreed that craving for an object of sexual gratification was a serious obstacle to liberation. In contrast to the more extreme ascetic traditions, most Buddhists went a step further to recognize that the problem lay not in the external object of desire itself, but rather in the subjective craving, which lay within oneself. The misogynist wing of the Buddhist community appears to have overlooked this distinction, however, and the Mahāyāna doctrine of nondualism can be seen, in part at least, as a response to just this type of confusion. The text just cited indicates the dispute that turned on this point, while also offering a powerful philosophical antidote. Neither ''men'' nor ''women'' in fact exist, at least not as intrinsically existing entities, nor consequently as objects of sexual clinging. If we nonetheless persist in our craving, then clearly the problem lies in the clinging, not in the nonsubstantial object onto which we project that clinging. And to cling, moreover, to one's *aversion* to such an object actually is just as deleterious as clinging to one's *craving* for it. Here we can see the spirit of the earlier principle of soteriological inclusiveness reemerging, though expressed now with a greater degree of philosophical and psychological insight and sophistication.

The three attitudes that I have discussed so far developed side by side for much of the first several centuries after the Buddha's death, and they are found in the *Nikāyas* and *Āgamas* as well as in the later Mahāyāna literature. Theoretically and chronologically, soteriological inclusiveness was the most basic of the three, though institutional androcentrism emerged fairly early, as social acceptability became an increasingly important issue for the order of monks. The roots of ascetic misogyny were pre-Buddhist, but it may have been the last of the three to have emerged in the literature, at least in its extreme, vituperative form. If true, that would suggest that the psychological problems it reflects were perhaps less severe when the monastic order was still more closely integrated into lay society in the early days. As monasteries became more autonomous and the monastic life more sheltered from contact with the outside world, however, the problems of psychological adjustment to celibacy may have become more central than the social problems that arose when mendicancy and social interaction were still part of the ideal.

In any case, the tension among these three attitudes is a recurrent theme in the social history of the early community, reaching its culmination in a controversy that became quite heated by the first century CE. The dispute concerned the question of whether a woman could become a buddha. Under the influence of androcentric and misogynist views many Buddhists—from both Hīnayāna and Mahāyāna schools of thought—rejected this possibility even if they were willing to allow for the existence of woman arhats. The question was never conclusively resolved, but in their attempt to reaffirm the early principle of soteriological inclusiveness some factions of the Mahāyāna were inspired to develop that original principle toward a much more actively egalitarian view, an affirmation of nondualistic androgyny, which had strong roots in the newly emerging Mahāyāna philosophy of emptiness.

Soteriological Androgyny

Finally then we come to the fourth attitude we must consider, one that formulated the goal of Buddhist practice psychologically as a dynamic state of nondualistic androgynous integration. As this fourth voice did not become fully articulated, in the written literature at least, until sometime after the sixth or seventh century CE, it is a development significantly postdating the period we have discussed so far (fifth century BCE–fourth century CE). The texts and practice traditions in which it does find expression, moreover, are not part of the core tradition shared by all forms of Buddhism. Strictly speaking, this development thus falls outside of my intention to focus on attitudes toward women in early Buddhism. Even so, it warrants our attention here, both because of the crucial shift in perspective it presents, but also because it has significant roots in those earlier Buddhist attitudes and doctrines we have been considering, a point that is too easily overlooked.

The innovative aspect of this fourth attitude lies in its dramatic revalorization of the feminine—its reassessment of the soteriological relevance not just of the feminine, in fact, but of socially defined gender characterizations in general, a reevaluation of all those qualities and expectations culturally ascribed to male and female. We must be careful not to overlook the relationship between this view and the position of soteriological inclusiveness considered earlier, but we must also note the significant evolution presented in this new stance. Rather than simply seeing sexual and gender differences as irrelevant and ultimately insignificant, this fourth attitude takes a more actively positive stance. The differentiation so characteristic of ordinary relative existence is seen not merely as something to be left behind in pursuit of the ultimate. Instead, differences are acknowledged as provisional, as not ultimately real, and they are further affirmed as potentially powerful means of soteric transformation.

The underlying assumption expressed in this view is that all beings, to differing degrees, consciously or unconsciously, manifest the full range of characteristics conventionally identified as gender specific. Certain psychological characteristics are conventionally distinguished as feminine or masculine, but the emphasis is on the soteriological potential of those differences rather than on the social limitations they often reflect. Femininity and masculinity are seen as dialectically interactive modes of all human existence—mutually complementary and equally essential to the ideal state, a state of androgynous integration. The soteric task is first to recognize those psychological traits or energies that dominate one's current state and then to use the power of that energy to bring the repressed and undeveloped aspects into full expression. Like Jung's archetypes, these psychological traits can take either positive or demonic expression, and those most likely to be destructive unless positively transformed are the ones conventionally associated with the opposite sex.

This new ideal of a dialectical androgyny finds its fullest expression after the sixth century CE in the Vajrayāna literature of later Indo-Tibetan Buddhism, although its origins can be discerned already in the Perfection of Wisdom literature of the early Mahāyāna movement, which probably dates from around the beginning of the Common Era. Much of the symbolism and imagery associated with this development came into Buddhism from the subcurrent of tantrism that eventually worked its way into the mainstream of both Buddhism and the various Hindu traditions. Even though some might wish to argue that the origins of this attitude thus are non-Buddhist, we must not overlook the distinctively Buddhist interpretation and transformation of these tantric themes and motifs. The new mythopoetic soteriology of Vajrayāna Buddhism clearly owes as much to older Buddhist philosophical principles as it does to the "new" tantric symbolism that we find emerging in Buddhist literature only later.

We see the beginnings of this new attitude already in the explicit feminization of liberating wisdom as Prajñāpāramitā in the Perfection of Wisdom Literature. Wisdom always had been a prime Buddhist virtue, to be sure, and it has been primarily expressed with a grammatically feminine noun (*prajñā/paññā*). In the early Mahāyāna literature, however, that grammatical gender begins to take on more explicitly psychological overtones when we find the ultimate virtue of wisdom, *prajñāpāramitā,* presented as "the mother of all Buddhas."

> The Buddhas in the world-systems in the ten directions
> Bring to mind this perfection of wisdom as their mother.
> The Saviours of the world who were in the past, and also
> those that are [just now] in the ten directions,
> Have issued from her, and so will the future ones be.
> She is the one who shows this world [for what it is], she is
> the genetrix, the mother of the Jinas [= Buddhas]. . .[34]

The femininity of this key virtue is no longer coincidental, and not surprisingly it is readily personified in the form of the goddess Prajñāpāramitā and later Tārā. But we should be careful not to assume that we are dealing with an exclusive or dualistic sexual dichotomy in this affirmation of the feminine aspect of liberating wisdom. In a provocative study of this theme in the *Aṣṭasāhasrikā Prajñāpāramitā Sūtra,* Joanna Macy astutely observes that the specific qualities associated there with feminine wisdom are not those typically ascribed to the feminine in more rigidly static and dualistic conceptions of sexual differentiation.[35] Wisdom is a teacher of the Buddhas, the genetrix and nurse of six perfections. Macy points out that her "evident compassion is not seen as a cradling, cuddling, or clasping to the bosom"; it is a function rather of her ability to see with clarity. Similarly there is little talk of sheltering, housing, or enclosing, because the point of this wisdom is to attain a way of being in the world unbound by any position or fixed attachment.[36] What makes this affirmation of the feminine distinctly Buddhist, then, is the rejection of an exclusive bipolarity or dichotomy between the traits identified as feminine and masculine.

The interactive or dialectical aspect of gender imagery we find in these early Mahāyāna texts is reflected further in a significant shift in terminology that gradually took place within that branch of the tradition. Wisdom and compassion had always been linked in Buddhist thought, and one of the central themes of the Mahāyāna as a revitalization movement within Buddhism was the assertion that there could be no truly liberating wisdom that was not inherently compassionate. In Sanskrit both of these terms, *prajñā* and *karuṇā*, are feminine in gender. As nondualistic androgyny began to emerge as the new ideal, that older pair of terms was supplemented, indeed virtually superseded by an equivalent pair: wisdom (*prajñā*) and skillful means (*upāya*), the latter understood as compassion in action and rendered, not coincidentally, with a word masculine in gender.

If the origins of the soteriological androgyny can be seen in early Perfection of Wisdom *sūtras*, we must turn to the tantric literature of Vajrayāna Buddhism to find the mature expression of this attitude. The psychosexual imagery assimilated into Buddhism with the development of Vajrayāna provides a rich elaboration of the nondualistic bipolarity incipient in the Prajñāpāramitā. Basic psychological states of mind, especially those conducive to or disruptive of liberation, were symbolized as both masculine and feminine deities, each with its own consort of the opposite sex; and enlightenment, the optimum mode of existence, was depicted in terms of a sexual union representing the androgynous ideal. The Vajrayāna masters recognized that the power of underdeveloped and unintegrated psychic energy could be both destructive and transformative, and they devised an intricate psychotherapeutic practice of visualization exercises that enabled properly initiated practitioners to manifest and then positively integrate even the most demonic aspects of their psyche. The liberating potential of those chthonic forces was typically represented by the female *ḍākiṇī*, the elusive "sky dancer" encountered sometimes as a demoness or hag and sometimes as a tantalizingly bewitching beauty.[37]

ng the various voices we have encountered in this survey of Buddhist attitudes toward women and the feminine, certainly this last one has spoken most alluringly to the concerns of modern feminism. Not surprisingly this attitude in Buddhism has attracted much attention from those who are currently seeking an alternative to the sexual dualism underlying many other religious traditions, all the more so because the view repudiates the institutional androcentrism and ascetic misogyny that prevailed throughout much of the history of Buddhism. Still, we should be careful not to overidealize what we find here. The potential for a truly androgynous soteriology based on an attitude of equivalence undoubtedly is great in light of this development; but we should ask how much of that potential in fact has been realized in practice. Who, we might well wonder, has really benefited the most from this revolution in Buddhist soteriology? In theory the shift to an androgynous ideal should have undermined the repression of female spiritual practice sanctioned by the androcentrism and misogyny of the monastic establishment; and indeed one does find in the later tradition, especially in Tibet, many more instances in the literature of women practitioners and masters. Still we must also recognize a persistent androcentric focus even in the elaboration of this feminine ideal. If the goal is androgynous integration, any valorization of the feminine is primarily of benefit to the male practitioner—even though it also may alter his behavior toward women as well. The feminine sky-dancers or *ḍākiṇīs* are a powerful representation of the repressed feminine aspects of the male psyche, to be sure. But are the corresponding needs of the female practitioner addressed so thoroughly and so richly? It is precisely the *ḍākiṇīs* that come to play a prominent role in this new view after all, not their masculine counterparts, the *ḍāka*.[38] But then perhaps that is a side of the tradition yet to emerge.

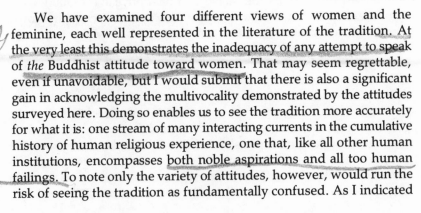

We have examined four different views of women and the feminine, each well represented in the literature of the tradition. At the very least this demonstrates the inadequacy of any attempt to speak of *the* Buddhist attitude toward women. That may seem regrettable, even if unavoidable, but I would submit that there is also a significant gain in acknowledging the multivocality demonstrated by the attitudes surveyed here. Doing so enables us to see the tradition more accurately for what it is: one stream of many interacting currents in the cumulative history of human religious experience, one that, like all other human institutions, encompasses both noble aspirations and all too human failings. To note only the variety of attitudes, however, would run the risk of seeing the tradition as fundamentally confused. As I indicated in the introduction to this chapter, the picture I wish to paint is not one of confusion or ambivalence, but rather one of contending interests and concerns variously expressed by different factions within the early community, each vying to assert its specific concerns. This is not to demean the Buddhist ideal clearly expressed in the principle of soteriological inclusiveness and androgynous integration. It is, however, an attempt to view that ideal in the context of actual human affairs, the only realm in which ideals become meaningful.

Critics of Buddhism will rightly find much to censure in what I have surveyed here. Buddhist women have unquestionably suffered abuses of androcentrism and misogyny, abuses quite comparable to those recently documented in the other major institutionalized religions. For advocates of the Buddhist tradition to deny those parallels would be naive. When these all too familiar expressions of human failing are viewed in the broader perspective of Buddhist thought, however, a positive note also must be heard. And it can only be heard if we acknowledge the multivocality I have sought to underscore in this study. Recognizing the institutional and psychological pressures that militated against the basic principle of inclusiveness asserted by Śākyamuni, one can only be struck at the persistence with which that ideal nonetheless was sustained, to be reexpressed in ever more comprehensive terms. Although the ideal expressed in that principle only rarely has been actualized within the tradition, it consistently has remained the guiding ideal. For non-Buddhists much can be learned from this tradition's experience in attempting to sustain that ideal. For Buddhists themselves, the ideal offers much that is yet to be realized.

Notes

Unless otherwise noted I have used the translations of the Pali Text Society (PTS), with occasional emendations for the sake of clarity and terminological consistency; references for those passages are to the PTS editions, which will allow easy access to both the original text and the translations, which are cross referenced.

1. Ambivalence is a recurrent theme in modern scholarship on this issue, see for example Cornelia Dimmitt Church's "Temptress, Housewife, Nun: Women's Role in Early Buddhism," in *Anima* no. 2 (1975): 53–58, esp. p. 54a; and Nancy Auer Falk's "The Case of the Vanishing Nuns: The Fruits of Ambivalence in Ancient Indian Buddhism," in *Unspoken Worlds: Women's Religious Lives in Non-Western Cultures,* ed. Nancy Auer Falk and Rita M. Gross (San Francisco: Harper & Row, Publishers, 1980), pp. 207–224.

2. Biographical details of the members of the early Buddhist community mentioned here and later are scattered throughout the canon and its commentaries; for a summary account see the appropriate entries in the Pali Text's Society's *Dictionary of Pāli Proper Names,* ed. B. P. Malalasekera (London: Luzac & Co., Ltd., 1960).

3. *MN,* vol. 1, pp. 298-305; this *sutta* is also noteworthy because Dhammadinnā discusses the nature of feelings, telling Visākha that the problem with the three kinds of feeling—pleasant, painful, or neutral—is that they carry a tendency toward attachment, repugnance, and ignorance, respectively. These negative tendencies are not inherently latent in all instances of feeling, however, so the point, she goes on to indicate, is not to eliminate the feelings, but to get rid of the disruptive tendency that normally accompanies the feelings.

4. For more on the roles women actually played, see I. B. Horner's *Women under Primitive Buddhism* (London: George Routledge & Sons, 1930); Falk, "Vanishing Nuns"; and Janice D. Willis, "Nuns and Benefactresses: The Role of Women in the Development of Buddhism," in *Women, Religion, and Social Change,* ed. Yvonne Yazbeck Haddad and Ellison Banks Findly (Albany: SUNY Press, 1985), pp. 59-85. For developments in East Asian Buddhism, see Nancy Schuster's excellent survey, "Striking a Balance: Women and Images of Women in Early Chinese Buddhism" also in *Women, Religion, and Social Change,* pp. 87-111.

5. Along with other historians of religion I use the term *soteriology* here to refer to the attempt to provide a systematic account of liberation in any sense, whether through the agency of a salvific figure or not. I also use the form *soteric* in reference to anything that has to do with the goal of liberation itself rather than the system that explains it.

6. The *anāgāmin* or "nonreturner" is one who will reach arhatship in the current lifetime, which raises an interesting ambiguity in this text. Is the Buddha saying here that there were nonreturners among these victims of the fire (and that their religious careers were cut short—or were brought to a sudden conclusion—by an untimely death)? Or is he speaking of the future, saying that some of them will become nonreturners in their next lives, which might be either as women or as men. The latter interpretation might help to explain the use of the neuter plural to refer to the women in this one passage, a grammatical peculiarity noted but not explained by the PTS translator, F. L. Woodward. In either case, the significant point for our purposes is that the path was open to women, even to lay practitioners like these royal courtesans.

7. One commentary explains that "women, when boiling rice, cannot tell if it is cooked without testing it between two fingers", cf. *Dictionary of Pāli Proper Names,* p. 1310.

8. The story of Somā's encounter with Māra, along with those of other female disciples, is found in the "Suttas of the Sisters" chapter of the

Saṃyutta Nikāya (*SN,* vol. 1, pp. 128–135), where the charge of spiritual incompetence is but one of the tribulations faced and overcome by the female practitioners. The *Psalms of the Sisters* (*Therīgāthā,* XXXVI) offers a slightly modified and less interesting version of Somā's story, one that appears to incorporate a stock passage from the accounts of Gautama's encounter with Māra instead of the key concluding verse found here.

9. It is important to note that early Buddhist cosmogonic myths place more emphasis on explaining the socioeconomic origins of the caste system and the social contract origins of kingship than on attributing the decline from a Golden Age to sexuality in general or to femininity specifically. Whereas there are some intriguing parallels to Western Gnosticism, as we shall see later, the contrast to Judeo-Christian cosmogonies in this important regard is sharper than Diana Paul, for example, suggests in her analysis of the *Aggañña-suttanta, Women in Buddhism* (Berkeley, Calif.: Asian Humanities Press, 1979), pp. xxvi–xxviii. Frank Reynolds provides a more balanced discussion of the *Aggañña-°* and the *Pāṭika-sutta* as examples of early Buddhist cosmogonic myths in "Multiple Cosmogonies and Ethics: The Case of Theravāda Buddhism" in *Cosmogony and Ethical Order,* ed. Robin W. Lovin and Frank E. Reynolds (Chicago: University of Chicago, 1985). Richard Gombrich argues, quite convincingly, that these stories are best understood as satirical spoofs of conventional Brahmanical views of society and kingship, though the later Buddhist tradition of course has taken them at face value; see his comments regarding "The Buddha on Kings and Politics" in *Theravāda Buddhism* (London: Routledge and Kegan Paul, 1988), pp. 81–86.

10. For a useful survey of current theoretical positions on this distinction and other issues in feminist studies, see Caroline Walker Bynum's introduction to *Gender and Religion: On the Complexity of Symbols* (Boston: Beacon Press, 1986), which she coedited with Stevan Harrell and Paula Richman.

11. See Nancy Schuster Barnes, "Buddhism," in *Women in World Religions,* ed. Arvind Sharma (Albany: SUNY Press, 1987), p. 106, for example.

12. There is one text sometimes adduced as evidence for a more explicitly egalitarian attitude. The *Saṃyutta Nikāya* (I, 82–83, *Kindr. Say.,* pp. 110–111) reports that when Pasenadi, the King of Kosala, was unhappy on hearing that his queen had given birth to a daughter rather than a son, the Buddha pointed out to him that a daughter may prove to be an even better offspring than a son. This is so, he argues, because she may grow up to be wise and virtuous and also because she may bear a son who will perform great deeds and rule great realms.

13. This is a central theme throughout her *Subordination and Equivalence: The Nature and Role of Women in Augustine and Thomas Aquinas* (Washington, D.C.: University Press of America, 1981; org. published in French, 1968).

14. The tradition accepts the story as factual, of course, in spite of inconsistencies with other texts that suggest that the Buddha's wife may have been the first nun. Chronologically Pajāpatī is not the most likely candidate, as it is said that she became a nun only after the death of her husband, King Suddhodana, by which time the Buddha already is supposed to have had many women followers. Pajāpatī would, however, be the obvious choice for a mythologized version of the event, however, both because of her prestige as the Buddha's foster mother and because a similar story is told of Mahāvīra, the founder of the Jains, and his aunt (or cousin). The first modern scholar to reject entirely the historicity of the story was Maria E. Lulius van Goor, in her critical study of the early order of nuns, *De Buddhistische Non: Geschetst naar Gegevens der Pāli-Literatuur* (Leiden: Brill, 1915), which was subsequently followed by E. J. Thomas and other historians of early Buddhism. I. B. Horner was more reluctant to reject the story entirely, although she notes the problems, adding apologetically that the prophecy of the decline of the Dharma after 500 years may have been an addition by the monks who "would naturally try to minimise the importance which he gave to women" (*Women under Primitive Buddhism,* p. 105).

15. Based on recent research on the early development of theories regarding the "decline of the Dharma" (Jpn: *mappō*), I feel that this Pali redaction of the story was formulated after the split between the Sarvāstivādins and the Vibhajyavādins, but probably before the Mahīśāsakas subsequently split off from the main Sthavira line; in other words, most likely between 237 and 200 BCE. An even later date has been suggested by Kajiyama Yuichi, who argues that this version of the story is an ex post facto "prophecy," composed 500 years after the Buddha's death to explain a decline that already had occurred. He thus dates this version of the story from roughly the beginning of the Common Era (*Shinran,* pp. 321–322), a date very late for a work included in the Pali canon. In her recent Ph.D. thesis, "The *Candragarbha-sūtra* in Central and East Asia: Studies in a Buddhist Prophecy of Decline" (Harvard University, 1988), Jan Nattier argues for an earlier date, pointing out the significant fact that this story seems to be found only in the literature of schools affiliated with the Sthaviras and not with the Mahāsāṅghikas (pp. 3–8). She feels that this redaction of the story thus must date no earlier than the Council of Pāṭaliputra (ca. 340 BCE), which marked that first schism, and no later than the division between the Sthaviras (Vibhajyavādins) and the Sarvāstivādins, which most likely occurred before the end of Aśoka's reign, probably in 237 BCE according to P.H.L. Eggermont (*The Chronology of the Reign of Asoka Moriya* [Leiden: Brill, 1956]). Following Nattier's sound lead, I would place the origin of the Pali version recorded in the *Cullavagga* somewhat later still, in light of the differences I shall note later between the Theravāda and the Sarvāstivādin versions of the story (see especially notes 17–21). These differences are sufficient, I feel, to argue for at least two different Sthavira traditions, the less elaborated version preserved in the Vinaya of the later Mūlasarvāstivādins and the Pali version of the Theravādins. This would suggest the more elaborate Pali version

developed some time after 237 BCE, when the Vibhajyavādins split off from the Sarvāstivādins, but before the Mahīśāsaka split, around 200 BCE. The Pali version appears to show significant development over the Sarvāstivādin Sanskrit version, but even allowing some time for that development to occur, the Pali redaction still seems to have been completed at least 200 years before the end of the Dharma predicted in the text. This date seems more plausible than the much later date suggested by Kajiyama, moreover, as it seems more likely that the anonymous editors would have reason to predict an imminent end (that is, one they expected within 100–200 years) rather than feeling the need to explain an end that had in their opinion already occurred.

16. The same Pali version is also found in a slightly truncated form in the *Aṅguttara-nikāya (IV;* VIII.VI.51–52). The only other version surviving in an Indic language is a somewhat different Sanskrit version from the Sarvāstivādin Vinaya. This Sanskrit text was edited by C. M. Ridding and Louis de La Vallée Poussin, ("A Fragment of the Sanskrit Vinaya: Bhikṣuṇīkarmavācanā," *Bulletin of the School of Oriental Studies* 1, no. 3 [1919]: 123–143), who point out that this Sanskrit version agrees closely with the Tibetan *Bhikṣuṇīvibhaṅga* (India Office, Stein Tib. MSS., No. 30), except for the section on the Patanīyas (folios 23b–29b). Their edition of the Sanskrit text recently has been translated by Frances Wilson in Diana Paul's *Women in Buddhism,* pp. 77–94.

17. The Sanskrit version is much simpler in structure: the events all take place on the same day at the same loction and are narrated in the first person by the Buddha, in contrast to the more detailed third-person historical account we find here. The inclusion of more elaborate details and the more complex and symmetrical narrative structure in the Pali version suggests that it represents a more developed redaction of the story, one tailored to serve specific needs.

18. In the Sanskrit version the Buddha says that the monastic life with shaved head and the robes of a mendicant would be suitable for Pajāpatī alone. He does not respond directly to her entreaty on behalf of the other women, and he does not say anything about being wary.

19. This detail, with its suggestion of defiance or of a fait accompli also significantly is absent in the Sanskrit account.

20. Here we find perhaps the most significant differences in the Sanskrit version of the story. First of all, there is nothing of Ānanda's switch of tactics, no direct challenge regarding the principle of soteriological inclusiveness. In the Sanskrit version, Ānanda simply repeats Prajāpatī's original request, whereupon the Buddha responds that going forth from home under the rule of the Dharma is not suitable for women. If it is undertaken, the Dharma will not be long enduring, he adds, citing analogies similar to those that follow later in the Pali version. But then he goes on to say that he will expound eight rules that will overcome the obstructions that prevent women from maintaining

the threefold instruction throughout life as nuns, adding finally the analogy of prophylaxis. The prophecy of decline thus is more vague and seemingly more avoidable in the Sanskrit version: it lacks the specific reference to a decline after 500 rather than 1000 years and it also reverses the logical order of the prophecy and the prophylactic measures, suggesting that the decline can be prevented.

21. As indicated in the previous note, the details narrated in the Pali version as separate events (Scenes 3–6) are collapsed in the Sanskrit version into a single exchange between the Buddha and Ānanda, without any further communication or mediation involving Prajāpatī. The rules in that version are the same, though in a different order, culminating rather than beginning with the rule about seniority; see Wilson's analysis in Paul, *Women in Buddhism,* p. 103, n. 8.

22. Several other narrative details occurring in the Pali version help support such a reading. Rather than as an unlikely act of defiant disobedience, the peculiar assertion that Pajāpatī and her followers donned yellow robes after the Buddha's initial rebuff might be read as a tacit acknowledgment that an order of nuns did in fact exist for some time before the community had to confront the social problems that it involved in a more formal manner. And the similarly incongruous detail about Pajāpatī's second thoughts regarding the seniority issue (see note 24) is probably best understood as an attempt to have one single figure in the narrative voice a divergence of opinion among the nuns. Or perhaps the latter view is the position initially taken by most of the nuns, whereas the compliant acceptance reflects part of the official compromise.

23. *Cullavagga* X; 263–264. Exhortation (*ovāda*) was the special ceremony in which a duly deputed senior monk formally questioned the nuns regarding their observance of the eight special rules for nuns (*garudhammā*) mentioned earlier. Subsequently the number of nuns who could go for exhortation at the same time was further reduced from four or five to two or three. For similar reasons, a rule was also added that monks should not go to the residence of nuns to perform the exhortation.

24. The importance placed on the need to conform to social expectations is underscored further by an intriguing coda appended to the Pali version of our story. Though initially she had accepted all eight of the special rules as readily "as a youth fond of ornaments would accept a garland," Mahāpajāpatī apparently had second thoughts. Later, we are told (*Cullavagga* X; 257), she asked Ānanda to go back to the Buddha to see if he would relent on the first rule regarding seniority, a concession that would have allowed nuns far greater status and prerogatives within the monastic community and one that would thus no doubt have significantly altered the subsequent history of the order of nuns. The reply was negative, not surprisingly, justified on the grounds that such a sexually egalitarian application of seniority was totally unprecedented. If it was not allowed among the other groups of religious wanderers,

as lacking in care as they unquestionably were, how could it be allowed by the Buddha, Ānanda is told. The allusion is no doubt to the Jains, who had split into two irreconcilable factions over the question of whether women could become liberated as women rather than first being reborn as male monks.

25. "Vanishing Nuns," pp. 208–210. A prominent exception to this observation can be seen, however, in the story of the courtesan who becomes a nun reported in the famous sixth-century Tamil epic, the *Maṇimēkalai.* In her excellent study of this tale, Paula Richman argues that it was skillfully composed to present the idea of female renunciation in favorable terms to a Tamil audience having little precedent for or familiarity with this then novel northern Indian religious ideal. Richman's dissertation research on this topic is summarized in "The Portrayal of a Female Renouncer in a Tamil Buddhist Text" in *Gender and Religion.*

26. Cited in the *Śikṣāsamuccaya,* trans. Cecil Bendall and W. H. D. Rouse (Delhi: Motilal Banarsidass, 1971), p. 77.

27. There is some evidence that this account may have been a relatively later addition to the canon, a possibility that would support my view that ascetic misogyny developed later in Buddhism than the attitudes of soteriological inclusiveness and institutional androcentricity.

28. Karen Lang, "Images of Women in Early Buddhism and Christian Gnosticism," *Buddhist-Christian Studies* 2 (1982): 97. The attempt to establish some direct link between Mahāyāna Buddhism and Gnosticism has been a perennial theme in comparative studies of the history of religion, from the publication of Isaac Jacob Schmidt's pamphlet "Über die Verwandtschaft der gnostisch-theosophischen Lehren mit den Religionssystemen des Orients, vorzüglich dem Buddhaismus (sic)" in 1828 up to the more recent efforts of Eliade, Tucci, and Conze; for a useful survey of the as yet inconclusive fruit of these endeavors, see Edward Conze's "Buddhism and Gnosis" in *Further Buddhist Studies,* (Oxford: Cassirer, 1975), pp. 15–32.

29. The most blatantly misogynous texts of the Pali literature are found in the *jātaka* stories, an (originally) noncanonical Buddhist appropriation of popular animal tales and hero legends. This relative (even if not exclusive) contrast between views in the *sutta* literature versus those in the more popular genres further supports my thesis that misogyny initially was resisted by the early tradition, but eventually found more of a home among those later factions of the community who defined their soteriological goals more in terms of ascetic purification than in terms of psychological enlightenment.

30. *T* 310, XI.543–547; trans. in Paul, *Women in Buddhism,* pp. 27–50.

31. See Kajiyama Yuichi, "Women in Buddhism," *The Eastern Buddhist* 15, no. 2 (Autumn 1982): 53–70; and Barnes, "Buddhism," pp. 105–133. In both cases, the criticism is directed in particular toward the depiction of the tradition presented in Diana Paul's *Women in Buddhism.*

32. *T* 310, XI.543; trans. in Paul, ibid., p. 29.

33. Trans. José I. Cabezón in "Women and Illusion: Toward an Aesthetics in Buddhism," a paper presented at the 1987 meeting of the American Academy of Religion, Boston, p. 10.

34. *Prajñāpāramitā-Ratnaguṇasaṃcayagāthā* XII, 1–2; trans. Edward Conze, *The Perfecton of Wisdom in Eight Thousand Lines and Its Verse Summary* (Bolinas, Calif.: Four Seasons Foundation, 1973), p. 31.

35. Joanna Macy, "Perfection of Wisdom: Mother of all Buddhas," *Anima* 3, no. 1 (1977): 75–80; reprinted in *Beyond Androcentrism,* ed. Rita Gross (Missoula, Mont.: Scholars Press, 1977).

36. Ibid., p. 77a.

37. A useful and very accessible introduction to the theme of spiritual androgyny especially as it occurs in the stories of female masters in Vajrayāna may be found in Reginald Ray's chapter on "Accomplished Women in Tantric Buddhism of Medieval India and Tibet" in *Unspoken Worlds,* ed. Falk and Gross. Ray's primary source, the traditional hagiographic songs and histories of the eighty-four siddhas or masters has been now been translated by Keith Dowman in *Masters of the Mahamudra* (Albany: SUNY Press, 1985), and in *Sky Dancer* (London: Routledge & Kegan Paul, 1984) the same translator provides the hagiography of Ye shes 'tsho rgyal, Tibet's most famous *ḍākiṇī* and female Buddha. This latter figure is also the subject of an excellent essay by Anne C. Klein "Nondualism and the Great Bliss Queen" (*Journal of Feminist Studies in Religion* 1, no. 1: 73–98), a study of the philosophic tradition underlying the dynamic, nondualistic masculine-feminine imagery exemplified in the visualization practices of Vajrayāna Buddhism. Further stories of female masters in Tibet are collected in Tsultrim Allione's *Women of Wisdom* (London: Routledge & Kegan Paul, 1984), along with the author's reflections on her own experiential encounter with this tradition as a Western woman practitioner.

38. This important notion that religious symbols are polysemic with regard to the gender of the user or perceiver is the central theme of the cross-cultural studies collected in *Gender and Religion.*

2

The Female Mendicant in Buddhist Srī Laṅkā

Tessa Bartholomeusz

During every full moon celebration (*poya*) in Srī Laṅkā,[1] the Buddhist temples are filled with those who desire to hear discourses from monks and "take" the Eight or Ten Precepts[2] for the duration of the day. No matter how small or remote the temple may be, the compound is gaily decorated, and alive and buzzing with *dhamma* talks, the chanting of *gāthās*, or advice on meditation. The most striking feature of the *poya* celebrations, however, is not the colorful banners draped around the Bo-Tree, nor the candles as they flicker, illuminating the saffron robes of the monk, but the preponderance of women and young girls who flock to the temples clad in white.

In a reminiscence of the picture we have from the Pali Canon, the Buddhist women of contemporary Laṅkā far outnumber men in actively participating in temple life. It thus is a paradox that membership in the *saṃgha* (monastic order) is not available to women in Laṅkā and other Theravāda countries. Yet, even though ordination is presently denied them, it is estimated that 5000 women have donned the ochre robe and assumed the vocation of the clergy.[3] These women are not *bhikkhunīs* (fully ordained members of the *saṃgha*) nor are they *sāmaṇerīs* (novices). They nevertheless exemplify the ancient order of nuns in Laṅkān society.

In this chapter, I will explore the tradition of the female renunciant in Buddhist Laṅkā, linking the classical tradition to living practice. I shall discuss the various movements to restore the tradition, and the gender values they reflect.

Nuns in Ancient Laṅkā

Though at present there are no recognized *bhikkhunīs*[4] in Laṅkā, or in any other Theravāda country, such has not always been the case. In fact, the chronicles of Laṅkā, especially the *Dīpavaṃsa* (fourth century), and the *Mahāvaṃsa* (sixth century), and its later section, the *Cūlavaṃsa* (twelfth century), attest to the prosperous life of the *bhikkhunī — the fully ordained nun. According to the Dīpavaṃsa,* for instance, not only were there *bhikkhunīs* in all parts of the island in ancient days, many of them were extremely gifted in matters pertaining to the *dhamma*: "the *bhikkhunīs,* well versed in the whole of the sacred Scriptures, unconquerable, the resolutions of whose minds were pure, who were firmly grounded in the true faith and *Vinaya* (discipline), came from Rohaṇa together with twenty thousand *bhikkhunīs* honoured by illustrious King Abhaya. They taught the *Vinayapiṭaka* in Anurādhapura."[5] Although the numbers, by comparison to the monks, do not inspire confidence, there must have been many renowned *bhikkhunīs* during the early Anurādhapura period in Laṅkā (300 BCE–500 CE).

The chronicles also record the inception of the *bhikkhunī sāsana* (dispensation) in the island. According to the *Mahāvaṃsa,*[6] the *bhikkhunī saṃgha* was introduced to Laṅkā by Sanghamittā, the daughter of the Indian King Aśoka, and the brother of the monk, Mahinda. Mahinda, who had journeyed to Laṅkā to convert the inhabitants of the island, is said to have introduced the order of monks there in the middle of the third century BCE.

Many flocked to hear the *dhamma* from the Indian *bhikkhu,* including the womenfolk. According to the legend, Queen Anulā, and her retinue of 500 maidens, were the first to attain to the level of *sotāpatti,*[7] having heard the wisdom of the Buddha from Bhikkhu Mahinda.

Mahinda, having arrived in Laṅkā with the quorum of monks needed to initiate a Laṅkān into the *bhikkhu saṃgha,* duly bestowed *pabbajjā* (admission to the order) on a local inhabitant, thereby establishing the *bhikkhu sāsana* in Laṅkā. Queen Anulā and her retinue, similarly desiring initiation into the *saṃgha,* also requested *pabbajjā* from Mahinda. But Mahinda, aware of the Buddha's injunctions, made the following remark: "It is not allowed to us, . . . to bestow the *pabbajjā* on women."[8] He then explained that his sister, Sanghamittā, would be able to initiate the queen into the *saṃgha,* for a quorum of ten *bhikkhunīs,* as well as ten monks was needed to initiate the female candidate. Mahinda dispatched a message to his sister in North India, who began the long journey to Laṅkā with eleven *bhikkhunīs,* also bringing with her a branch from the sacred Bo-Tree.

In the meantime, Queen Anulā and the other women who were desirous of ordination were sequestered on one side of the capital in the *upāsikāvihāra;* that is, the home built especially to accommodate these pious lay women (*upāsikās*). Moreover, while awaiting the arrival of Bhikkhunī Sanghamittā, they accepted the Ten Precepts incumbent on the novitiate and donned the yellow robe of the clergy. Thus, in all respects, the life-style of the Queen and the others was similar to that of the *sāmaṇerī* (female novice), though formal initiation had not been bestowed on them. They remained in this "marginal" state, finding themselves on the boundaries of two groups—the laity and the *saṃgha*—for six months. Upon the arrival of Bhikkhunī Sanghamittā, the queen and her retinue were granted *pabbajjā* and higher ordination. In this way, the *bhikkhunī sāsana* was established in Laṅkā in roughly 250 BCE.

Since that time and until the eleventh century, literary and epigraphical sources suggest that the *bhikkhunīs* of Laṅkā supported Buddhism in many ways and that the institution prospered. According to various inscriptions, the *bhikkhunīs* were responsible not only for teaching the *dhamma,* but for ordinary religious and social duties as well. One inscription suggests that the *bhikkhunīs* nursed the sick in a hospital in Anurādhapura,[9] and Chinese records indicate that they were also involved in missionary activities. According to one such record, Laṅkān *bhikkhunīs* were responsible for introducing the *bhikkhunī saṃgha* in China around 430 CE.[10]

The *Cūlavaṃsa,* the continuation of the Mah*āvaṃsa,* records one of the last literary references to the *bhikkhunī* in ancient Laṅkā. Based on the chronology of history supplied by the *Cūlavaṃsa, bhikkhunīs* can be accounted for up to the end of the tenth century. According to the chronicle, Mahinda IV (956–972) was a patron of the *bhikkhunī saṃgha* and built them a *vihāra* (monastery). In addition to this literary reference, an inscription of the period indicates that King Mahinda IV was responsible for building kitchens and medical halls for the *bhikkhunīs* and for repairing existing structures that belonged to them.[11] The fact that the king was interested in building for the female monastics, and updating their property, suggests that though the historical record of them ends during his reign, their numbers were increasing. However, the occupation of the island by the Cōḷas of South India proved catastrophic for Buddhism in general; during the Cōḷa occupation of the eleventh century, even the *bhikkhu saṃgha* became defunct.

In the year 1070, however, King Vijayabāhu, having succeeded in defeating the Cōḷas, set about restoring Buddhism, which included the restoration of ordination for *bhikkhus.* When he realized that the proper quorum of *bhikkhus* required to confer ordination could not be gathered, he sent a message to the king of Burma who, in turn, sent a delegation of monks to Laṅkā. As a result, higher ordination for monks was restored, and the *bhikkhu saṃgha* began to prosper once again. Unfortunately, no steps were taken to reestablish the *bhikkhunī sāsana,* even though Burmese inscriptions attest that the order of Buddhist nuns continued to thrive there until at least the thirteenth century.[12] The reason for King Vijayabāhu's lack of interest in resuscitating the defunct *bhikkhunī saṃgha* may be found in the Pali Canon, which contains disparate and conflicting models for religious action for women. In fact, even the story of the establishment of the *bhikkhunī saṃgha* by the Buddha has traditionally been interpreted as suggesting that he did not consider the mendicant life-style an appropriate one for women.

Though the Buddha eventually did accede to his foster mother's wishes to become a member of the *saṃgha,* according to the *Vinaya* texts it was not without Ānanda's appeals to the Buddha on her behalf. Whether or not the canonical version of the establishment of the order of nuns is accurate, however, the message of the story is that the Buddha was reluctant to admit women into his *saṃgha.* On the other hand, as the canonical version of the story continues, the Buddha does affirm to Ānanda that women are as capable as men of achieving the soteriological goal of the Buddhist path — *nibbāna.*[13] These conflicting attitudes toward women and renunciation in the canon have doubtlessly contributed to the ambivalent attitude toward the *bhikkhunī saṃgha* since its inception.

Recent studies of ancient and modern noncanonical Theravāda Buddhist texts have indicated that similar ambiguities continue concerning the ideal role for women in South Asian Buddhism. Charles Keyes, in his study of popular Thai texts, has concluded that gender notions derive from the texts that formulate the Buddhist world-view. Based on textual studies, Keyes suggests that Thai culture regards women to be more "natural" than men in their role of supporting the religion: "While a man must reject his 'nature' (that is, his sexuality) in order to pursue the Path, a woman must first realize her 'nature' (becoming a mother) as a prerequisite to her traversing the Path."[14] In other words, it is the religious duty of women to nurture the religion by providing sons for the *saṃgha.* Such a notion, of course, is antithetical to the meaning of renunciation.

In the canonical literature, the image of woman as mother-nurturer and the embodiment of evil is as striking as in the popular Thai texts on which Keyes focuses. For instance, loving kindness — represented by a mother's affection for her child — often is evoked as a paradigm for human relationships.[15] However, images of woman as temptress are equally as prominent. Regarding the image of woman as temptress and the embodiment of evil in the Pali Canon, Lorna Rhodes Amarasingham states:

> In the great tradition, certain meanings are given to women: sensuality, desire and attachment. And since these imply suffering, death, and rebirth, women become images also of the impermanence and inevitable corruption of life. And most importantly, because women embody birth, they become a metaphor for the karmic energy that maintains suffering in the world.[16]

Nevertheless, innumerable statements in the Pali Canon affirm the position of the Buddha; namely, that women are able to realize the liberating goal of the path through renunciation. Contemporary Theravādin Buddhist society, however, holds that the spiritual activities of women should be realized within the role of mother.[17] In short, though one view of the Pali Canon attests to the ability of women to progress along the path, Buddhist society has encouraged a different view of the canon; namely, that women need not renounce family life to be spiritual. Thus, the ambiguous and conflicting images of women found in the canon, linked as they are with religious assumptions, can account for the low priority given to the resuscitation of the *bhikkhunī sāsana* in the eleventh century.

From the late tenth century until the final decades of the nineteenth century, there are no records — literary or epigraphical — to suggest that there were female renunciants of any type in Laṅkā. Toward the turn of the twentieth century, however, during a period of religious revival in Laṅkā, a new trend emerged among the Buddhist laity, the ramifications of which are apparent today. During the latter decades of the nineteenth century, interest in the revival of the tradition of the female Buddhist renunciant in Laṅkā was rejuvenated. To understand this renewed interest, it is necessary to recall the cultural and social milieu in which it was spawned.

Nineteenth Century Laṅkā

Nineteenth century Laṅkā was marked by change, on the one hand, and revival, on the other. The first few years of the nineteenth century witnessed a change in government, which was to have lasting repercussions then unbeknownst to the people of Laṅkā. Unlike the Portuguese and the Dutch before them, the British were able to take control of the entire island and win the support of the people. To accomplish this, the British drafted a "Convention" in 1815 that, among other things, guaranteed the protection of Buddhism in Laṅkā. The Fifth Clause of the Kandyan Convention, dealing specifically with Buddhism, read as follows: "The religion of the Boodhoo professed by the chiefs and the inhabitants of the Provinces is declared inviolate, and its Rites, Ministers, and Places of Worship are to be maintained and protected."[18] In other words, the traditional *saṃgha*-state relationship, which had existed between the king and the clergy since the inception of Buddhism in Laṅkā, was to be upheld by the English governor who, by virtue of the Convention, had assumed the responsibility of the deposed king.

Throughout the history of Buddhism in Laṅkā, the king, as political authority, has acted to ensure that the monks abide by the *Vinaya*, following up on allegations of laxity and corruption. This incursion of political authority into *saṃgha* affairs, or "purification of the *saṃgha*," is evident as early as the Anurādhapura period.[19] According to Laṅkan Buddhist history, it is evident as late as the eighteenth century, when the king sponsored the reestablishment of the higher ordination of male monastics with Siamese help.[20] In fact, all matters of the *saṃgha*, from higher ordination proceedings to the appointment of ecclesiastical office, at one time or another, have been litigated by the king. Such was the backdrop set for the British when they entered the scene in the late 1700s.

In keeping with the terms of the Kandyan Convention, the British eventually took custody of the Tooth Relic of the Buddha, on which the authority of the king had rested since the fourth century, and began to assume the duties of the king with regard to Buddhism. However, after a few decades of state patronage, many of the British in Laṅkā began to resent the involvement of a Christian government in Buddhist affairs and voiced their dissatisfaction to the state.

The sentiments of many of the British living in Laṅkā incited the queen of England to act and, in the 1840s, she directed the government to withdraw from all direct interference in the Buddhists' religious observances.[21] The state's new relationship with Buddhism, or the "disestablishment of Buddhism"[22] in Laṅkā, had far-reaching repercussions, influencing laity and clergy alike. The honor and power to which the chief *bhikkhus* were entitled, by virtue of their office, was no longer enforced by law. As a result, they had to "do their best to assert their authority in relation to their subordinates,"[23] including the laity.

Aside from the crisis experienced by the ecclesiastical establishment, another result of the new policies of the British was that the state no longer performed "purifications" of the religion. Thus, pious monks and laity lost the state as the recourse they traditionally had to rectify *saṃgha* problems. Therefore, when the need arose to purify the *saṃgha,* the laity were forced into a position of having to carry out the task without help from the state.

Purification in the literature[24] can be understood only in the context of the king as the protector and defender of the religion. In spite of the traditional meaning, however, purifications of a sort continued to exist in Laṅkā, even after the fall of the king and the disestablishment of Buddhism by the British. Whether considered in its traditional meaning, or in its broader application, however, *purification* implies not only purging, but restoration and revitalization as well.[25]

After Buddhism was disestablished—that is, after its links with the government were severed—the laity launched massive efforts to breathe new life into the religion in innovative and revolutionary ways. At such a time—when the clergy functioned as a matter of habit[26]—the laity thus were motivated to purify the religion themselves, thereby assuming the responsibility of the state and the *saṃgha.*

This type of purification, the incursion of the laity in monastic affairs, often resulted in the appropriation of the vocation of the clergy by the laity. In fact, donning the robe by pious laity, one of its manifestations, led to interest in the resuscitation of the *bhikkhunī saṃgha.* In other words, the reemergence of the female mendicant around the turn of the twentieth century, after a lapse of several hundred years, came into being as a part of the changes related to the disestablishment of Buddhism, on the one hand, and its revitalization, on the other.

As specific examples of this type of purification of Buddhism in the 1890s illustrate, many lay people assumed the vocation of the monk, thereby blurring the traditional distinction between clergy and laity in Laṅkā. This blurring of the roles of the *bhikkhu* and laity in the 1890s was a preamble to the rise of the unordained "nun" in the twentieth century.

Women and Laṅkān Buddhism in the 1890s

Criticism of the clergy in the latter decades of the nineteenth century abounds in the newspapers and other publications of that era. Among those who voiced their opinions was an ex-monk by the name of Subhodānanda, who advocated a status drawn on the life-style of the clergy, on the one hand, and the laity, on the other. In an 1898 editorial, Subhodānanda admonished people to observe the Ten Precepts of the particularly pious Buddhist and novice monk and to wear the yellow robe while in lay life. Writing from an *upāsakārāmaya,* that is, a monastery (*ārāmaya*) for pious laymen (*upāsakas*), Subhodānanda invokes Queen Anulā's life-style, prior to her ordination, as a suitable one for all Buddhists.[27] To my knowledge, this is the first record, since the days of the *Mahāvaṃsa,* of lay people donning the robe and sequestering themselves in a monastery without changing formal status.[28] By adopting this life-style for himself, Subhodānanda contributed to the blurring of distinction between the laity and clergy.

Those who defied traditional Laṅkān Buddhism, that is, the established *bhikkhu saṃgha,* were not always men; in fact, many of the most interesting figures have been women. Several articles in a Siṅhala biweekly indicate that there were instances of laywomen "going forth from home into homelessness," without changing formal status. Though many of the articles are supportive of such a practice, others are very critical.

An 1899 article, about a laywoman named Jitadharmadūtā Silavatī Upāsikā who kept the Ten Precepts, makes it clear that there were women preachers at the time. Silavatī, who had made a pilgrimage to Anurādhapura from Galle in a rickshaw, was stopping at resthouses and exhorting the crowds.[29] She must have had quite a reputation as a preacher to be invited by persons living as far away as Anurādhapura.

A later article suggests that Silavatī, or someone like her, became the object of attention by at least one writer in 1899. Critical of the appropriation of the monastic vocation by laywomen, the writer makes the following remarks:

> It has been prohibited for *upāsakas* and *upāsikās* who observe the Ten Precepts to don the yellow robes, and attachment to money is also prohibited. In spite of this, I have seen in many places those who observe the Ten Precepts wearing yellow robes, while preaching and collecting money. This *upāsikāwā* [laywoman] collects money at the various places including Colombo in which she preaches. We would like to know what becomes of this money. The answer to the question is that she puts it in the bank in her daughter's name and will use it in the future for an *ārāmaya* [convent]. This lady collects money by preaching in many parts of the country.[30]

Whether critical or simply informative, these sources demonstrate that the idea of the *upāsikā* and *upāsaka* undergoing a change of name, life-style, residence, and appearance, in favor of those traditionally associated with the ordained Buddhist clergy, had been established by the late 1890s.

Other writers from the same period encouraged the laity to assume a more active role in Buddhism by appropriating the life-style of the clergy. One writer introduces the following proposition: "It is no doubt that the producing of pure, knowledgeable *upāsikās* and *upāsakas* will spread the *sāsana* [Buddhist religion] in the world. I don't think anyone would contest this fact. Therefore we should set up schools in the hope of setting up *ārāmayas* [cloisters] of *upāsikās* and *upāsakas.*"[31] The writer, who considered that Buddhism was in need of reform, considered that reform was the responsibility of the laity—pious *upāsikās* and *upāsakas*—both of whom should be trained properly in cloisters. What is strikingly absent from the proposition is the mention of the ordained clergy, who were traditionally held to be responsible for the spread of the Buddhist religion. No longer did the charge of the doctrine lay with the monks.

Another writer condemned the revolutionary activities of men and women who appropriate the vocation of the clergy, but remarks that "it is no doubt that women donning the yellow robes and shaving their heads will at some time establish a *bhikkhunī sāsana*"[32] in Laṅkā. Thus, though it is generally assumed[33] that the first recorded instances of women donning the yellow robe and "going forth" (that is, becoming "nuns") in the modern period are of the early twentieth century, the newspaper articles of the 1890s indicate that such a trend was evident and fairly common a decade earlier.

The editorials, which suggest that robed women with shaved heads were a part of the landscape in Laṅkā during the 1890s, also characterize the period as one in which a great Buddhist revival was underway. This revival, which began as a reaction to the threat of religious and cultural effacement, due to the disestablishment of Buddhism, is unique in that the laity made the largest contribution to its vitality.

The Buddhist-Christian controversies, which began in the 1860s, marked the advent of a new era, one in which the laity, especially, felt it necessary to defend Buddhism against Christianity and the colonial powers that were its purveyors. With the arrival of Colonel Olcott of the American Theosophical Society in 1886, the burgeoning Buddhist revival was given shape and direction.

The main agenda of the Theosophical Society in Laṅkā was the establishment of Buddhist schools on the island. Hundreds of the most elite members of Laṅkā society rallied around the Colonel, and by the end of his first tour of Laṅkā, many schools for boys had been opened.[34] However, few efforts were made to establish Buddhist schools for girls. Yet, with the arrival of the American Countess Canavarro in Colombo in 1897, at the request of the Anagārika Dharmapāla, schools for girls became a part of the agenda of Laṅkā's elite, as did the resuscitation of the *bhikkhunī saṃgha.*

Theosophists, Educators, and Nuns

In the days in which Buddhism flourished in Laṅkā—the period of Laṅkān Buddhist history invoked by the Buddhist Theosophists—the *bhikkhus* and *bhikkhunīs* were depended on to provide a proper religious education.[35] In addition to this historical fact, it was widely held among the Christians and the Buddhists of Laṅkā that women were the supporters of religious life on the island. In the 1888 report of the Wesleyan Mission of Laṅkā, the following remarks are made about women and Buddhism: "the greatest force of Laṅkan Buddhism is not the Bo-Tree, the priesthood, the wealth of temple lands, or even in the sacred books. The dominant force for Buddhism in the Island is Woman."[36] This "dominant force" collected itself into what was eventually to become the Women's Educational Society, the chief aim of which was the following: "to open, as soon as funds are available, an institution at Colombo for the higher education of Siṅhalese girls. . . under European supervision and to establish as many girls' schools as possible in the country.'[37] Interest in the revival of Buddhist education, inasmuch as it focused on the education of young women, naturally led to interest in the revival of the *bhikkhunī saṃgha,* the traditional conveyors of Buddhist education to the female gender in Laṅkā. Such an interest, coupled with the revolutionary appropriation by pious laywomen of the robe and vocation of the clergy, resulted in the first attempt, in recent history, to reestablish the tradition of the female renunciant in Buddhist Laṅkā.

The person who led the movement to revive female mendicancy in Laṅkā during the 1890s was the Anagārika Dharmapāla who, by then, had become the symbol of national and religious pride. Writing in 1897, the Anagārika gives a synopsis of his interest in the Buddhist order of nuns: "In 1890 in the month of July, I believe, I suggested the resuscitation of the *Bhikṣunī* Order in Laṅkā. Seven years later the idea suggests itself again. I wrote to Mr. James Dias of Pandura about it."[38] Contrary to suggestions that "Dharmapāla did not anticipate the recent movement of 'nuns' in Laṅkā,"[39] his diaries and travel articles indicate that he was, indeed, fascinated with the idea of female Buddhist mendicants, and continued to be for decades.[40]

The circumstances of Dharmapāla's renewed interest in the *bhikkhunī saṃgha* in 1897 are fascinating. According to his diary, Dharmapāla's earlier interests were rejuvenated after meeting a colorful American countess in San Francisco, who was just as eager as he to resuscitate the *bhikkhunī* lineage in Laṅkā.

Countess Miranda de Souza Canavarro, a Catholic and the American wife of the Portuguese ambassador to the United States, had spent many years as a keen student of Theosophy and the occult sciences. But it was not until she met Dharmapāla in 1897 that she was able to completely renounce lay life, and immerse herself in the study of Asian religions.[41] At Dharmapāla's request, the Countess became a Buddhist in a public ceremony in New York City on August 30, 1897; and, having renounced husband, wealth, and home, she set sail for Laṅkā the next day.[42] It was planned that together, along with the aid of the Colombo Theosophical Society and the Women's Educational Society, they would not only reestablish a proper Buddhist education for children, but the *bhikkhunī sāsana,* as well.

In fact, writing in June of 1897, prior to the countess's conversion to Buddhism, Dharmapāla wrote the following concerning his plans for their future: "Received under registered cover a long letter from Mrs. Canavarro. . . . Replied to her that there is work to be done in reestablishing the Order of Nuns in the Island."[43] It appears that Dharmapāla had finally found the person who could fulfill his desires of restoring women to their rightful place in Buddhism.

As soon as she arrived in Laṅkā, the Countess began to work diligently for the Theosophical Society, establishing schools for young girls. But more important, however, she and members of the Theosophical Society, as well as the Anagārika's Mahā Bodhi Society, set about trying to find a location for what would be the first *upāsikārāmaya* (house for pious Buddhist laywomen) in recent history.[44]

Though the *upāsikārāmaya* had very auspicious beginnings[45] and was patronized by the local elite,[46] it failed within three years of its inauguration. Nonetheless, it is the first project of its kind in recent history and can be fully documented.[47]

The *upāsikārāmaya,* named after Bhikkhunī Sanghamittā, opened on April 30, 1898. According to its organizer—the Countess Canavarro who later became known as Sister Sanghamittā—the establishment of the *upāsikārāmaya* was a historic event. In a letter written to an American confidant, the countess makes the following claim: "I have established the first Buddhist convent in Laṅkā for 1400 years." She continues with a description of her new order: "liberal views are entertained by the founders, there is freedom from dogmatism, and no vows are given by those who enter, but a desire to give."[48] Though initially the Countess did not envisage that her order of Buddhist "nuns," the Sanghamittā Sisterhood, would be closely regulated, the printed pamphlet of the history of the order suggests that it was.[49] In fact, the pamphlet was a type of *Vinaya,* which not only gives a history of the Sisterhood, but contains its rules as well.

Though the women who resided with Sister Sanghamittā at the *upāsikārāmaya* never became *bhikkhunīs,* photographs of the convent and its residents,[50] as well as the printed account of the Sisterhood[51] and eyewitness accounts,[52] suggest that the members wore the ochre robes of the ordained clergy. In addition to this appropriation of the raiment of the *bhikkhunī,* the members of the order took clerical names,[53] lived cloistered in a convent, and preached the *dhamma.*[54] Thus, Sister Sanghamittā and the Siṅhala, Burgher, and Western women who became "nuns" under her supervision, exemplified the ancient *bhikkhunī saṃgha* in many ways.[55]

The Anagārika Dharmapāla, who founded the convent,[56] later had misgivings about the Countess, who, according to his diaries, claimed to have reestablished the *bhikkhunī sāsana* in Laṅkā. Three years after arriving on the island, the Countess Canavarro departed for America in a cloud of controversy. Though she was not successful in cementing a relationship with her teacher, the Anagārika Dharmapāla, she had nonetheless organized, established, and presided over the first Buddhist "nunnery" in Laṅkā in recent history. Undaunted, however, she continued her career as a Buddhist "nun" in America, while actively participating in the American branch of the Mahā Bodhi Society.[57]

Though an American was the Mother Superior of the Sanghamittā Convent, many Laṅkān women renounced lay life under her tutelage. Moreover, as the newspapers of the 1890s indicate, women like Silavatī "went forth" independent of the Countess's efforts to reestablish the *bhikkhunī sāsana* in Laṅkā. These women, whether students of the Anagārika Dharmapāla and the Countess Canavarro or itinerant mendicants, were all a product of the disestablishment of Buddhism and its concomitant, the Buddhist revival in Laṅkā.

Contrary to the assumption that renewed interest in female monasticism in Laṅkā was an import from Burma,[58] the archival evidence suggests that such was a response to the changing face of Buddhism in Laṅkā toward the turn of the twentieth century. In other words, the appropriation of the life-style and vocation of the clergy by women in the 1890s is a direct result of cultural change in Laṅkā and, therefore, truly Laṅkān.

This first attempt in recent history to reestablish the tradition of female renunciation in Colombo indicates that women, as well as men, contributed to the Buddhist revival in Laṅkā. Moreover, it is clear from the Anagārika's diary entries that he believed the revitalization of the religion could be consummated only if women were restored to their rightful place in Buddhism. His egalitarian views, which shaped the course of the revival in the 1890s, helped give birth to institutionalized female renunciation in the modern period.

The second documentable attempt to reestablish the tradition of female mendicancy in Laṅkā occurred in the hill capital of Kandy in 1907. Not unlike the attempt of the Anagārika and the Countess in 1897, the people involved in the effort in Kandy were also drawn from the affluent and educated classes. In fact, Catherine de Alwis, the organizer of the Kandy *upāsikārāmaya,* which was later renamed after its patron, Lady Edith Blake, was from one of the most affluent families on the island.[59] It is interesting that she, like the Countess Canavarro, was formerly a Christian and converted to Buddhism later in life.

Female Renunciants in Twentieth Century Laṅkā

According to written biographies and oral histories, Catherine de Alwis, swept by the tide of change in Laṅkā, secured for Buddhist women a more active role in the religious arena. Sister Sanghamittā and the Anagārika had attempted to do the same thing a decade earlier, but their efforts focused on the resuscitation of the *bhikkhunī saṃgha,* whereas Catherine's efforts were geared toward the revitalization of the laywoman's role in Buddhism. The following passage, which indicates that Buddhism was in need of reform, describes Sister Sudharmachārī's (Catherine de Alwis's) contribution to the religion: "The *Buddha sāsana* rests upon four beams, viz., the *bhikkhu, bhikkhunī, upāsaka* and *upāsikā.* Out of the four beams, the beam of the *bhikkhunī* has completely collapsed, leaving the *Buddha sāsana* shaking and unstable. It is proper to say that Srī Sudharmacārī Māniyo[60] helped greatly in restoring the beam of *upāsikā* which was on the verge of collapsing."[61] The four "beams," to which the writers refer, are the four categories of worshippers the Buddha describes in the discourses.

Though the dialogues of the Buddha suggest that he may have been reluctant to establish the *bhikkhunī saṃgha,* he nonetheless regarded it as an essential support of the religion. However, Sudharmacārī Māniyo and the organizers of her *ārāmaya* focused on the "*upāsikā* beam"; Sudharmacārī believed that it, like the *bhikkhunī saṃgha* hundreds of years earlier, was on the brink of destruction.

Recalling the days when Buddhism flourished in Laṅkā and using the stories in the *Mahāvaṃsa* as their "charter,"[62] Sudharmachārī's biographers also recall the paradigm of Queen Anulā as the pious laywoman par excellence, though the historical allusions are incorrect:

> It is said that the birth of a great man or great woman will bring about a great renaissance when things all over the world are in decay. During the reign of great kings like King Devānaṃpiyatissa and King Duṭṭhagāmani, the *upāsikārāmaya* which were in the thousands were being destroyed and were existing in name only. At a time like this, the great Sudharmacārī Upāsikā Māniyo built the Srī Sudharmacārī Upāsikārāmaya in Katukele, Kandy. By doing so, she restored the *brahmacāri* [celibate] *upāsikārāmaya* [houses for pious laywomen].[63]

The tradition of elderly women who, having fulfilled their family responsibilities, wear white on a permanent basis while keeping the Eight or Ten Precepts, instead of the Five incumbent upon all Buddhists, has been maintained for centuries in Laṅkā. These elderly women, not unlike all pious Buddhist laywomen, are referred to as *upāsikās*. However, it was not the tradition of the elderly *upāsikā* to which Sudharmacārī was giving new life. Rather, Sudharmacārī, using the *upāsikā* Anulā's life as a paradigm, donned the robe of the clergy, kept the Ten Precepts, and lived cloistered, in spite of having no formal status.[64]

The type of life-style that Sudharmacārī Māniyo believed she was resurrecting—she did not recognize Anulā's status prior to ordination as "liminal"[65]—is symbolized by the raiment she chose. She donned the ochre robe, which symbolized her commitment to the *dhamma*, but her blouse was white, the color associated with the laity. The symbolism is, in many ways, a commentary of her position in Theravāda Buddhist society, a position which can best be described as marginal.[66]

Though her biographies indicate that she intended to revive the *upāsikā* "branch" that, according to the Theravāda Buddhist Canon, includes the moral accumulation of wealth and family responsibility,[67] Sudharmacārī nevertheless helped to broaden the definition of *upāsikā* in Laṅkā. No longer was it reserved for elderly lay women who had withdrawn from social responsibility toward the end of their lives. Rather, *upāsikā* was also used as a designation for those who maintained dual social connections, clergy and laity, but who did not represent either. In other words, Sudharmachārī institutionalized a unique position for women in Laṅkān Buddhist society.

Though Sudharmacārī's "nunnery" was well patronized during its formative years and the life-style she exemplified was considered worthwhile, the contemporary female renunciants of Laṅkā do not share the same prestige. Today, women follow Sudharmacārī's footsteps, shave their heads and don the robes, yet find themselves, in most cases, impoverished. The contemporary female mendicants' lack of membership in the *saṃgha* sends a negative message to the Buddhist society that cares for their material needs, creating economic hardship. Paradoxically, the majority of the female mendicants do not want to be ordained into the *saṃgha* in spite of their plight.

The *upāsikārāmaya* that Sudharmacārī founded in 1907 continues to function today. Within its walls, eight "Mothers of the Ten Precepts" (Siṅhala: *dasa sil mātāvo*) who trace their lineage to Sudharmacārī Upāsikā, preach the *dhamma,* meditate, teach Sunday School, counsel the members of the community, and chant *pirit* (efficacious verses). In short, their function in society is the analogue of the ancient *bhikkhunī.* Nonetheless, like Sudharmacārī, they claim that they do not seek the resuscitation of the *bhikkhunī sāsana,* but an appropriate life-style in which to attain *nibbāna.* Their views are shared by the majority of the 100 *dasa sil mātāvo* whom I interviewed, though others offered alternatives why the resuscitation of the *bhikkhunī saṃgha* is not warranted.

Though most *dasa sil mātāvo* have exchanged their white blouses for ochre colored ones, symbolizing a complete break from lay life, a majority of them do not rally behind scholars and other lay people who are trying to reestablish the order of nuns with the help of the Chinese.[68] Many of them expressed a desire to remain free from the control of the monks, which would be impossible with the advent of the *bhikkhunī saṃgha* in Laṅkā. They relate their autonomy with power, declaring that if they were granted *pabbajjā,* they would lose the independence they have gained by renouncing lay life. In other words, as one *dasa sil mātā* related to me, they would go from "one oppressive situation to another" if they become ordained members of the *saṃgha.*[69]

Due to the Eight Chief Rules that Mahāpajāpatī Gotamī accepted when she established the order of nuns, the *bhikkhunī saṃgha* fell under the control of the monks, a position many of the *dasa sil mātāvo* do not desire for several reasons. They would resent such subjugation, in view of their feeling that they are at least equal to the monks in regard to the purity of their practice. Others claim that the Eight Chief Rules would be undesirable for other reasons. Scholarly *dasa sil mātāvo* suggest that the Buddha never proclaimed them—that they are the addition of the editors of the *Cullavagga.* They argue that a fully enlightened being could not be capable of subordinating the *bhikkhunī,* to the *bhikkhu, saṃgha.* Still others fear that because many of the rules require the *bhikkhunī* to come in close contact with the *bhikkhu,* such might cause the downfall of the religion.

Many *dasa sil mātāvo,* without citing the Eight Chief Rules, simply remark that it is difficult enough to keep the Ten Precepts, much less the 311 *Vinaya* rules incumbent upon the *bhikkhunī.* Others offered that they would accept ordination if it were possible, but in light of the *Vinaya* injunctions concerning ordination, the resuscitation of the Theravādin *bhikkhunī saṃgha* is not feasible. This group agrees with the traditional monks of Laṅkā who claim that it is impossible to revive the order with the help of the Chinese. According to them, the *bhikkhunī sāsana* in China is presently Mahāyāna and, therefore, incompatible with the Buddhism of Laṅkā. These *dasa sil mātāvo* believe that only Buddha Maitreya, who is awaiting in Tuṣita Heaven for rebirth on earth, can restore the order when he takes birth in approximately 2500 years.

However, a few of the *dasa sil mātāvo* whom I interviewed adamantly insisted that they deserve ordination into the *saṃgha*. They argue that because *bhikkhunī* ordination has not been an option for them, they suffer as a result. According to this group of renunciants, their low status in Siṅhala Buddhist society is a direct result of their lack of membership in the *saṃgha*. They claim that, if ordination were bestowed upon them, they would be deemed worthy by society of the same alms as monks. Because a woman cannot enter the *saṃgha*, they, therefore, cannot serve as a "field of merit," the giving to which, according to the canon, reaps merit for the donor. Thus, their socioeconomic struggle can be attributed to their lack of formal status in Theravāda Buddhism. As these renunciants point out, when economically depressed people make donations to the clergy, they choose to support the *bhikkhu saṃgha* that, according to the canon, is the best "field of merit."

On the other hand, though the female renunciants are not as economically secure as the monks, a situation with its roots in the aforementioned doctrinal reasons, they are nevertheless accorded the same respect. This is evinced especially by the language used in reference to them—by monks, laity, and the female mendicants themselves. For instance, the "ordination" of a *dasa sil mātā* is referred to as either *mahaṇa wenna* or *pävidi karanna*, the same terms used for the ordination of a novice monk. In addition, the robes worn by the female mendicants and the monks are both referred to as *civāra*, and the midday meal of both is called *dānaya*. These and other actions on the part of the laity toward the *dasa sil mātāvo* suggest that though they do not serve as a formal "field of merit," they nevertheless provide an attenuated one; recognized as the female counterpart of the *saṃgha*, they are powerful symbols of the Buddha's *dhamma* in Laṅkā.

In wearing the yellow robes and acting in a clerical capacity toward the laity, the *dasa sil mātāvo* represent themselves in the same category as full-fledged members of the *saṃgha*. The laity, in turn, regard them as such, though they are restrained in supporting them fully.[70] Thus, the attitudes of the laity toward the *dasa sil mātā,* in many ways, reflects the Buddha's egalitarian point of view, insofar as he regarded pious women as worthy of veneration as pious men.

On the other hand, the majority of monks whom I interviewed—in Laṅkā, monks carry the authority of religious truth—do not hold the *dasa sil mātāvo* in high esteem, thereby sending a negative message to the community. As it is believed that the monks represent the Buddha himself, their views become authoritative.

Citing the story of the establishment of the *bhikkhunī sāsana* by the Buddha, these monks argue that the "going forth" of women was never encouraged by the Buddha and, therefore, motions to reinstate the *bhikkhunī saṃgha* in Laṅkā are summarily squashed by them.

The attitudes of the conservative monks is best exemplified in the following translation of an "ordination" of a *dasa sil mātā,* which I witnessed recently in Laṅkā.[71] In the text of the speech, the presiding monk, who is the head of the Amarapura Chapter in Laṅkā and thus very powerful, made these subtle remarks:

> At the time of the Buddha, he allowed that if a person demonstrates good qualities, and observes the Three Refuges, that person can become ordained. Even today, Monks are ordained by observing the Three Refuges. Since they have to be abided by properly, there are two ways to observe the Refuges. The first way is marked by pronouncing the Refuges like this: "*Buddhaṅ saraṇaṅ gacchāmi,*" etc.[72] The second way to observe them is by substituting the *n* with an *m* in the following way, "*Buddhaṃ saraṇaṁ gacchāmi,*" etc.[73] The second way is reserved for the Monks, while lay people and *dasa sil mātāvo* must observe the Refuges in the first way. Also when the Ten Precepts are "given," there are two ways to give it. The Precepts are the same, though the way they are chanted is different. *Dasa sil mātāvo* and lay people chant the *gihi* [householder] *dasa sil,* while monks chant the *pävidi* or *pabbajjā* ("going forth") *dasa sil*. . .[74]

Clearly this monk, not unlike the majority of the members of the *saṃgha* in Laṅkā, does not consider the *dasa sil mātāvo* worthy of the rite of passage of male monastics. Nonetheless, the *dasa sil mātāvo* are as active, in the religious life of Laṅkā, as the full-fledged members of the *saṃgha.*

Conclusion

In this article, I have highlighted different attitudes toward the renunciation of women in Srī Laṅkā and suggested that there has not been a single Buddhist attitude in this regard. In the earliest period of

Siṅhala Buddhist history, the chronicles record that not only was ordination bestowed upon women, the renunciant life-style was encouraged as well. In the medieval period of Laṅkān history, however, when the *bhikkhunī saṃgha* was not restored, even though the king resuscitated the order of monks, renunciation is not viewed as a necessary religious role for women. This lack of interest represents one view of women in the canon, the view holding that renunciation is not necessary for the performance of their specific religious duties.

In the modern period, with the "disestablishment of Buddhism" and the concomitant Buddhist revival, the egalitarian view of gender of the early Buddhists once again emerges, and the cause of women becomes paramount with thinkers such as the Anagārika Dharmapāla, and other members of the Theosophical Society. This trend remains until the present day as exemplified by the recent establishment of a separate department in the Ministry of Buddhist Affairs to care for the needs of the *dasa sil mātāvo*.[75]

Contrary to the attitude of the state toward the *dasa sil mātāvo* is the attitude of the traditional clergy. Their views demonstrate how powerful "myth"[76] can be—in this case, the discourses that produce a negative image of women—for creating a world-view. Opposed to these conservative ideas that many of the monks of contemporary Srī Laṅkā entertain, however, is the response of many Theravādin Buddhist monks living abroad. Many Laṅkān monks in America, emphasizing the egalitarian portions of the Pali Canon, have argued recently that Buddhism is as much for women as it is for men. The Venerable Hävanpola Ratnasāra, in a revolutionary event that took place in May 1988, in the Los Angeles Dharma Vijaya Buddhist Vihāra, ordained a Thai woman as a *sāmaṇerī,* in spite of protestations from Srī Laṅkā. Calling on the aid of the Mahāyāna Buddhist community, the monks at the Vihāra ordained Sister Dhammamittā with the necessary quorum of ordained nuns drawn from the Chinese, Korean, and Vietnamese orders. At the conclusion of the ordination, the Venerable Ratnasāra made the following optimistic address to the crowd: "It is both a religious and a human right for an individual to follow the religious path—no one should have the right to interfere or deny that right. The state of women in Buddhism must be viewed afresh. We find no reason to deny ordination to women and decided to open the door for the restoration of the Theravāda *bhikkhunī order* in America."[77] Whether the Venerable Ratnasāra's fellow monks in Srī Laṅkā will be persuaded by his point of view remains to be seen. Yet, in spite of the ongoing debates in the monastic and scholarly communities of Srī Laṅkā concerning ordination for women, the *dasa sil mātāvo* very seldom involve themselves, choosing instead to meditate, teach the *dhamma,* and strive to attain *nibbana.*

Notes

A Fulbright-Hays Doctoral Dissertation Abroad Fellowship, granted for the study of Buddhist nuns in Srī Laṅkā, enabled me to conduct the research on which this article is based. I am grateful to H. L. Seneviratne and Karen Lang for their helpful comments on drafts of this article. In this work, I maintain the convention of using Pali terms when discussing Buddhism in Srī Laṅkā; however, Siṅhala and Sanskrit words will be used when quoting from sources that use them.

1. Srī Laṅkā will be referred to as Laṅkā throughout this paper; though Srī Laṅkā has had many appellations, including Ceylon and Zeylan, Laṅkā is the name used throughout history by the Siṅhala Buddhists themselves and, therefore, will be used here.

2. The Ten Precepts include abstinence from destroying life; abstinence from stealing, abstinence from impurity; abstinence from lying; abstinence from intoxicating liquors; abstinence from eating at inappropriate times; abstinence from dancing, singing, music, and seeing shows; abstinence from using garlands, scents, unguents, and ornaments; abstinence from the use of high beds; and abstinence from gold and silver.

3. Interview with the president of the All Ceylon Buddhist Congress in Colombo, Srī Laṅkā on January 30, 1989. The Ministry of Buddhist Affairs, however, claims that there are fewer female renunciants in Srī Laṅkā—approxmately 3000.

4. Even though several contemporary female mendicants have received the higher ordination from the Mahāyāna Buddhist community, their new status is not recognized by the Theravādin *bhikkus* of Srī Laṅkā. See later.

5. Hermann Oldenberg, trans., *The Dīpavaṃsa* (New Delhi: Asia Educational Services, 1982), p. 205; for the Pali text, see p. 98.

6. See G. P. Malālasekera, *The Pāli Literature of Ceylon* (Colombo: M. D. Gunasena & Co., 1958), pp. 4–8 for a discussion of the value of the Buddhist chronicles in the scholarship of South Asia, and pp. 24–31 for an analysis of the Sanghamittā story.

7. The first of the four Buddhist levels of attainment, commonly referred to as *stream enterer.*

8. Wilhelm Geiger, trans., *The Mahāvaṃsa* (Colombo: Ceylon Government Information Department, 1950), p. 98; for the Pali text, see Wilhelm Geiger, ed., *The Mahāvaṃsa* (London: Luzac and Company, 1958), p. 112 (15.19–23).

9. Don Martino de Zilva Wickremasinghe, ed., *Epigraphia Zeylanica,* vol. 2 (London: Oxford University Press, 1928); see pp. 19–22 for a discussion of the relevant pillar inscription.

10. H. Sylvain Levi, "Chino-Siṅhalese Relations," translated from the French by John R. Seneviratne. *Journal of the Ceylon Branch of the Royal Asiatic Society* 24 (1915–16): 107.

11. Wilhelm Geiger, ed., *The Cūlavaṃsa* (London: Luzac and Company, 1980), p. 154 (LIV.47).

12. Mi Mi Khaing, *The World of Burmese Women* (London: Zed Books, 1984), p. 78. At this time, the proper quorum of *bhikkhunīs* could have been summoned from Thailand to reestablish ordination into the *saṃgha* for women. After the thirteenth century, however, the *bhikkhunī saṃgha* became an impossibility to restore because it had become defunct in all South Asian countries by that time.

13. Max Muller, trans., "The Cullavagga," *Vinaya Texts,* in *Sacred Books of the East,* vol. 19 (Varanasi: Motilal Banarsidass, 1950), p. 322; for the Pali text, see H. Oldenberg, ed., *The Vinaya Piṭakam,* vol. 2 (London: Luzac and Company, 1964), pp. 254, 255.

14. Charles Keyes. "Mother, Mistress, but Never a Monk: Buddhist Notions of Female Gender in Rural Thailand," *American Ethnologist* 11, no. 2 (May 1984): 229. However, Keyes argues that "Thai Buddhist culture does not relegate women to a religiously inferior status relative to men" (p. 223).

15. H. Saddhatissa, trans., *The Sutta Nipāta* (London: Curzon Press, 1985), p. 16 (v. 7); for the Pali text, see Dines Andersen and Helmer Smith, eds. *The Sutta Nipāta* (London: Luzac and Company, 1965), p. 26 (v. 149).

16. Lorna Rhodes Amarasingham, "The Misery of the Embodied: Representations of Women in Sinhalese Myth," in *Women in Ritual and Symbolic Roles,* ed. Judith Hock Smith and Anita Spring (New York: Plenum Press, 1978), p. 104.

17. Keyes, "Mother, Mistress," p. 233. Though Keyes's research focused on Thai culture, this proposition has wider application.

18. Cited in Tennakoon Vimalananda, *The State and Religion in Ceylon since 1815* (Colombo: M. D. Gunasena and Co., 1970), p. 202.

19. S. J. Tambiah, *World Conqueror and World Renouncer* (Cambridge: Cambridge University Press, 1976), pp. 162–178.

20. Ibid., pp. 162–178.

21. Cited in Vimalananda, *State and Religion,* p. 94.

22. Kitsiri Malalgoda, *Buddhism in Siṅhalese Society, 1750–1900: A Study of Religious Revival and Change* (Berkeley: University of California Press, 1976),

p. 125. By *disestablishment,* Malalgoda is referring to the relinquishment of authority in matters regarding Buddhism by the state.

23. Ibid.

24. By literature, I mean not only the texts that record the purifications, but the scholarship that interpreted them (for example, Tambiah, *World Conquerer,* pp. 162–178).

25. For purification as a type of revitalization, see Tambiah, ibid., p. 164, where one of the kings discussed is said to have asked the following: ''Whom should I employ in order to restore the *sāsana*?''

26. See B. G. Gokhale, ''Anagarika Dharmapala: Toward Modernity through Tradition in Ceylon,'' in *Tradition in Theravāda Buddhism,* ed. Bardwell L. Smith (Leiden: E. J. Brill, 1973), p. 30. According to Gokhale, during the mid-1800s, ''the monastic order functioned more as a matter of habit than any conscious aspiration or design.''

27. ''Letter to the Editor,'' *Lakmiṇipahana* (August 6, 1898).

28. See Michael Carrithers, *The Forest Monks of Sri Lanka* (Oxford: Oxford University Press, 1983), pp. 104–116 for a detailed analysis of the movement that Subhodānanda later inspired. However, Carrithers does not mention this phase of Subhodānanda's career nor does he refer to the article.

29. ''Dasa Sil Upāsikāwak,'' *Sarasavisaňdaräsa* (July 14, 1899).

30. ''A Dasasil Upāsikāwak Who Dons Yellow Robes,'' *Sarasavisaňdaräsa* (September 15, 1899).

31. ''Upāsakas, Upāsikās through Buddhist Schools,'' *Sarasavisaňdaräsa* (December 13, 1899).

32. ''Questions Which Should Be Addressed,'' *Sarasavisaňdaräsa* (December 23, 1898).

33. See, for instance Lowell Bloss, ''The Female Renunciants of Sri Lanka,'' *The Journal of the International Association of Buddhist Studies* 10, no. 1 (1987): 7–32; Richard Gombrich and Gananath Obeyesekere, *Buddhism Transformed: Religious Change in Sri Lanka* (Princeton, N.J.: Princeton University Press, 1988), p. 287; and Elizabeth Nissan, ''Recovering Practice: Buddhist Nuns in Sri Lanka,'' *South Asia Research* 4, no. 1 (May 1984): 32–49.

34. Gregory Tillett, *A Biography of Charles Webster Leadbetter* (London: Routledge & Kegan Paul, 1982), p. 49.

35. U. D. Jayasekera, *Early History of Education in Ceylon* (Colombo: Department of Cultural Affairs, 1969), p. 112.

36. ''The Wesleyan Mission Report,'' cited in *The Buddhist* (1889): 295.

37. "A Retrospect and an Appeal," *The Buddhist* (1889): 247.

38. Quoted from the Anagārika Dhamrapāla's diary entry for July 13, 1897. The diaries are in the possession of the Mahā Bodhi Society of Srī Laṅkā, Maligakānda Pāre, Maradāna, Srī Laṅkā. Though not available to the general public, portions of the diary have been printed in various issues of the *Journal of the Mahā Bodhi Society.*

39. See Gombrich and Obeyesekere, *Buddhism Transformed,* p. 287.

40. See H. Dharmapāla, "Burma and Buddhism," *The Buddhist,* (June 26, 1891): 210, for a detailed, eyewitness account by the Anagārika of "nuns" in Burma. Also see his diary entries for 1897–1900, which document the rise and fall of the Sanghamittā Upāsikārāmaya. Later diary entries of the Anagārika, written while in Burma, for example, April 16, 1907, describe his meetings with female renunciants in Rangoon.

41. "Buddha's Fair Pale Convert," *The New York Journal* (August 31, 1897).

42. "Woman Vows to Follow Buddha," *New York Herald* (August 31, 1897).

43. Quoted from the Anagārika's diary entry of June 14, 1897.

44. See the Anagārika's diary entries for October–December, 1897. Also see "Lady Miranda Upāsikā," *Sarasavisaňdaräsa* (October 12, 1897).

45. "The Opening of the House of the Sanghamittā," *Sarasavisaňdaräsa* (May 3, 1898).

46. For instance, D. Baron Jayatillake who founded the YMBA in Colombo was involved in the project. See the Anagārika Dharmapāla's diary entry for December 30, 1898.

47. Space prohibits providing all the details of the history of the Sanghamittā Upāsikārāmaya, though it is fully documented in my dissertation, "Women under the Bo-Tree" (University of Virginia, 1991).

48. Canavarro, Miranda de Souza [Sister Sanghamittā], *Letters to Paul Carus* in the Special Collections–Morris Library, Southern Illinois University at Carbondale. This letter is dated December 1899.

49. See "The Order of the Sanghamittā Buddhist Sisterhood" (Colombo: Clifton Press, 1899). According to the *List of Books Printed in Ceylon* [entry 4334, 1899] 200 copies were published; however, I believe, only one survives.

50. See "A Modern Instance of World Renunciation," *The Open Court* 13, no. 2 (February 1899), pp. 110–115. The Countess Canavarro and the other Buddhist sisters are featured in this American publication. The article is complete with photographs.

51. "The Order of the Sanghamittā Buddhist Sisterhood," p. 3.

52. See "The Donning of the Yellow Robes by Upāsikās," *Sarasavisaňdaräsa* (January 3, 1899), where a columnist writes the following: "I have seen the woman from America, Canavarro Upāsikāwa, donning the yellow robes."

53. The Countess lists the lay and clerical names of four of the members of the her nunnery in "The Order of the Sanghamittā Buddhist Sisterhood," p. 2. One of them is a distant relative of mine.

54. The Siṅhala *Sarasavisaňdaräsa*, owned and operated by the Buddhist Theosophical Society, devoted much space to the Countess and her activities in Ceylon. See, for instance, the February 14, 1899, issue, which characterized her as a great preacher.

55. According to information provided by the pamphlet, there were ten "nuns" at the convent at the date of publication. The communities of four of them can be identified: Sister Sanghamittā and Sister Padmavatī were Americans, whereas Sister Upalavathie and Sister Dhammadinnā, a Siṅhalese and a Burgher, respectively, were Laṅkān.

56. "The Order of the Sanghamittā Buddhist Sisterhood," cover page.

57. See *Letters to Paul Carus*. From among the 150 letters written from Sister Sanghamittā to Paul Carus, a majority of them were written while she was working for the AMBS in Chicago.

58. Gombrich and Obeyesekere, *Buddhism Transformed*, p. 276.

59. Biographical data was collected from the following publications: "Srī Sudharmachārī," in *Sinhala Vīrayo*, ed. V. S. Dharmabhandu (Colombo: S. B. Fernando, 1949), pp. 315–317; "Srī Sudharmachārī Upāsikā Mǟniyan: Her Biography," ed. Srī Sudharmā Society (Kandy: Editor, 1939); "Mahanuwara Katukelle Srī Sudharmā Upāsikārāmaya," ed. Srī Sudharmā Society (Kandy: Editor, n.d.). These sources are available only in Siṅhala.

60. Mother, in Siṅhala; ǟ is pronounced like the *a* in cat.

61. "Srī Sudharmachārī Upāskiā Mǟniyan," p. 1.

62. See Bronislaw Malinowski's definition of myth as charter in *Magic, Science and Religion and Other Essays* [Garden City, N.Y.: Doubleday Anchor Books, 1954], pp. 144–146. Says Malinowski, "the function of myth, briefly, is to strengthen tradition and endow it with a greater value and prestige by tracing it back to a higher, better. . .reality of events."

63. "Srī Sudharmachārī Upāsikā Mǟniyan," p. 1. There is nothing in the chronicles or the epigraphical evidence to suggest that there was ever more than one *upāsikārāmaya* in Ceylon. This, of course, housed Queen Anulā and her retinue of 500 while awaiting the inception of the *bhikkhunī sāsana*.

64. See Edith Blake, ''The Sacred Bo Tree,'' *The Nineteenth Century and After* 74 (July–December 1914): 671; and Edith Blake, ''A Buddhist Nun,'' *The Buddhist Review* 7 (1915): 52, for an early description of Sister Sudharmachārī's life as a nun.

65. See Victor Turner. "The Center Out There: Pilgrim's Goal," *History of Religions* 12, no. 3 (1973): 199. Turner defines liminality as "an interval between two distinctive periods of intensive involvement in structured social existence."

66. By *marginal,* I am referring to Sudharmachārī's dual status as clergy and laity, as well as to the fact that, during the time of her career, very few women donned the ochre robe. Today, however, female renunciants are a common sight in every region of the island, and they clearly are considered clergy by those who support them.

67. See the ''Sigālovāda Suttanta,'' in *Dialogues of the Buddha,* trans. T. W. and C. A. F. Rhys Davids (London: Luzac and Company, 1957), p. 184; for the Pali text, see *The Dīgha Nikāya,* vol. 3, ed. J. Estler Carpenter (London: Luzac and Company, 1960), pp. 180–193.

68. It will be remembered that Laṅkān nuns established the *bhikkhunī sāsana* in China.

69. For more on the relationship among power, independence, and renunciation, see Tessa Bartholomeusz, *Women Under the Bo Tree,* Chapter 8.

70. During the first two decades following independence in 1948, the female mendicant became a prominent feature of the Siṅhala countryside. This trend continues to the present, though many female renunciants intimated that few women these days are showing interest in renouncing lay life. Nonetheless, due to economic hardships that all have faced from the recent turmoil in Laṅkā, the vocation of the *dasa sil mātā* is becoming more mainstream. In short, because it is very expensive to provide *dānaya* to the *saṃgha* in the traditional elaborate style, the laity look to the *dasa sil mātāvo,* rather than the *bhikkhu saṃgha,* to act as a ''field of merit.'' Thus, the *dasa sil mātā* in contemporary Srī Laṅkā society is not a marginal being, but rather provides a mainstream function, vivifying the ancient order of nuns. Though she is not a member of the *saṃgha,* she is effectively Buddhist clergy. For more on the changing status of the *dasa sil mātā* in Lankan society, see Bartholomeusz, ibid., Chapter 8.

71. Ordination of Soma Ranasinghe at Susilaramaya, Maharagama, May 25, 1989.

72. I go for refuge to the Buddha, the *dhamma,* and the *saṃgha.*

73. When chanted deliberately and in unison, the *m* ending of the Pali words resounds more than the *n* ending, and thus has a very dramatic and triumphant effect.

74. Madhihe Panyasee Mahā Thera "gave" Soma the *dasa sil* (the Ten Precepts), having delivered this sermon.

75. Interview with Abhaya Weerakoon, Secretary to the Minister of Buddhist Affairs, November 28, 1988, Colombo, Sri Lanka.

76. See note 62.

77. I would like to thank the Venerable Walpola Piyānanda for lending me the videotape of the ordination and for his hospitality at the Vihāra.

II

Gender and Contemporary Buddhist Culture

3

Buddhism and Abortion in Contemporary Japan: Mizuko Kuyō and the Confrontation with Death

Bardwell Smith

The fact of death is the central human preoccupation. Other preoccupations are often skillful diversions from coping with one's mortality. In Reinhold Niebuhr's words, the human problem is not that we are finite but that we have trouble living with our finitude. To put the matter more directly, the central problem of life is not death but learning how to die. This chapter is about the confrontation with death set within the context of present-day Japan. It deals with the reality of death in the form of abortion, miscarriage, or stillbirth. It is not about abortion or infant death *in general,* but about the experience of mortality in personal terms. In particular, it is about the mother's experiencing of death, whether or not this death has been willed by her. And, it is also about factors within Japanese society that contribute to the dilemma surrounding abortion specifically.

Second, this chapter deals with various Japanese Buddhist reactions to the widespread modern phenomenon of abortion and raises questions about these responses. The primary response to this phenomenon is known as *mizuko kuyō*: *mizuko* meaning water child or children, referring normally to an aborted fetus (induced or spontaneous) but also to stillborn infants and those who died soon after birth. *Kuyō* itself is a memorial service conducted in most cases by Buddhist priests for the spirits of *mizuko* and intended in part as consolation to the mother, as the one most directly affected, but often with other members of the family in mind as well. Understanding the many features of this widespread movement throughout Japan provides one example in the modern period of how diversely Buddhism and gender are found to be interrelated.

Although based on research that began intensively in 1986 and will extend through 1994, this chapter is not primarily a report on that research but an initial attempt to view the contemporary phenomenon of *mizuko kuyō* against a wider socioreligious background in modern Japan. Once the field research, being done collaboratively with Elizabeth Harrison, has been completed, we shall begin to formulate in greater detail our understanding of the diverse ingredients within this movement.[1]

The primary research is of several kinds. It includes extensive interviews with temple priests and women who have experienced the loss of a fetus or child. We have also distributed over 3000 questionnaires to worshippers who have participated in memorial services (*kuyō*) for aborted or stillborn children (*mizuko*). Beyond this, we have access to data being collected on *mizuko kuyō* by sociologists at two major Japanese universities and to more than 1500 questionnaires completed by women at an important temple in Kyoto. Finally, we have collected sizeable amounts of published materials in Japanese that deal with abortion and *mizuko kuyō* directly or seek to relate those to wider social and religious issues of both a contemporary and historical nature. These materials will be analyzed in the projected volume based upon this research.

The General Context

In the *Japanese Journal of Religious Studies,* published by Nanzan University in Nagoya, two articles on *mizuko kuyō* have appeared in recent years, one by Anne Page Brooks (1981) and, in December 1987, a translation of an essay published two years before in Japanese by Hoshino Eiki and Takeda Dōshō.[2] Surprisingly, this is the extent of serious research on the subject yet to appear in English. The article by Anne Brooks is a good overview of the scene. The essay by Hoshino and Takeda is helpful in placing *mizuko kuyō* within the general conceptual framework of Japanese attitudes toward the spirits of the dead, in providing reasonably current statistics on abortions in Japan, and particularly in making careful distinctions between the meaning of abortion or infanticide (*mabiki*) within traditional life in Tokugawa Japan (1603–1867) and the meaning of *mizuko kuyō* today. This paper is addressed to the contemporary scene. Although the differences between traditional and contemporary Japanese social systems are complex, among the major assertions of the Hoshino article is the following: that with the gradual devolution of the traditional family system in modern urban areas the responsibility for abortion, which used to be shared by the local community in Tokugawa or Edo Japan, must now often "be borne in secret completely by the individual."[3]

It is precisely this "broken connection," as Robert Jay Lifton uses the term, that needs examining, not only with respect to earlier family systems and communal forms of support but also compared with former ways of relating death to life.[4] Arising out of his extensive interviews with survivors from several contexts (including Hiroshima, the Chinese cultural revolution, and the Vietnam War), Lifton's studies have focused on the importance and difficulty of grieving, on the process by which one confronts death (or "death equivalents"), and on symbols relating death to the continuity of life.

> Images of death begin to form at birth and continue to exist throughout the life cycle. Much of that imagery consists of death equivalents—image-feelings of separation, disintegration, and stasis. These death equivalents evolve from the first moments of life, and serve as psychic precursors and models for later feelings about actual death. Images of separation, disintegration, and stasis both anticipate actual death imagery and continue to blend and interact with that imagery after its appearance.[5]

Lifton's research makes clear the importance of psychoanalytic studies that take seriously the human life process as well as an individual's feelings, such as anxiety, guilt, rage, and violence, which often accompany the confrontation with death or any of its equivalents. At the same time, his research indicates the equal importance of images of continuity, or life equivalents such as connection, integrity, and movement. Whereas modern existence is frequently the experience of broken connections of various sorts, Lifton believes that life-promoting connections are possible *provided* one confronts and learns to handle factors within human community that resist the facing of death, or death equivalents, such as injustice, collapse of communal order, profound disillusionment, and the like. Lifton's twofold approach (that is, of realism in the face of death equivalents and hope if these are seriously encountered), is central, implicitly, to the theme of this chapter and the issue of Buddhism and gender.

Thus far, no attention has been paid to the implications of these sorts of findings on the widespread modern social and religious phenomenon known as *mizuko kuyō*. This seems ironic, because at the heart of this phenomenon lies both the experience of death and difficulties encountering this death. Lifton's research confirms my own suspicion that the problems experienced with abortion in Japan are not only more serious than often is acknowledged, but that complex factors exist within Japanese society related to abortion which are rarely discussed. It is part of this chapter's purpose to identify some of these.

As is commonly done by the media, one can easily dismiss the phenomenon of *mizuko kuyō* as another form of *shōbai* or business enterprise. Without question, there has been the tendency for it to become commercialized in many circles. Along with this there has been the inclination of some priest-practitioners to capitalize on feelings of guilt and fear that women frequently experience following abortion and to attribute many subsequent personal and family problems to the decision to abort. Our findings also reveal the problematic nature of economic support for many temples, thereby forcing some priests into activities even they may question. The present economic basis of temple support in Japan thus, in our estimation, is an important subject on which careful research needs to be done. As far as we are aware, no systematic studies exist.

But on whatever grounds one can legitimately question certain forms of *mizuko kuyō* practice, one quickly encounters the emotional problems that significant numbers of women attest to following abortions (in some cases years afterward). Our interviews reveal both the diversity of these experiences and the varied ways in which temple priests and sympathetic lay people have responded. The more deeply one looks, the more evident it becomes not only that widespread abortion creates genuine problems within Japanese society but that this society in fact has made it almost inevitable that these problems exist. Whereas problems connected with abortion are hardly unique to Japan, there are peculiar features here that one does not find elsewhere, or in earlier times within Japan. Hoshino and Takeda are right, for instance, in stressing that although early death was common in previous times there are new ingredients in the modern experience: for one thing, the very number of abortions today; for another, the more private nature of the experience and hence the greater emotional burden upon individuals. In Lifton's sense, the experiencing of this death becomes even more difficult within the framework of a vastly broken religious and cosmological world-view. The old connections are more problematic today. And this raises the interesting question as to whether the extraordinary public attention being paid to *mizuko* (whether aborted or stillborn) in Japanese society has arisen partly because the "image" of *mizuko* itself may have become yet another symbol of the broader social sense of disconnection.

The basic thrust of this chapter therefore is to begin raising questions about what lies behind the complex phenomenon of *mizuko kuyō*. First, it will discuss the anomalous situation of birth control in Japan, in which abortion is the most effective of the widely used methods, with the result that the number of abortions is unusually high for a society like Japan. The very lack of significant procreative choices for most Japanese women contributes to the many problems not being adequately faced by the medical profession or other segments of Japanese society. Therefore, the chapter also looks at the emotional needs women frequently have following abortion and asks what these represent. Third, as the *kuyō* or memorial service is the most common response offered by Buddhist temples, its general nature is examined briefly. Furthermore, because ritual and cosmology are necessarily related, the chapter discusses certain forms of traditional Buddhist cosmology, especially the omnipresent Jizō figure and the concept of the six paths (*rokudō*) and asks about the appeal of these ancient ideas within a modern and "broken" era. Finally, the chapter concludes by questioning whether the present Buddhist response addresses itself to certain deeper and often unstated grievances felt by Japanese women. In the context of this discussion other forms of ritual that seek to confront resentment and anger in particular will be mentioned. A concern of this kind is akin to Lifton's conviction that the life-cycle process and the rituals related to it help to create forms of renewal, with social as well as personal meaning, *only* when they address the pervasive experience of broken connections, in Japan or anywhere else.

The Paradox of Abortion: A World of Necessity and Sorrow

To enter the world of abortion is to observe a scene of resolution undermined by doubt, a scene of both conflict and relief. As one perceptive viewer of this world has put it: "This is the heart of the struggle. The quality of life pitted against life. Whichever we choose, we lose. And that, too, is part of being human. That too is the dilemma of abortions."[6] It is no longer surprising to hear American or European women, who have gone through an induced abortion and who affirm a woman's right to do so, express the emotional difficulty of such an experience, even to hear them reliving spiritual or psychic pain for years after the fact. It is clearly more anguishing still to absorb, through miscarriage or stillbirth, the death of a child one wished to have, let alone the death of an older child. Each instance is unique, though support from those who have encountered similar sorrow helps in offsetting isolation. The pain of grieving, inevitably personal, becomes more bearable when it can be shared, when it becomes less private.

In modern Japan the world of abortion is both similar to that of some other countries and very different. Although abortion has been legal in the United States only since 1973, Japan passed the Eugenic Protection Law in 1948 (with revisions in 1949 and 1952), making abortion legally possible for the first time. And yet, approaches to birth control exist here that are radically different than those found in most modern societies. As many studies reveal, there are but three primary methods of birth control practiced in Japan. *One* is the rhythm method, which lacks reliability. The *second* is the condom, which can be reliable if used properly, but this means of contraception frequently keeps the woman in a position of dependence on the male partner. The *third* method is by far the most effective, namely, abortion, thereby setting the stage for widespread emotional unrest—especially when adequate contraceptive alternatives are minimal. It therefore is accurate to say that the procreative choices available to Japanese women are remarkably slight.

Because of fears about side effects, oral contraceptives are not normally available; and because of their reluctance to be fitted by male gynecologists, Japanese women do not commonly use the diaphragm. It is possible that some form of abortificant (preventing the fertilized egg from becoming implanted in the uterus) may be available on the Japanese market in a few years if it proves free of serious side effects. The result would be a considerable lowering of the incidence of abortions and thus should be welcomed. The present conservative estimate of abortions per year is about 1 million, which is twice the officially reported number. More liberal estimates put the figure at close to 1.5 million. At any rate, obstetrician-gynecologists (Ob-Gyns) have a tremendous economic stake in abortions, deriving a large share of their income from this practice. The fewer reported, the less income declared. A clear conflict of interest exists: abortions pay off for the profession.

The most thorough analysis of birth control and abortion in Japan is by Samuel Coleman, *Family Planning in Japanese Society,* the data for which goes through 1976.[7] Although written in English, this study uses primarily Japanese sources along with the author's own research conducted over a period of twenty-eight months in Tokyo. This analysis spells out the inadequacies of family planning methods and sex education in Japan. The consequences of this situation appear not only in the general unavailability of modern contraceptive means but in the continued lack of reliable information provided to men and women regarding safe and effective methods of family planning. "Few private practice Ob-Gyns provide contraceptive counselling and methods for their patients. The most striking omission of this service appears among abortion cases, where contraceptive counselling should be a matter of routine."[8] The topic of sexual relations remains a taboo subject for discussion in most schools and in family circles (even between husband and wife, at least in early stages of marriage, let alone between parents and children). The result is naivete, embarrassment, misinformation, and an alarming rate of unwanted pregnancies within marriage and, increasingly in the past ten years, outside of marriage as well. It is common for women to have had at least two abortions by the time they are forty years old. Coleman speculates about what might alter this picture and believes that change will be prompted only from the bottom up, not from government or from the medical profession (primarily men in this case) with its vested interests.

Other, even more fundamental, differences in the Japanese social and cultural scene compound the problem of whether to keep or abort a pregnancy. It is perhaps true that the average relatively young, politically liberal Japanese professional woman, married or not, might have few qualms about an abortion if she wishes not to have the child. That category of person in Japan, however, is a tiny minority. As is well known, the vast majority of women are family bound, normally getting married in their middle to late twenties. For them, this path is deeply imbedded in their self-image and in social expectations. Within this customary pattern are two children, with a family beginning as soon as possible. For the married woman who does not wish to work full-time, therefore, the issue of abortion is not one she faces at the start. *Before* she is married, however, or *after* her complement of two children, the issue is real. At these times the lack of adequate family planning methods makes abortion a statistical probability if pregnancy occurs. The fact that women often have small procreative choice contributes not only to frustration but to considerable resentment, however diffused or obliquely expressed. Our findings reveal that women, trapped in this fashion, have strong feelings, even if these are seldom voiced in public. Indeed, frustrations mount precisely because so few contexts exist in which to discuss such matters.

At the most basic level, therefore, Japanese women possess insufficient procreative choice. Huge numbers become pregnant against their wishes or because of ignorance of adequate family planning methods. Husbands and wives rarely discuss matters of this kind in ways that help to open up communication on such issues, let alone correct the problem. As a result, women experience considerable frustration, and only after one or two abortions do they begin to assert their needs and rights in this arena. Japanese society does little to help in the areas of family planning and sex education. The medical profession would seem to be notably recreant in its responsibility to serve the needs of women who may neither want to get pregnant nor wish abortion to be their primary option. Often one hears the rationalization that more contraceptive means are not made available because this would simply encourage teenagers to become sexually promiscuous "like their Western counterparts." (Actually, women frequently express the same fear about their husbands: the safer sex becomes, the more he will play around.) As the statistics given in the Hoshino article make clear, the teenage years are one of two age brackets in which there have been sharp increases (almost double) in the number of abortions during the period 1974–1981, which simply means that more unmarried people are having sexual relations but without adequate birth control protection.

A Spectrum of Reactions to the Abortion Experience

Even if a woman favors having an abortion, it does not mean she will go through this experience unscathed. Even with perfect assent she may later, much to her own surprise, encounter feelings of guilt, and if not that, then often a sense of sadness, brought about by something deeper than hormonal adjustments. Thoughts of "what might have been" surface in almost every person. The experience, in other words, is rarely simple relief, as though the object removed were an intruder, with no connection to the woman.

At a still-deeper level is the unexpected awareness that one's need to mourn this loss is very real and not unnatural. This is not simply because Buddhism teaches that human life begins at the instant of conception. Actually, it is more likely the reverse: Buddhism's teaching may be the endorsement of a profoundly human experience, namely, that nothing less than a human life is at issue. One question revolves around the symbolic nature of what are called *mizuko,* for in the case of *mizuko* there is obviously a fundamental inversion of the typical and expected sequence in the ancestor-descendent continuity. A child here dies before its parents. This naturally raises religious questions in Buddhism about what happens to the *mizuko,* as well as psychological questions as to how one experiences the loss, how one grieves. Even this prospective experiencing of family bond becomes an avenue for discovering hidden connections in life (in Lifton's sense) and a source of deep meaning. If so, whenever ambivalence exists in the decision to abort, mourning becomes the acknowledgement that something of consequence has occurred, that one is never quite the same again. It is therefore to acknowledge death, even a death which one has willed. Once more, therefore, in the words of Magda Denes, "That. . . is the dilemma of abortions."

At a still more painful psychic and spiritual level, there is the encountering of a reality so filled with sorrow that much deeper healing is required. One experiences a rupture or brokenness that tears at one's inner nature. Many Japanese words convey this quality of affliction: *nayami, kurushimi* and *modae,* each of which suggests anguish, ache, torment, agony. Perhaps the most appropriate term would be *kumon,* incorporating the Japanese *kanji* of *kurushimi* and *modae,* doubling their intensity. An apt Western equivalent might be Kierkegaard's "sickness unto death"; that is, a form of spiritual malaise for which there is no remedy without cost. There remains only the possibility of healing through deep suffering.

The earliest Buddhist example of this may be the story of Kisa Gotami who lost her only child, a young son. Her grief was such that she could not face the reality and refused to bury the child. Days ensued and the neighbors became alarmed, urging her to visit the Buddha. Although sympathetic, he advised her to make the rounds of each house in the village, requesting a grain of mustard seed from any family where death had not occurred. At the day's end she returned, with no mustard seeds. The universality of pain suddenly hit her. In Lifton's sense, she had in some authentic way confronted mortality itself. She could then bury her son and, although continuing to mourn his passing, became able to release her attachment to grief. As this happened, her own capacity for compassion emerged.

It is appropriate now to provide some sense of what the Buddhist memorial service called *mizuko kuyō* entails. To begin with, the term *kuyō* literally means "to offer and nourish." In this sense, it is the offering up of prayers for the nourishment of the spirit of the aborted or stillborn child. Also, as mentioned earlier, it is intended to console the parents, especially the mother, though not infrequently one finds fathers coming with the mother or even by themselves. This service may take place once, or once every month, or it may occur annually on the anniversary of death. Also, one may request a private service or include one's suffering with a service for many *mizuko.* This latter is more common. As one would expect, in Japanese Buddhism, because of the sectarian variety, there is no one pattern to this service. And, because the very existence of a memorial service for an unborn child had no precedent until the past three decades in Japan, one finds considerable variation in content and emphasis. Although debate occurs in denominational circles among priests about all aspects of the *mizuko kuyō* phenomenon and about the service in particular, no official stated policy exists nor any recommended form of service.

On the other hand, the number of common elements are significant, as the general pattern that is followed bears some resemblance to what is used in regular services for the recent dead and even more to the memorial services for ancestors known as *senzo kuyō*. In general, priests conduct the service on behalf of those requesting it and face the altar during most of the service. At the beginning, the names of one or more forms of the Buddha and various bodhisattvas are invoked. Parts of several Mahāyāna *sūtras* are chanted, often including the *Heart Sūtra* (*Hannya-shin-gyō*) or the *Kannon Sūtra* (or *Kanzeon Bosatsu Fumon-bon* from the *Lotus Sūtra*), as well as selected *wasan* or songs of praise in behalf of figures such as Jizō Bosatsu. Frequently, the congregation joins in this chanting, but not always. Central to these services is the offering of light, food, flowers, and incense to the Buddha in behalf of the child and as tokens of the larger offering of one's life. In most cases, some sculpted representation of Jizō or of an infant symbolizing a *mizuko* is bought by the family and left in a specially designated place within the temple grounds. Quite frequently a *kaimyō,* or posthumous Buddhist name, is given the child; and this is inscribed on an *ihai* or mortuary tablet, which is left in a special chapel within the temple or taken home and placed in the family *butsudan,* or Buddhist shrine.

Clearly much more is involved in the memorial and grieving process than the externals of ritual. Often, for instance, a sermon is given, which tries to put the experience of those who attend into a wider human and Buddhist context. Furthermore, normally, a certain amount of counseling precedes and also may follow the service. In some cases there may be contact with other women who have already gone through a similar experience. On the other hand, for reasons of privacy, it is common for people to have these services performed at a temple where their identity is not known. Again, this supports the claim made by the Hoshino article that here we are dealing with a phenomenon in which there often is little, if any, communal support.

To provide another example both of the sorrow of losing one's child and of a *kuyō* in the child's behalf, a look at a well-known Noh play, *Sumidagawa,* is instructive. Written by Jūrō Motomasa (1395–1459), son of Zeami Motokiyo, this play is in the genre called *kyōjo-mono* or "mad woman" piece. The scene is set at the banks of the Sumida River in what is now Tokyo. A ferryman is about to take an unnamed traveler to the other shore when an obviously distraught woman appears, also seeking passage across. Unknown to the others, she is the widow of Lord Yoshida of Kita-Shirakawa in Kyoto and the mother of a twelve-year old boy who was abducted the year before by a srave trader. Ever since, she has searched with "frenzied longing" for her lost son, Umewaka-maru. As the boat makes its way across, the woman divulges her mission, and the ferryman realizes that she is the mother of the boy whose death anniversary is just then being memorialized on the opposite shore by villagers who remember well his valor in the face of sudden illness and death.

One needs to see this play to appreciate the emotion portrayed by the mother as she takes part in the memorial service for her son.

> Before the mother's eyes the son appears
> And fades away
> As does the phantom broomtree.
> In this grief-laden world
> Such is the course of human life...
> Now eyes see how fleeting is this life.

On stage, the ghost of Umewaka-maru emerges from the burial mound, disappears, and reappears again. Each time the mother tries to touch him, but she cannot cross the boundary of life and death. The child speaks to her and echoes the villagers' chanting of the *nembutsu*. She reaches for his hand again.

> The vision fades and reappears
> And stronger grows her yearning.
> Day breaks in the eastern sky.
> The ghost has vanished;
> What seemed her boy is but a grassy mound
> Lost on the wide, desolate moor.
> Sadness and tender pity fill all hearts...

One is struck by how effectively the play creates in the viewer genuine feelings of loss and grief. The play not only incorporates a *kuyō* service but in a dramatic sense becomes one itself. By its very length on stage it draws out these feelings of grief in extended catharsis. The tragedy of the child's death remains, but of central importance is the way in which this has been faced in full, not glossed over or denied. A grief not encountered is a grief denied, and one thereby retains the "frenzied longing" in one guise or another. Only through realizing that the apparition is a ghost can she begin to accept his death and regain her sanity.

Confrontation with Death and Death Equivalents

Alongside the direct encounter with grief is the necessity of confronting feelings such as anger, guilt, or despair which frequently accompany the experience of another's death. For, as Lifton's research makes evident, these feelings may derive from significant exposure to what he calls *death equivalents;* that is, the sense of profound separation, fragmentation, and immobility or stasis. Sigmund Freud, in his rich essay "Mourning and Melancholia," makes a related point in distinguishing between two conditions whose symptoms often appear alike. "In mourning it is the world which has become poor and empty; in melancholia it is the ego itself. The patient represents his ego to us as worthless, incapable of any achievement and morally despicable."[9] As Freud knew, a gradation exists between these, not a sharp line. The clearest distinction is that the symptoms of mourning fade in time whereas the low esteem of melancholia persists. Freud also observed that in melancholia is a strong ambivalence toward the person who has died; an inner struggle occurs "in which love and hate contend with each other." Indeed, he correlates "obsessional self-reproach" with this ambivalence, regarding it as "the motive force of the conflict."

With Freud's thesis in mind it is reasonable to suggest that women who become pregnant against their wishes and who may also feel guilty over having to abort are prime candidates for a type of inner conflict that includes not only diffused resentment but self-reproach as well. This combination of repressed anger, guilt, and diminished self-esteem has many ramifications in the lives of women. This is not to imply that they are caused mainly by the problems over birth control and abortion. If anything, it is the reverse, namely, that problems arising there are attributable to less than satisfying relationships between men and women in so many areas of Japanese social life. The literature on women and the Japanese family is filled with portrayals of tensions within the home. The reality may be better or worse than the image, but it is certain that the widely read novels of Enchi Fumiko, Ariyoshi Sawako, and other women writers present a bleak picture.[10] In them one finds vivid portrayals of the kind of fragmentation and disconnectedness Lifton cites as death equivalents. Although the absence of realistic procreative choices discussed earlier, often leading to the necessity of abortion, is sufficient cause for frustration, the deeper causes are rooted within the whole social structure in which women have little opportunity to participate in the decision making that affects important areas of their lives. It must be acknowledged that Japan is hardly alone in this, as the women's movement, in its various forms throughout the world, makes clear.

A recent anthropological study by Takie Sugiyama Lebra, *Japanese Women: Constraint and Fulfillment,* provides a view different but not opposed to that of the Japanese women novelists just mentioned.[11] Her discussion of the well-known phenomenon of the close mother-child relationship is pertinent here. Referring to the mother's existence as filiocentric, in which she tends "to see a mirror image of herself in the child," Lebra calls the relationship one of "double identity" (herself and the child as one entity).[12] The most vivid expression of this relationship is suggested by the term *ikigai,* or that which is worth living for. In this case, the mother's worth is inherently related to her child. On one level this can mean genuine caring; on another level it suggests preoccupation, which is the usual connotation. What I am proposing here is that a correlation may exist between this heavy investment of self-esteem in her child and the ambivalence and dissatisfaction so many women feel (even if rarely expressed publicly) about their situation within Japanese society in general and their subjection to frequent abortion in particular. It would not be surprising if considerable melancholia (in Freud's sense) were present in the psyche of Japanese women, arising from a high level of ambivalence about their status in a male-governed society, a situation in which they develop various strategies to compensate for a sense of relative powerlessness. If so, Japanese women would not be alone, but they may have devised unique ways of approaching their dilemma. In another paper I have discussed this subject.[13]

At this point I turn to the concept of *redressive ritual,* as one means of confronting situations of frustration caused by broken connections of one sort or another. My thesis is that rituals of this kind can assist in providing imagery not only of death and death equivalents but also imagery of life's continuity, as Lifton uses these terms. In the process, people are assisted to confront threatening situations or broken connections both more deeply and more constructively.

In his last few years the anthropologist Victor Turner wrote at length on the topic of performative ritual and its relation to four phases of social drama (breach, crisis, redressive action, and outcome). His basic assumption is that society and social dramas are combative, filled with conflict, "agonistic," yet not yet settled, indeterminate.[14] Breach and crisis are chronic possibilities, not exceptional circumstances. The third phase, redress, implies the possibility of encountering conflict and moving through and beyond it, either to resolution or to recognition of stalemate. Although the latter may be unsatisfactory, it is at least honest. The phase of redress "reveals that 'determining' and 'fixing' are indeed processes, not permanent states or givens. . . .

Indeterminacy should not be regarded as...negation, emptiness, privation. Rather it is potentiality, the possibility of becoming. From this point of view social being is finitude, limitation, constraint."[15] Turner sees ritual (and theater) as able "to mediate between the formed and the indeterminate" for these especially entertain the subjunctive mood, thus employing a serious engagement of new visions of reality.

There is a distinct similarity between the Turner thesis of ritual's potential within conflictive situations and Lifton's psychoanalytically based research into how one copes with life's broken connections. In both, there is the recognition of the commonness of conflict and of situations of fragmentation. In both, there is the stress on encountering these and learning how to experience them anew. In Lifton's words, there is a "three-stage process available to the survivor of actual or symbolic death encounter, consisting of confrontation, reordering, and renewal."[16] Within the second of these stages one discovers the possibility of "converting static to animating forms of guilt" or anger or despair. Using an anthropological approach, Victor Turner elaborates a theory of the therapeutic nature of "rituals of affliction" (as distinguished from the "prophylactic rituals" of life crises and seasonal festivals) and thereby takes his notion of redress a step further. Central to rituals of this kind is "divination into the hidden causes of misfortune, conflict, and illness (all of which in tribal societies are intimately interconnected and thought to be caused by the invisible actions of spirits, deities, witches, or sorcerers)," along with curative rituals that seek to move the afflicted person through and beyond the causes of this affliction.[17] As Turner well knew, these phenomena were not limited to tribal societies, and he had plans to study their presence in Japanese life before he died.

One could place *mizuko kuyō* precisely in the genre of rituals of affliction, for the sources of anguish are not only within each person's experience but within a larger cultural and social environment. Again and again, our research reveals how frequently women in Japan, in seeking explanations for repeated illness, financial troubles, or tensions within the family, begin to attribute these to an earlier experience of abortion. This search for causation is entirely understandable and analogous to Western explanation of evil from Job to Camus (questions of theodicy). One is struck, however, by how often abortion is cited as the cause for personal and social misfortune in Japan today. The simplest form of this is to view such misfortune as the punishment or evil spell (*tatari*) caused by the spirit of an aborted child. As the Hoshino and Takeda article states, "In traditional society the spirits of the children were not considered as possible purveyors of a curse, whereas in contemporary society the spirits of children are considered as the same as the spirit of an adult, and thus have the potential for casting a curse."[18] Although this is but *one* way of explaining the diverse phenomenon of *mizuko kuyō*, it is a common explanation offered by some proponents and cited by most critics.

It is our judgment, however, that behind the attribution of misfortune to abortion is a much larger issue, namely, the attempt to understand what underlies the confusions and fragmentation of a culture whose connections with its past are simultaneously broken and yet in many ways still alive. For this reason one needs to look at the forms of ritual and cosmology that are resorted to repeatedly in Buddhist temples and to ask whether these are potentially means of enabling men and women to confront the deeper and more systematic causes of what Lifton means by death equivalents. One problem, of course, is that in the modern period men and women live with several, often conflicting world-views. On the other hand, world-views are always in process and traditional forms of cosmology and ritualistic expression respond in various ways to newly experienced human needs. This is again to put the anguish so often experienced after abortion into a larger cultural framework and to seek for more complex factors behind this widespread phenomenon.

Paths to Healing through Cosmology and Rituals of Affliction

In an essay on Thai Buddhist healing, Stanley Tambiah discusses the inevitable relationship between ritual and cosmology. "In the rituals we see cosmology in action. Ritual is symbolic action that has a telic or instrumental purpose—to effect a change of state. The cosmology and ritual are closely connected because the cosmological concepts and categories are translatable into an action medium that employs symbols of various kinds—verbal, visual, auditory, graphic, tactile, alimentary, and so on."[19] To anyone familiar with Japanese Buddhist ritual that will be an apt description. Of particular importance here is ritual's instrumental purpose in effecting a change of state. In the case of some worshippers, the cosmological symbols as experienced in a ritual setting will be taken with a certain literalness. The ritual state is the real state. For most, the symbols will refer to something else, imperfectly understood but also real in some sense. For any one, their meaning in an age of broken connection becomes problematic. And yet, this happens frequently in history.

Within all forms of Buddhism, for instance, both Theravāda and Mahāyāna, there is reference to the six worlds or paths or destinies known as *rokudō* in Japan. These are paths within the realm of desire (the ego world), far removed spiritually from the realms of buddhas and bodhisattvas, and are composed of six graduated levels: the world of gods or heavenly beings, humans, *asuras* (warlike spirits who can also protect the Buddha Dharma), animals, hungry ghosts, and those who inhabit the many hells. Even if not taken literally as places, their meaning is metaphorically symbolic of real states of existence which all beings experience in one way or another. In the language of Japanese proverbs: "the Six Roads are right before your eyes"; "Hell and Heaven are in the hearts of man"; and "there is no fence to the Three Realms, no neighborhood to the Six Roads" (meaning "beyond there is only *nirvāṇa;* and short of that there is nowhere to escape"). In modern parlance, Sartre's play *No Exit* or Arthur Miller's *Death of a Salesman* might serve to convey analogous visions of entrapment, the central difference being that none of the six worlds or paths is a permanent place of residence. Each person is reborn or finds himself or herself in one or another because of previous karma, remaining a pilgrim in these realms until all sense of a separate independent self (what the French call *la moi,* the idea of "me") is extinguished. Because progress along these paths is slow and arduous, Buddhism provides symbols of hope and sources of grace. Foremost among the bodhisattvas who have vowed never to rest until all beings are rescued are Kannon and Jizō. Because Jizō is especially central to *mizuko kuyō* he will be singled out here.[20]

Jizō is omnipresent in Japan, from now-deserted but once-used mountain trails, to crossroads throughout the land, to tiny neighborhood shrines, to chapels and main altars in larger temples. He is the foremost protector of children, particularly those who have died early. As such, he is intimately identified with those who have been aborted, who never came into this realm of existence. Jizō Bosatsu is therefore the single most important figure in the drama of young children, infants, and unborn fetuses in Japanese Buddhist cosmology, and in ritual related to this. He is known as *migawari,* one who suffers in behalf of others, one who can transform his shape infinitely to rescue those in dire straits. He is the only bodhisattva who is associated with all six worlds, being present in each simultaneously, though he identifies especially with those in the three unhappy conditions (*san-akudō*): the realms for animals, hungry ghosts, and those in hell.

In other words, Jizō identifies with those in any kind of suffering. He is an apt paradigm for worlds where strife, discouragement, and passion reign. In such a world he represents the possibility of hope; he is the epitome of compassion in a realm where this is rare. In Turner's language he is the liminal figure par excellence; he is the androgyne who represents male and female equally. He is in the midst of life and death, present symbolically in the womb and tomb alike. Moreover, he is the alternative to chaos, but challenges all forms of order implicitly by his compassion, settling for nothing less than rescue from defeat and ultimate liberation. He thus is both antistructure *and* the hope for communitas (in Turner's words) beyond all present structures. In Lifton's sense, Jizō assists in the confrontation of death and death equivalents. Serene in appearance, he nonetheless confronts demonic and other forms of hellish experience.

He is thus potentially a symbol toward which all redressive action points. Within pan-Buddhist cosmology he is said to be the connecting link between Gotama (the last historical buddha) and Maitreya (*Miroku*), the buddha to be. This in-between age typically is depicted in Buddhism as one devoid of buddhas. It therefore epitomizes a time of broken connection; it is separation, disintegration, and stasis per se. It is the time once called *mappō,* the last days of the law, when conditions worsen, when hope seems impossible, and skillful means of rescue have powerful attraction. For these many reasons, Jizō's symbolic importance to the believer is clear. *Mizuko kuyō* needs to be viewed partially within this cosmological context, ancient but still alive. On the other hand, these are the words of conventional piety, and they may not reach those whose sense of broken connection is more than personal and who view the disorder of the modern world with greater seriousness.

As one seeks to understand a phenomenon as widespread and complex as this, is it possible that the Jizō and *mizuko* figures can be viewed as opposite yet virtually inseparable symbols at this point? And, in their dialectical relationship as life-death paradigms respectively? If Jizō is clearly the salvific boundary figure between all forms of life and death, one symbolic meaning of *mizuko* lies in its representation of radical isolation, a figure with no connection to anything living or dead, one whose ''spirit'' remains in limbo unless freed ritualistically to reenter, to be reborn within this world.

A traditional term in Japanese Buddhism for someone who has died without relatives is *muenbotoke,* one who has lived but who dies with no connections. This term was used for anyone who died without descendents to make offerings for his or her spirit. It was regarded as the ultimate desolation and also as a potentially dangerous circumstance because the person's spirit had not finally been put to rest.

Its very restlessness was highly threatening, a concept that has been pervasive throughout East Asia, as well as elsewhere, since ancient days. As Emiko Ohnuki-Tierney has expressed it: "The freshly dead hover at the margin of culture and nature, the point at which the latter threatens the former...the world of the ancestors and the world of the living."[21] They therefore are in a condition of limbo, which always has been seen as both polluting and dangerous to the Japanese. Whereas it would be too simple to equate the *mizuko* with the *muenbotoke,* there is a sense in which they are genuinely homologous. Each represents a radical disconnection from its origins, and the departed spirit of each has not received proper treatment in the ancestral tradition. Indeed, in the case of the *mizuko* the point is precisely to put them *into* the ancestral lineage. It is also the function of ritual to assist in the process of transforming potentially malevolent or demonic forces into ones capable of being protective and benevolent to the living. In the classical Buddhist sense, all mortuary ritual has this continuing transformation as central to its purpose.

It is but one step of the imagination to propose further that the condition of *muen,* or not-relatedness, is a pervasive experience in the modern world and certainly within Japan. In this vein, the symbolic power of the *mizuko* or the *muenbotoke* lies in the fact that they are not metaphors abstracted from living human existence, but indicators of what that existence commonly experiences. Perhaps only in this sense can one come to understand the rather extraordinary preoccupation with abortion manifested by so many Japanese women and with the various ways to encounter the meaning of this experience (as illustrated in *mizuko kuyō*). Further, this may also help one to understand the immense weight put upon the mother-child relationship, in which the average woman seeks to find her deepest identity. Without disparaging this bond, it is ironically a tie that tends to undermine the sense of wider, more corporate relationships with others within a pluralistic world. The price paid for forging a relationship so potentially narcissistic is not only that it may backfire (in cases of failure) but also that it fails to encourage broader, transpersonal bonds across lines of social difference. In other words, its very limited nature contributes paradoxically to the world of broken connection instead of helping to heal this condition in more basic ways. The current privatism of urban Japanese family life may be an attempt to construct connections of a closely personal sort, but most evidence suggests that this is rarely the outcome, either for parents or for children, and that it serves primarily to increase the sense of brokenness and isolation from a larger social fabric.

This, of course, is what Lifton is arguing on a more general level, and what he means by the term *broken connection.* His discussion of this condition is on many levels. Fundamentally, it deals with images of death and life and the symbolically broken connection between them. "Much more elusive is the psychological relationship between the phenomenon of death and the flow of life. Psychological theory has tended either to neglect death or to render it a kind of foreign body, to separate death from the general motivations of life. Or else a previous deathless cosmology is replaced by one so dominated by death as to be virtually lifeless."[22] It would be gratuitous to claim that a condition of nonrelatedness is the only experience men and women have in Japan or anywhere else. In fact, one might observe the very high premium put on relationships, especially close emotional relationships, in modern society. Again, there are innumerable forms of this within Japan. Yet it would be plausible to say that this emphasis exists, to a significant degree, precisely because so many of the old connections in traditional societies lack compelling power. This is not to romanticize these connections, but, in Lifton's words, "something has gone seriously wrong with everyone's images and models."[23]

In our research on *mizuko kuyō* we have come to realize that what is of central importance in any analysis of nonrelatedness or broken connection in Japan is the steady deterioration of traditional ancestral bonds. This cannot be overemphasized. Although these still exist in many forms and in certain circumstances they remain powerful, they are not strong enough to offset the more powerful experience of a people's increasing deracination from its past. Again, this phenomenon is worldwide. Half a century ago Walter Lippmann labeled this process as *the acids of modernity.* This is not to suggest that new forms of ancient traditions are not possible, only that the condition of disconnection is extreme. At the core of his research on survivors in many important contexts Lifton has observed a factor that has no precedent in history and that certainly affects the Japanese mind deeply, more so than that of any other people except perhaps the Jewish community (because of the Holocaust experience). The following words are telling:

> The broken connection exists in the tissues of our mental life. It has to do with a very new historical—one could also say evolutionary—relationship to death. We are haunted by the image of exterminating ourselves as a species by means of our technology. Contemplating that image as students of human nature, we become acutely aware that we have never come to terms with our "ordinary"—that is, prenuclear—relationship to death and life-continuity. We seem to require this ill-begotten imagery of extinction to prod us toward examining what we have steadfastly avoided.[24]

I wish to conclude this section by suggesting that many ingredients within the Japanese world-view are potential catalysts in this confrontation with both death and its equivalents and with the continuity of life and its equivalents. If the imagery of benevolent grace is powerfully expressed within Japanese religions, so too is the dark side of human existence with imagery of fury and malevolence. Although scarcely unique in this respect, the Japanese consciousness has managed to keep alive (whether in traditional or modern form) the awareness that these elements within the human and nonhuman scene (in worlds visible and invisible) are constants within psychic and spiritual existence. Japanese art and mythology are rich in depicting demons (*oni*), ghosts (*yurei*), raging deities (*araburu kami*), ferocious guardians at temple gates, and menacing divinities like Fudō-san who epitomizes sternness in the face of evil. In fact, Jizō and Fudō are often seen as complementary figures, two seemingly opposite forms of encountering tough reality. At least two features about these "dark" portrayals of the spirit world are central. First, they attest to the ambiguity of all existence, which clearly can be malevolent but is not *inherently* so. And second, intrinsic to all Buddhist mythology is a transformationist motif, meaning that (for those who seek wisdom and compassion) the most malign of forces can be transmuted into benevolent protective figures. Metaphorically, all of these forces suggest an august realism about the basic Japanese world-view; that is, an absence of sentimentality about the destructive potential within all existence, and at the same time, a basis for believing that even the most painful forms of nonrelatedness or separation are not the final or deepest expression of human experience. The key question here, of course, is how this might relate to the issue of abortion in modern Japanese society.

Redressive Ritual and Social Disorder: A Concluding Paradigm

If the symbols of *mizuko* and *muenbotoke* have a homologous relationship, and if these represent human experience in some universal sense, then the question naturally arises of how ritual in particular can assist persons and communities to confront obstacles to the possibility of transformation and renewal. When one considers the full ritualistic process, as Arnold van Gennep did in his classic work *The Rites of Passage* (1909), one typically sees it as a movement from symbols of discontinuity to those of transition to those of continuity (or reincorporation).[25] In this final section my focus is on the first phase only, in part because I see it as crucial to the others and as frequently neglected in much modern expression of ritual. I have in mind *mizuko kuyō* in particular, for I also believe this same ritual has the potential to effectively help persons to face forms of *social* disconnection as well as the inner anguish they may feel personally after having lost a child or experienced deeply negative feelings following abortion.

For this purpose I return to Turner's idea of redressive ritual as one way to understand the deeper potential of a phenomenon such as *mizuko kuyō*. Central to any redressive ritual is its attempt to "include divination into the hidden causes of misfortune, conflict, and illness."[26] It is one thing to settle for the same explanation for all personal turmoil or family problems (attributing these to "vengeful spirits"), and it is another to allow for, even to smoke out, multiple interpretations. In the case of *mizuko kuyō* a major problem is to get society to conceive of a wider diagnosis. To pursue this wider diagnosis is to encounter the complexity of real existence. As Victor Turner writes, this openness to plural interpretation is evident "in ritual procedures, from divination to shamanistic or liturgical curative action, in which many invisible causes of visible afflictions are put forward by ritual specialists as they try obliquely to assess the main sources of discord in the communal context of each case of illness or misfortune."[27]

Such a diagnosis takes more time, though its value lies not only in inviting a richness of contending interpretations, but even more in its involvement of a wider community of people who then puzzle about their own implication in the misfortune at hand. As a way of gaining a certain perspective on the Japanese scene I wish to provide an example along similar lines from another culture with which I am familiar.

An eloquent discussion of this process is given by Bruce Kapferer in *A Celebration of Demons: Exorcism and the Aesthetics of Healing in Sri Lanka.*[28] More often than not in cases of spirit possession it is unclear why someone has become possessed or who the possessing spirit is. In other words, the diagnosis is part of the cure, is even intrinsic to the cure. It becomes a means of widening the circle of involvement both sociologically and cosmologically. In Śrī Laṅkā, "demonic spirits" are not viewed as foreign to the natural or human realms but permanent ingredients within a more universal sphere. Demons, so-called, are allowed their place. Symbolically, they personify the possibility of disorder, confusion, and injustice, but they are seen within a deeper framework of social and cosmic order, not as independent of this order. The demonic element therefore is recognized as inherently present within a world of pain, not some intrusion into it.

This recognition is identical with Turner's view of existence as conflictive and agonistic. The demonic element may be found anywhere within the social and natural order, but its existence is not granted free play. It too is part of contingent reality. Demonic possession thus symbolizes the inversion of true order, somewhat like the death of a child represents a fundamental inversion of typical expectation. Also, this demonic possession manifests itself within normal human contexts of family and neighborhood. And, exorcism (which is one form of redressive ritual) is designed as the means of reestablishing harmonious order, but only *after* the roots of disharmony have been confronted and displaced. The relationship of order to disorder (the demonic) thus is ritualistically the same as that of life to death, for unless the threats of fundamental disorder and death are confronted (personally and communally) in symbolic, psychological, and liturgical ways one is avoiding the dark side of existence and hence the situation remains paralyzed by it.

In the process of encouraging over many days multiple diagnoses of the illness at hand, the Śrī Laṅkān exorcist invites those close to the victim (family, neighbors, friends) to assess *why* so-and-so has become afflicted. In the hands of a skillful practitioner, the speculations grow more and more complex and many plausible explanations are rehearsed. There are even acknowledgments by those who perceive how they may have contributed to a poisoned and disordered climate (not unlike what can happen in group counselling if candor emerges). At a certain point, the exorcist deems the time ripe for the ritual itself to begin; without that preparation, diagnosis would be premature. It would have settled on causes within the patient alone, raising no questions about the social environment in which he or she exists. All possibility of confronting the wider picture would have been neglected, and the ritual's impact would be severely limited. Whenever the social roots of the disease or of the broken connection are ignored, the communal involvement in healing is also diminished.

There are important implications in the preceding example for how one may approach the anguish of losing a child and the ritual of *mizuko kuyō* in Japan. Although afflictions take infinite shape there is a clue here in how one tries to assess what lies beneath the surface and who else may be involved in creating the situation at hand. On one level, through *mizuko kuyō* thousands of women are being helped to go through the mourning process after the turmoil of abortion, miscarriage, or stillbirth. That certainly has great value. On the other hand, there remains a need to address the specific factors that make abortion so frequently necessary. These are rarely being addressed, in part because doing so would reveal other sources of conflict and pain; but their very avoidance may also contribute to what Freud called *melancholia* and to diminished self-esteem. Although women can become skilled in coping with difficult aspects of a male-oriented society, the very strategies they employ successfully may serve to perpetuate the basic problems.

As mentioned earlier, this chapter is not intended as a descriptive report on our research. Although admittedly speculative, it is one effort to see the *mizuko kuyō* phenomenon within a broader socioreligious background than is normally done. It is also an attempt to place it in the context of other research, notably that of Robert Jay Lifton and Victor Turner, as theirs has been concerned with issues very similar to what I find here. If one adopts the metaphor of social drama, as Turner and others do, then what one finds in relations between men and women in Japan is precisely what Michel Strickmann intriguingly calls a *theatre for the unspeakable* when discussing an ancient Taoist ritual in which resentment and anger against a dead parent are expressed, though obliquely through a priest. Thus the *form* of filial piety is maintained, but very unfilial emotions are given expression. The ritual is therapeutic, though not basically redressive.

It is a truism that whenever deep feelings cannot be expressed either with sufficient candor or in some effective ritualistic manner, then anger and frustration go underground. If indeed this is true, then the important phenomenon of *mizuko kuyō* must finally be seen within a larger context. When analyzed in this fashion, it illuminates more aspects of Japanese society and religion than one would initially suspect. The significance of any ritual and its healing powers usually will vary with the level of depth at which affliction is perceived and the extent to which the social fabric is seen as connected to the suffering of individuals, particularly when the extent of that suffering is so widespread. This paper represents the first stage of trying to outline certain connections between the momentum behind this movement and various features of the present Japanese social system and its economic values. It helps to illuminate also some of the very real tensions that Japanese Buddhism needs to address as it exists in an increasingly gender-conscious period of time.

Notes

This essay is a revised form of an article originally published in the *Japanese Journal of Religious Studies* 15, no. 1 (1988). Reprinted with permission.

1. This research is being conducted collaboratively with Elizabeth Harrison, who is a doctoral candidate at the University of Chicago, working in Tokugawa intellectual history. For several years, while living in Kyoto, she was a research associate at Ryūkoku University. Currently (1989–91), she is teaching East Asian history and Japanese religion at Carleton College and in 1991 she joins The East Asian Studies faculty at The University of Arizona. The project has been funded by grants from the Fulbright Commission and the Faculty Development Fund, Carleton College.

2. See Anne Page Brooks, "Mizuko Kuyō and Japanese Buddhism," *Japanese Journal of Religious Studies* 8, nos. 3–4 (1981); and Hoshino Eiki and Takeda Dōshō, "Indebtedness and Comfort: The Undercurrents of *Mizuko Kuyō*," *Japanese Journal of Religious Studies* 14, no. 4 (1987).

3. Hoshino and Takedo, ibid., p. 314.

4. Robert Jay Lifton, *The Broken Connection: On Death and the Continuity of Life* (New York: Basic Books, 1983).

5. Ibid., p. 53.

6. Magda Denes, *In Necessity and Sorrow: Life and Death in an Abortion Hospital* (New York: Penguin Books, 1976), p. 245.

7. Samuel Coleman, *Family Planning in Japanese Society: Traditional Birth Control in a Modern Urban Culture* (Princeton, N.J.: Princeton University Press, 1983), pp. 38–41.

8. Ibid., p. 40.

9. Sigmund Freud, "Mourning and Melancholia," *The Standard Edition of the Complete Psychological Works of Sigmund Freud,* trans. James Strachey in collaboration with Anna Freud (London: Hogarth Press, 1964), vol. 14, pp. 247–268. This quote is from p. 254.

10. See Fumiko Emchi, *Masks* (trans. Juliet Winters Carpenter (Tokyo: Charles E. Tuttle, 1984); and *The Waiting Years,* trans. John Bester (Tokyo, New York, and San Francisco: Kodansha International, 1980). Those by Sawako Ariyoshi are *The Doctor's Wife,* trans. Wakako Hironaka and Ann Silla Kostant (Tokyo, New York, and San Francisco: Kodansha International, 1981); *The River Ki,* trans. Mildred Tahara (Tokyo, New York, and San Francisco: Kodansha International, 1981); and *The Twilight Years,* trans. Mildred Tahara (Tokyo, New York, and San Francisco: Kodansha International, 1984).

11. Takie Sugiyama Lebra, *Japanese Women: Constraint and Fulfillment* (Honolulu: University of Hawaii Press, 1984).

12. Ibid., p. 165.

13. Bardwell Smith, "The Social Contexts of Healing: Research on Abortion and Grieving in Japan," forthcoming in Michael A. Williams, et. al., eds., *Innovation in Religious Traditions: Essays in The Interpretation of Religious Change* (New York and Berlin: Mouton de Gruyter, 1991).

14. Victor Turner, *Dramas, Fields, and Metaphors: Symbolic Action in Human Society* (Ithaca, N.Y., and London: Cornell University Press, 1974), pp. 38–44.

15. Victor Turner, *From Ritual to Theatre: The Human Seriousness of Play* (New York: Performing Arts Journal Publications, 1982), p. 77.

16. Lifton, *Broken Connection,* p. 177.

17. Victor Turner, ''Dewey, Dilthey, and Drama: An Essay in Anthropology of Experience,'' in *The Anthropology of Experience* (Urbana and Chicago: University of Illinois Press, 1986), p. 41.

18. Hoshino and Takeda, ''Indebtedness and Comfort,'' p. 316.

19. Stanley Jayaraja Tambiah, *Culture, Thought, and Social Action: An Anthropological Perspective* (Cambridge, Mass.: Harvard University Press, 1985), pp. 103–104.

20. Jizō is the Japanese name for this figure. In Chinese he is known as Ti-tsang; in Sanskrit, Kṣitigarbha.

21. Emiko Ohnuki-Tierney, *Illness and Culture in Contemporary Japan: An Anthropological View* (Cambridge: Cambridge University Press, 1984), p. 70.

22. Lifton, *Broken Connection,* p. 4.

23. Ibid., p. 3.

24. Ibid., p. 5.

25. Arnold Van Gennep, *The Rites of Passage* (reprinted Chicago: University of Chicago Press, 1960).

26. Victor Turner, ''Dewey, Dilthey, and Drama,'' p. 41.

27. Bruce Kapferer, *A Celebration of Demons: Exorcism and the Aesthetics of Healing in Sri Lanka* (Bloomington: Indiana University Press, 1983).

28. Victor Turner, ''Liminality and the Performative Genres,'' in *Rite, Drama, Festival, Spectacle,* ed. John J. MacAloon (Philadelphia: Philadelphia Institute for the Study of Human Issues, 1984), p. 25.

4

Buddhist Women of the Contemporary Maharashtrian Conversion Movement

Eleanor Zelliot

I am the daughter of Bhim
and the granddaughter of Gautama
Marathi folk song

This line from a village woman's folk song expresses the thrust of the modern Buddhist conversion movement in India. Today's Buddhists are the followers of Bhim, that is to say Dr. Bhimrao Ramji Ambedkar, whose conversion to Buddhism in 1956 was the capstone of a long battle for civil rights and human dignity for India's Untouchables.[1] Although Ambedkar died within two months of the initial conversion ceremony in Nagpur, over 4 million Indians, many from his own untouchable Mahar caste of Maharashtra, followed him into Buddhism. In the thirty some years since the conversion movement began, the Buddhists of Maharashtra[2] have evolved a Buddhism that meets their needs and encourages their aspirations. As in the case of other modern conversions (perhaps all conversions through history?), the Buddhist movement must be seen in the context of the religion that was rejected for the new faith.

The role of women in this mass conversion to Buddhism has not been previously studied, nor have the special views they may hold been the subject of systematic research. In this chapter, I can use only my general impressions from many visits to Buddhist homes in Maharashtra, statements by Buddhist women from several levels of education, notes on the work of an English Buddhist woman who has worked for several years with Buddhist women in India, and a poem about the Buddha's wife that I find a meaningful glimpse into the way a highly educated woman who has been schooled in Hinduism views the myths of her new religion.

As a preamble, however, something must be explained about the background of the Buddhist conversion and the caste that figures most prominently in the story, the Mahars of Mahrashtra. The largest of the untouchable castes of the Marathi-speaking area, indeed almost 10 percent of the population, the Mahars in the modern era attempted to raise their low status and demanded the lifting of the many restrictions placed on them. From the 1890s on, various individuals and groups have submitted petitions to the government for civil rights, organized for support and education, and attempted to enter temples or otherwise claim full membership in Hinduism. B. R. Ambedkar, a Barrister and Ph.D. from Columbia University by the grace of several reformist princes,[3] took charge of this movement in the early 1920s, creating among his followers a powerful unity and a great will to change. Over the years he also created educational institutions, political parties, a system of government educational and occupation benefits for Untouchables, and the Buddhist conversion movement. He served on the all-India level as independent India's first law minister and the chairman of the drafting committee of the Constitution of India. His people have a sense of being lifted from a despised and persecuted life to one of freedom and self-respect by his example.

Ambedkar's death in 1956 deprived the movement of any one accepted leader, but since that time, local leadership has continued a number of innovations. A literary movement has been one of the most important facets of Marathi literature for the past fifteen years, and the publishing of *dalit* (downtrodden, ground down, the current term ex-Untouchables[4] use for themselves) literature[5] has spread to Karnataka and Gujarat. Educational institutions continue to be founded. The Buddhist movement, with no central organization in control, has developed according to the strength of local people. The Republican Party founded by Ambedkar has almost ceased to be an effective force, but Ambedkar's people are politicized and aware, even though the vast majority are still villagers. Ambedkar's influence continues, and the women of the Buddhist conversion movement are conscious of being "daughters of Bhim," acknowledging in the same metaphor their Buddhism as "granddaughters of Gautama."

Buddhist Women

My impressions of Buddhist women from all strata of society are (1) they are not necessarily the upholders of old religious traditions, as is the stereotype for Hindu women; (2) they often are as strong a force for change, and at times stronger, than the men; (3) their view of Buddhism is intensely personal, reflecting their experience and their present situation; (4) even though Buddhism may not be understood in a sophisticated way, it is clearly part of their identity.

In contrast to upper-class women of the Hindu faith, many Buddhist women seem not to cling to traditional rituals, even if "superstitions" still exist in their minds. Most of the *dalit* women worked and worked hard, both inside and outside the home. There was little time or money for rituals or elaborate preparations for festivals. Although there was no general belief that their place in life was the result of previous sin and their birth as Untouchables therefore individually earned, still there was a sense that, whatever the cause, life was hard and the gods could do little to lighten their load. The temple was closed to them, their food was not exchanged with higher castes on festive occasions, and some of the Hindu practices in which they shared (for example, possession by a god or a ghost or dedication of children to a god or goddess in exchange for some favor) were declared harmful in the early days of the movement.

Second, even though the literacy rate was abysmally low, some women seem to have understood early on the value of education. I have heard a great many educated Buddhist man say openly that they owe their learning to their mothers' strong will and constant encouragement. The Untouchables were a poor and generally despised community, and even now many are caught in the life-style of the poverty stricken and culturally deprived, but it is clear that the great counterbalancing message of Ambedkar, his constant challenge to be educated, to live clean, sober, and creative lives, had a strong effect. And his message that women are important, that they should be equal to men, or at the very least that the movement would not flourish without their advancement, had its effect.

The personal approach to Buddhism that, it seems to me, today's Buddhist women take is best illustrated by their own literature. I will begin with folk songs, move through material collected from women with little education, and close with statements from those who have benefited from the movement and government efforts at "compensatory discrimination,"[6] and so belong to the new "middle class."

Songs and Stories

The women's songs collected by Indira Junghare from a village near Nagpur are not as ideological or moralistic as the Buddhist men's songs, which speak of "five principles" and "making one's enemy one's friend."[7] Junghare found that the women make up their own songs whereas the men tend to pick up songs in Nagpur or from the innumerable small pamphlets of songs circulated among Maharashtrian Buddhists. One song sung by the women seems to have no message at all, except for the sense of unity and participation woven into every sentence:

Let's go to Buddha's temple, my friend!
To the temple, to the temple, to the temple.
A two-paisa incense stick, a three-paisa candle,
Tie them in your sari. Let's go to Buddha's temple!

Are you wearing a white sari and white blouse?
Are you ready to go?
Let's go to Buddha's temple...

We are getting nearer Bhima's town.
I am sure Narayanrao is there playing the *khanjiri*.
Let's go to Buddha's temple! To the temple, the temple.[8]

The same message with a sense of even wider participation is found in a song urging others to go to Nagpur on Dasara, the day of conversion to Buddhism in 1956, which still finds tens of thousands of Buddhists streaming into the city to the spot where the conversion took place. In this song, *Bhima,* of course, is Bhimrao Ramji Ambedkar, the *a* added to Bhim for the sake of meter, and *his task* undoubtedly means the raising up of the *dalit* as well as the spread of Buddhism.

Thousands of men and women will come there.
Thousands of men and women will come there.
A great pilgrimage for Bhima is held there.
A great pilgrimage for Bhima is held there.
Listen to what I say, listen to me, the servant of Buddha.
O friend, let's go there this year,
Let's go to Nagpur this year.

You wear the sari with the golden border
And I'll yoke the bullocks to the cart.
We have to finish Bhima's task,
We have to finish Bhima's task.

No one has relatives there.
Even though we're poor, we will give our share.
O friend, let's go there this year,
Let's go to Nagpur this year.
Let's go to Nagpur this year.[9]

Three interviews with illiterate women by Sumitra Bhave in Pune recently add some dimension to these songs. The first statement, that of Savitribai, denies any involvement in Hinduism and accepts Buddhism as part of her family identity, without question. I have paraphrased some of her statements:

> I don't make much fuss about God. I say its better to have a book so my daughter can read. I haven't fasted even once, as far as I can remember. Not even lit incense [for a god]. I still have the [goddess] basket my mother-in-law gave me but I don't even worship that... I do light incense before Buddha and Babasaheb [Ambedkar]....My niece [who committed suicide] used to put *kum kum* on the picture....Now my girls say to me "Ambedkar is our God."...I do celebrate Divali, Holi, Nag Panchmi. To celebrate a [Hindu holy] day is to make sweets. [Earlier Savitribai had said she did not know the religious stories of the Hindus.]...Our *dharma* is Buddha. Since I can remember it's been the Buddhist religion in our house....Sometimes I go to the [Buddhist] temple for Jayanti, Purnima. For naming ceremonies and weddings and *barsa* [the naming of a child on the twelfth day after birth] we do the Buddhist ceremony, sing Buddhist songs....[10]

Another Buddhist woman interviewed by Sumitra Bhave, Rakhma, adds the concept of morality to her comments on Buddhism:

> These days we are Buddhists: meaning we don't do god and all that. Once a year there is Jayanti—Buddha Jayanti, Ambedkar Jayanti. We do those. We make sweets on Divali—Dasara, but we don't do puja and all that nonsense....Once a bride's brother said at her wedding, "I won't stay if you put tumeric on the bride and groom." [Said with approval.] According to Buddhism, we threw all that out. Now we wear white garments. Before, my mother worshipped the gods. Then we threw them in the river. As it is, life is hard enough. Why should we have to look after gods too?...And who showed us the way? You must see either Buddha's image or Babasaheb's [affectionate but respectful title for Ambedkar] photo in our houses....Just keep your mind pure. Don't steal. Don't lie. If you see a cripple or a blind one, help them cross the street. If a child falls, pick him up. That's god, and whoever does that is god's man....In Buddhism, you don't kill even an ant, meaning you don't sin even that much; that's our religion. But then who can do all that?...[11]

A third woman, Savitri, combines respect for the mind with an unusual compassion for those who are rich and a deep resentment of those who do not value their democratic voting rights:

> God is in our minds. . . . The people who say "God, God" sin too. In the end it all depends on your mind. I don't do "God God" and I don't have bad thoughts either. . . . Even if someone brushes his teeth with gold, I say, let them have even better days! They've worked hard, haven't they?. . . What good is all this puja. One should live purely. Now look at this: some people of our caste get money from leaders for voting. I'll never do that. To sell your vote is like selling your soul![12]

Two middle-aged women with elementary school educations recorded their interpretation of the meaning of the Buddha for Maxine Berntsen in the small town of Phaltan in Maharashtra several years ago. Their telling of the story of the Buddha's finding enlightenment reveals the power of the oral tradition as well as their clear perceptions of the Buddha's message.

> Buddha came from a kingly family. He was the king's son. Then why did he take up this new *dharma*? Do you know where he spent all his time? In the house. He never felt the scorching sun outside. He didn't know the wind or the birds or the animals. He didn't know all the troubles and difficulties of men. He would sit on his throne and say, "Since I am happy the whole world must be happy." One day he asked his father, "Baba, may I go out for a walk?" His father said, "No, don't go. A guru told me not to let you go out for twelve more years, so don't go." But without telling his father the prince went out.
>
> He went in a tonga with his servant. Just after they had left the house they saw a corpse. "What is that?" the prince asked.
>
> "A man has died."
>
> "Do men die? What does *die* mean?"
>
> So the servant explained, "Now here are you and me. We've been born, we've grown up, we're alive. Now you are nineteen or twenty. Soon you'll be forty, then fifty. Your hair will all turn gray, you'll get tired, you'll sit wasting away. Finally you'll die and people will carry you away and bury you. That's how it is in the world."

[The storytellers go on to tell equally graphically of the Buddha's meeting a leper and an old man.]

> The prince had never seen any of these things. He went back to his house, to his lovely wife and his son Rahul. All day long he sat thinking, and at midnight he took leave of his wife and his son and went into the forest. There he remained, doing *tapaścarya* [religious austerities] all night, but he didn't find God. He did this according to Hindu *dharma*, mind you. . . . So what did he do next? He fasted until he was skin and bones and ready to die. . . . So he decided that one cannot find God by fasting. Then he went down by the river and sat

> under a banyan tree. He sat meditating on the world and the mind. Nobody has seen the gods so why do people say that they exist?
>
> After meditating on all this he wrote his thoughts down. He wrote that men—we ourselves—are God. There is no God in the world and nobody should put any hope in Him. Nobody should feel that if he fasts or does such things he will see God. A man should honestly follow his own path. The *atma* [soul] is God. As for us, *saṃgham saraṇam gacchāmi*—I go for refuge to the *saṃgha*. I go for refuge to the *dhamma*. I go for refuge to the Buddha. That is what the Buddha taught. Be a friend to all and never hope in what we cannot see.[13]

Statements by Educated Women

The realistic and quite delightful interviews by Sumitra Bhave and Maxine Berntsen are unself-conscious in their interpretations of Buddhism. Two women who live in Bombay, who are well-educated, who are in touch with the history of the Ambedkar movement and sophisticated Buddhist literature as well, recount a more orthodox Buddhism. The first, Meenakshi Moon, sent a very long statement in response to my request that she write what Buddhism meant to her. She included a history of the sufferings of untouchables. Among her most interesting notes in this section is her opinion that in other countries revolutions and war changed the social status of the lowly but "in Bharat, the pollution of the Shudra was always observed." And so the conversion to Buddhism is the only path to freedom.

Moon gives a clear sense of the long road to Buddhism, beginning with a six year effort at Nasik to enter the Hindu temple, but "the Hindus would not listen." Then she notes the fearless statement of Ambedkar in 1935, "I was born a Hindu but I will not die a Hindu," which was followed by twenty-one years of study of Christianity, Islam, Sikhism, Jainism, various Hindu sects, and Buddhism. The commitment to Buddhism was based on the leading principles of Buddhism: equality, justice, brotherhood, and liberty. And in her discussion of Buddhism versus Hinduism, Moon links the untouchables, the poor, the Shudras, and women as victims of the Hindu system.

At the time of conversion, Ambedkar said, "Now I am free from hell. I feel as if I had started a new life." And Moon adds,

> At the time of the conversion the lives of we Dalits were totally revolutionized. We knew we must understand this *dhamma*. We began to read. We began to question: Buddhism means what? Hinduism means what? Why did we convert? What are the harmful customs of

Hinduism? Why were we burdened with untouchability for thousands of years? Who planted the seeds of inequality? Why even today are atrocities committed on Dalits and Buddhists? What benefit is there in this to Hindus?

A list of Buddhist tenets, paralleled with Hindu ones, is part of Meenakshi Moon's statement. I have omitted the Hindu parallels, except for point 2.

1. Gods are not worshipped.
2. The Pali Tipiṭaka and Dr. Ambedkar's *The Buddha and His Dhamma* are our books. (In contrast to the *Vedas,* the *Upaniṣads,* and the *Manusmṛti,* the law book that delimits the place and status of women and untouchables.)
3. Progress is in our own hands. The Buddhist religion proclaims equality; it condemns caste distinctions.
4. There is no rebirth.
5. The emphasis in the Buddhist religion is on intelligence.
6. We must be alert. Our faith is rational.
7. Buddhists do not practice untouchability.
8. In Buddhism, women have equal rights, every type of freedom.
9. The *pañca śīla* (five precepts) is the base of the Buddhist religion. Do not lie, steal, do violence, or commit immorality; respect your parents. Hold to the truth.

Meenakshi Moon is aware of matters that have not entered into the statements of less-educated women. She stresses that not only have Mahars converted, but untouchables from the Mang, Chambhar, and Bhangi castes have also. She takes pride in the "thousand Buddhist cave temples" that exist as testimony of Buddhism's previous glory. She notes that Buddhism is the religion of Japan, China, Thailand, and Śrī Laṅkā, and that India's foreign policy is based on the *pañca śīla* idea. She is very aware of the recent caste violence directed against *dalits* and Buddhists, and she fears that this violence may bring *dalits* back into Hindu practices as a sort of self-defense. She also mourns the selfishness of many Buddhists who have become well educated and well off and ignore those still at the bottom of society.[14]

Although Urmilla Pawar is a neighbor of Meenakshi Moon and, like her, married to a successful government official, her background is one of village life and greater poverty. I have been told that she herself once sold baskets door to door to get some income for her family. Now well educated and a writer of short stories, she began her statement on Buddhism with the story of her mother, "Unlearned, unlettered, a great devotee of god. Waking and sleeping she recited "Vithal, Vithal, Vithal, Vithal." Thirty-three crores of gods in the cow's stomach. . . she would satisfy her hunger and thirst by worshipping the gods."

But one day, Pawar recalls, there was a meeting on the school grounds. There was a proclamation. Everyone responded "Victory to Bhagwan Gautam Buddha. Victory to Dr. Ambedkar."

> All the older people came from the meeting and went straight to the godhouse. God's photo, the small images, the metal dish, the brass pot, the five-leaved container, the bells, the lamp, the sandlewood—all were thrown in a basket and taken out to the river. I asked, "Mother, where are you taking the gods?" She said, laughing, "To drown in the river." "Why?" "Because we are now Buddhists." "What does that mean?" Mother was silent.

Urmilla Pawar goes on to say that now as "we have studied, grown and looked with a sharp eye at the changing situation around us, we have gotten an answer to that question." And some of the answers she gives are these:

1. Subcastes became one: "like a vast spreading sea, the whole Mahar community became one."
2. The life of insult, bootlicking, and other peoples' leftover food was cast away; "we did whatever we could: sold bamboo baskets, supplied fuel from the forest, cut grass."
3. After the conversion "we began to get education. Because of the power of Dr. Ambedkar's example, because of the rational teaching of the Buddhist *dhamma,* because it was actually possible to go to school, we developed a thirst for learning."
4. "Our superstitions fell away, and we saw the cruelty and hypocrisy of god and ghost possession, the evil of giving our children to the gods as *murlis* and *devadasis* [women dedicated to the god Khandoba or the Goddess Yellama], as *vaghya* [men dedicated to Khandoba] and *potraj* [a servant of the village Goddess Mariai]."
5. "We learned self respect."
6. "We have learned that deeds which are good or bad must be done in this life, in this body. The idea that we suffered the sins of a past birth made us weak and made the rich and powerful hard men. That's why, instead of doing evil things, we should live by establishing bonds of love, equality and brotherhood with each other."

7. "We used to take the clothes from corpses to wear. Now we wear clean white clothes for Buddha Jayanti. These clothes have taught us two important things. One is that we should live cleanly—don't let your clean white clothes get dirty; second, in the same way that a stain on white clothes is apparent, any kind of stain on a person's character can be seen."

Pawar refers obliquely to the barring of Untouchables and women formerly from Sanskrit learning, saying with pride that after the conversion, people began doing *vandana* (the praise of Buddha) in each house. "Our uneducated ignorant women sang the *vandana* with all sorts of mistakes. Their pronunciation was not right. The Pali language is somewhere between Sanskrit and Marathi and it took some time before it would sit on the tongue properly, but now we have grasped the pronunciation very well." She speaks out of her own experience when she says, "The Buddhist religion is the path to self-respect, progress, uplift. It is the religion that will make our future bright. . . . We are not now living a parasitical life. We are self-respecting and self-reliant."[15]

The Teaching of Buddhism

The only sustained effort to teach Buddhism to women of which I am aware is the work of the Friends of the Western Buddhist Order. Founded by the Venerable Sangarakshita, an English Buddhist who spent many years in India, the FWBO functions in India as the Trailokya Bauddh Mahasangh Sahayyaka Gana (TBMSG) and does medical and educational work as well as teaching the *dhamma*. An English Buddhist whose religious name is Padmasuri went to work in Dapodi, near Pune, as a nurse-midwife in 1982, but as Indian personnel became available, shifted to "dhamma work" for the six months of every year she spends in India.

Padmasuri's description of giving a talk to a Buddhist group in India evokes the world of most urban Buddhists better than any other source I know:

> A lot of effort goes into organizing these programmes. They are usually held in the open air between slums. A stage is erected, bedecked with fairy lights. In the centre stands a Buddha *rūpa* [image], a photo of Dr. Ambedkar, flowers, candles and incense. The men and women sit separately, and front rows are taken up by wide-eyed children.

> Flower garlands are offered, introductory speeches given, the Refuges and Precepts chanted, then at the end of the talk which will last at least an hour with translation, there are more garlands and the last *vandana* is chanted. On three occasions I have been greeted at a programme by all the women dressed in white saris, holding candles, forming parallel lines through which I have walked having flower petals showered on me to the shouts of "Victory to the Buddha and Baba Saheb Ambedkar." In the daytime one would notice the crumbling shanties, the open gutters, the filth and poverty, but on occasions like this they are transformed into a fairy land of light and colour, and the smell of excrement and rotting waste is hidden by the sweet perfume of jasmine flowers and sandlewood incense. Sometimes the talks are in corridors of tenement blocks, or in school buildings, or in stifling hot *vihāras* [Buddhist temples] made of corrugated iron.[16]

In situations like this one, or in retreats specifically for women, Padmasuri's message of Buddhism falls upon many different sorts of ears. There is such receptivity, however, that she not only feels that "the *dhamma* is the only way for women to be emancipated" but that some women are ready for high levels of understanding of Buddhism. Recently two women were ordained as Dhammacharinis (lay-ordained women) in the Western Buddhist Order (TBMSG). To be ordained in the order is not to enter a monastic life or to leave one's family, but to be fully involved in the work of the *dhamma*. The ordination ceremony was held at the retreat center near the ancient Buddhist caves of Bhaja, with 500 in attendance, and the "mighty shouts of SADHU" reverberating around the valley to rejoice in the fact that two women had "Gone for Refuge."[17]

The life story of one of these women, Mrs. Kharat, now Vimalasuri, indicates something of the contrasts possible in the life of the *dalit*. One of nine children, Vimalasuri can remember a time when the family was so poor her mother broke stones on the road, but she had such a commitment to education that Vimalasuri was the only untouchable girl in school. As a married woman in Bombay, she was part of a "Buddhist Political group" strongly in favor of the Congress Party and even met Indira Gandhi at one time. But her chief interest was religion, and she went to see a monk in the local *vihara*, then to *Vipassana* meditation conducted by another monk, and then to a three-day retreat led by the TBMSG.

Five years later, after much reading and training, she received ordination as Vimalasuri, "pure and stainless heroine." She lives with her husband and three children in Bombay, leads a women's class, meditates daily, goes on retreats, and has brought her husband's family thoroughly into the movement.[18]

The second woman, Jnanasuri (heroine of knowledge), came to Buddhism from politics, after a good education and a "love marriage." During the 1982 agitation for the renaming of Marathwada University as "Dr. Ambedkar University," she spent a week in prison, and there found she had a natural ability to lead women. She taught some to meditate, sang songs about Ambedkar, did the cooking! Upon release, she shifted from politics to religion as her main emphasis, and by 1985 requested ordination. Now she lives with her husband, four daughters, and mother in Aurangabad; is administrator of the TBMSG social projects (including a boys' hostel attached to the Buddhist Centre); leads three classes in Buddhist doctrine a week; meditates daily; and leads occasional short retreats for women.[19]

The Meaning of Buddhism for Women

These songs, stories, and comments indicate a deep faith and commitment on the part of at least some Buddhist women, a pride in the rationality, morality, and equality of Buddhism. For others there is at least a clear sense of identity. However, it must be said that almost all the literature written by Buddhists in the conversion movement is by men, and the vast majority of leaders in local Buddhist groups are men. Of course, it is a Buddhist movement sprung from a Hindu culture in which men are the priests, the public ritualists, and usually the teachers; and the women's part is confined to *pūjā* in the home, celebration of holy days, and participation in such events as the pilgrimage to Pandharpur in the *bhakti* (devotional religious) tradition, and the Khandoba, or the goddess festivals. Given this context, it is difficult to say if women are more devout, more active, more perceptive of religious ideas than are men. What is clear is that women do not seem to be a force for a return to the Hindu tradition. It is also clear that they bring an intensely personal view to Buddhism, and a storytelling carryover from the Indian oral tradition, which may help the spread of Buddhism to the village population in a meaningful way. Further, it may be worth noting that there is an untouchable woman poet-saint in the most important literary tradition of the common people of Maharashtra, the *bhakti* movement, Soyrabai, the wife of the fourteenth century Mahar poet-saint Chokhamela. No Buddhist woman says that Soyrabai is an inspiration, because *all* the Hindu past has been set aside, not only that which limited and humiliated Untouchables. But Buddhist women come from a tradition in which they not only have been strong and useful in the home and in the work force, but also creative in literature and religion.

My chapter has many limitations. My material is from Maharashtra; and although there are strong groups of Buddhists in many urban centers in both north and south India, I cannot write knowledgeably of women's activities in Delhi or Ahmedabad or Hyderabad, although I have seen active women in these cities. Also, my material reflects a deep faith and commitment among Buddhist women that may not be true of all. I am sure many women still worship a god or a goddess out of belief or to be more acceptable to Hindu neighbors. I know that spirit possession, belief in black magic, and trust in a shaman can still be found. I am aware that some of the educated separated themselves from their still backward brothers and sisters. But in spite of all this, I am struck by the creativity of Buddhist women in Maharashtra, by the depth to which Buddhism has penetrated in the society, by the positive forces the conversion has released.

My final segment is not a statement of faith, but a literary and feminist response to the Buddhist movement. It is a poem about the Buddha's wife, and although it is not about doctrine or belief, I want to present it in its entirety here. Its author, Hira Bansode, is a well-educated woman, a government employee, and one of the most-published of the *dalit* women poets. She was president of the initial *saṃvādinī* (feminine colloquy) in 1986 of the newly formed Dalit Stri Sahitya Manc (the *dalit* women's literary platform.)[20]

One of her poems seems to me to open up new vistas, both in the creative ideas of the Buddhist women of Maharashtra and in the field of what women bring to Buddhism. The humanness of the Buddha, as opposed to the divine status of Hindu gods or the leave-the-world austerity of Hindu saints, is one message of the poem. But there is another message, which is more unusual. Hira Bansode, herself a married woman, looks at Yaśodharā, the Buddha's wife, as a tragic figure, an abandoned woman, and yet a woman who somehow is a part of the Buddha's final accomplishment.

Note the religious language Hira Bansode weaves into her song of praise to Yaśodharā, the Buddha's wife. The Buddha brings light, but the dark was "absorbed" by the wife he deserted to enlighten the world. The sky comes to *her* for refuge, a play on the "three refuges," the *dhamma*, the *saṃgha*, and the Buddha, to which all Buddhists go. The light image appears again in the phrase, "He was moving toward a great splendor," but the focus is on the woman the Buddha left behind in order to serve humankind. Yaśodharā is seen as sacrificing the crown of womanhood, her married life, for the Buddha's enlightenment. The faithful wives of the Hindu tradition, Sītā and Sāvitrī, are honored by all as ideal women. The wives of the great gods,

Pārvatī, Durgā, Kālī, Lakṣmī, Sarasvatī, and, in Maharashtra, Rukmiṇī, appear in temples. Only the Buddha's wife is ignored, her sacrifice unacknowledged, her influence not even considered.

In the last staza, Hira Bansode addresses Yaśodharā with the fond dimunitive *Yashu* and comforts her with the thought that at least one Buddhist woman has seen her behind the Buddha's closed eyelids, a part of that great mind.

Yashodhara[21]

Oh Yashodhara!
You are like a dream of sharp pain, life-long sorrow.
I don't have the audacity to look at you.
We were brightened by Buddha's light, but you absorbed the dark
Until your life was mottled blue and black, a fragmented life, burned out,
Oh Yashodhara!

The tender sky comes to you for refuge
Seeing your shining but fruitless life, and the pained stars shed tears.
My heart breaks,
Seeing your matchless beauty, separated from your love, dimming like twilight.
Listening to your silent sighs
I feel the promise of heavenly happiness is hollow.

Tell me one thing, Yashodhara, how did you contain the raging storm in your small hands?
Just the idea of your life shakes the earth and sends the screaming waves dashing against the shore.
You would have remembered while your life slipped by
The last kiss of Siddharth's final farewell, those tender lips.
But weren't you aware, dear, of the heart-melting fire
And the fearful awakening power of that kiss?
Lightning fell, and you didn't know it.
He was moving toward a great splendor, far from the place you lay...
He went, he conquered, he shone.
While you listened to the songs of his triumph
Your womanliness must have wept.
You who lost husband and son must have felt uprooted like the tender banana plant.

But history doesn't talk about the great story of your sacrifice.
If Siddharth had gone through the charade of *samādhi*[22]
A great epic would have been written about you!
You would have become famous in *purana* and palm leaf like Sita and Savitri.
Oh Yashodhara!

I am ashamed of the injustice.
You are not to be found in a single Buddhist *vihāra*.
Were you really of no account?
But wait—don't suffer so.
I have seen your beautiful face.
You are between the closed eyelids of Siddhartha.
Yashu, just you.

Hira Bansode

Notes

The initial folksong is from "Dr. Ambedkar: The Hero of the Mahars, Ex-Untouchables of India," a paper given by Indira Y. Junghare at the South Asia Conference, Madison, Wisc., November 1987.

My initial research on the Ambedkar movement was funded by a grant from the American Institute of Indian Studies.

1. For Ambedkar's accomplishments, see several of my articles: "Buddhism and Politics in Maharashtra," in Donald E. Smith, ed., *South Asian Politics and Religion* (Princeton, N.J.: Princeton University Press, 1966); "The Leadership of Babasaheb Ambedkar," in B. N. Pandey, ed. *Leadership in South Asia* (New Delhi: Vikas, 1977); entries for B. R. Ambedkar in the *Encyclopedia of Asian History* (New York: Scribners, 1988) and the *Encyclopedia of Religion* (New York: Macmillan, 1986). Full biographies include Dhananjay Keer, *Dr. Ambedkar: Life and Mission*, 3rd ed. (Bombay: Popular, 1971); and W. N. Kuber, *B. R. Ambedkar* (New Delhi: Government of India, 1978).

2. Although the majority of Buddhists converted in Dr. Ambedkar's movement live in Maharashtra, there are important groups in Gujarat, the Punjab, Madhya Pradesh, and Uttar Pradesh, as well as in most large Indian cities.

3. The non-Brahman princes of Baroda and Kolhapur made Ambedkar's education in America and England possible.

4. Since the practice of untouchability has been made illegal in the constitution of India, the term *ex-Untouchable* has come into use.

5. For a brief history of the Dalit literary movement, see Eleanor Zelliot, "Dalit—New Cultural Context of an Old Marathi Word," *Contributions to Asian Studies* 11 (1978): 77–97.

6. *Compensatory discrimination* is a term first used by Marc Galanter to describe the "reverse discrimination" in jobs and scholarships intended to bring ex-Untouchables up to higher castes' levels.

7. Indira Junghare, "Songs of the Mahars: An Untouchable Caste of Maharashtra, India." in *Ethnomusicology* 27, no. 2 (1983): 271–295.

8. Ibid., p. 287.

9. Ibid., p. 288.

10. Sumitra Bhave, *Tāvā culyāvar: āṭh dalit strīyāncyā ātmakathā* [The Pan Is on the Stove: Eight Dalit Women's Life Stories], (Pune: Strivani Prakash, 1987), p. 18. I have slightly changed the translations made for me by Jayant Karve of the selections from this book. Since this chapter was first written, an English edition of the book has appeared: *Pan on Fire: Eight Dalit Women Tell Their Story*, trans. Gauri Deshpande (New Delhi: Indian Social Institute, 1988).

11. Ibid., pp. 31–32.

12. Ibid., p. 10.

13. From Bebi Kamble and Ulpabai Chauhan, "Scattered Voices: Refuge in the Buddha," in *The Experience of Hinduism; Essays on Religion in Maharashtra*, trans. Maxine Berntsen, ed. Eleanor Zelliot and Maxine Berntsen (Albany: SUNY Press, 1988), pp. 291–294. Bebi Kamble has since seen her autobiography published in Marathi.

14. Statement by letter from Meenakshi Moon, December 1987, translated by Philip Engblom and adapted by Eleanor Zelliot. Meenakshi Moon has written a book of Buddhist stories for children in Marathi. She and Urmilla Pawar have recently written a book based on extensive field research on the role women have played in the Ambedkar movement: *Amhīhī itihās ghadawlā* [We Too Made History].

15. Statement by letter from Urmilla Pawar, December 1987, translated by Philip Engblom and adapted by Eleanor Zelliot.

16. Padmasuri, "Teaching the Dharma to Indian Women," *Dakini* 1 (1986): 13.

17. Padmasuri, "New Women, New Lives: Ordination into the Western Buddhist Order," *Dakini* 2 (1987): 10–12.

18. Ibid., pp. 11–12.

19. Letter from Padmasuri, October 13, 1987.

20. The *saṃvādinī* was publicized as possibly the first women's literary conference of any sort in Maharashtra. Meenakshi Moon and Urmilla Pawar were among the organizers of the group.

21. "Yashodhara" was first published in *Strī* (Davali issue, 1981), and reprinted in a collection of Hira Bansode's poems, *Phiryād* [Petition, Complaint] (Pune: Samaj Prabodhan Sanstha Prakashan, 1984). Translated by Jayant Karve, Philip Engblom, and Eleanor Zelliot.

22. This line is obscure. The context might be that many of the saints in the Pandharpur *bhakti* tradition, Dnyaneshwar, Eknath, and Tukaram among them, took *samādhi*; that is, ended their earthly existence voluntarily. Dnyaneshwar's sister and the wives of Eknath and Tukaram are known and honored, at least to some extent. However, the "charade of *samādhi*" seems to be more a criticism of Hindu practice than an actual reference to either saints or gods.

III

The Rhetoric of Gender in Buddhist Texts

5

Gender and Persuasion: The Portrayal of Beauty, Anguish, and Nurturance in an Account of a Tamil Nun

Paula Richman

Introduction

Because Buddhist doctrine posits an ultimate state (*nirvāṇa*) beyond all gender distinctions, the study of gender in Buddhist texts proves particularly intriguing. The term *gender* refers to culturally constructed ideas about what it means to be male or female; research on gender in religious traditions focuses on how those culturally constructed ideas manifest themselves in and shape religious texts, rituals, and communities. In particular, the issue of gender is crucial to an understanding of Buddhist monastic life, where males and females live in separate orders according to rules designed to discipline the passions, including sexual desire.[1] Although scholars have looked at the way Indian notions of gender shaped the development of the Buddhist *saṃgha* as an institution,[2] they have paid less attention to the role gender plays in the process by which individuals renounce the world and commit themselves to religious discipline.[3] This process is the subject of *Maṇimēkalai*,[4] a Tamil text about a courtesan's daughter who becomes a Buddhist nun.[5] Scholars believe that *Maṇimēkalai* was written ca. the sixth century C.E. in South India by Cīttalai Cāttaṉār, about whom little is known except that he was a wealthy grain merchant. In *Maṇimēkalai* Cāttaṉār undercuts, reverses, and extends conventional ideas about "masculine" and "feminine" behavior to give his account of a woman seeking to achieve the ultimate state beyond gender distinctions.

In this chapter, three ways in which Cāttaṉār uses and tinkers with Tamil gender constructs are explored. First, I chart Cāttaṉār's treatment of phrases about female beauty to demonstrate how he undercuts traditional ideas about the nature and value of sexual love. Second, I analyze Cāttaṉār's manipulation of the motif of the heroine's separation from her beloved to show how he reverses traditional ideas about the source of female anguish in an intimate relationship. Finally, I explicate Cāttaṉār's transformation of ideas about motherhood—both human and bovine—to reveal how Cāttaṉār has universalized the idea of maternal nurturance as a way of describing the Buddhist ideal of generosity.

Before turning to *Maṇimēkalai,* a few words about the use of the term *gender* are appropriate here. Many recent publications in the fields of cultural anthropology and psychology have focused upon the cultural construction of gender.[6] Social scientists generally agree that gender, that is, conceptions of what it means to be male or female, is inculcated as part of the process of socialization. It exists as one component of the set of concepts that constitute "culture." Gender-related religious symbols (such as "God the father" or "the bride of Christ") can also function as *part of* that socialization process itself, thereby reinforcing the normative understanding of gender in society.

Gender-related religious symbols, however, can act in many other ways in addition to simply mirroring or instilling acceptance of the order found in society. As Bynum comments in her introduction to a group of essays illustrating this point, symbols can be seen as

> not merely reflecting and shaping but also inverting, questioning, rejecting, and transcending gender as it is constructed in the individual's psychological development and sociological setting.... Gender-related symbols, in their full complexity, may refer to gender in ways that affirm or reverse it, support or question it; or they may, in their basic meaning, have little at all to do with male and female roles. Thus our analysis admits that gender-related symbols are sometimes "about" values other than gender.[7]

Scholars, therefore, cannot always assume that gender-linked religious symbols will function in a way that directly affirms the given social order. Sometimes they are used as a language for making statements of a theological nature—about the nature of reality, religious liberation, or transcendence.

One more element must be added to this discussion of gender-related religious discourse to adequately understand how notions of gender function in *Maṇimēkalai*. We need to adopt a less static and reified view of culture than many traditional anthropologists have done.[8] Keeping in mind that the "invention" of culture is ongoing, we must take notice of the ways in which individuals can shape their culture by manipulating conventional gender-related symbols to create new meanings.

Cāttaṉār is an individual who seeks to do just that. In *Maṇimēkalai*, he sets forth a new perspective for understanding reality. As part of his thoroughgoing critique of ordinary understanding of reality, Cāttaṉār uses gender-related symbols, language, and imagery to undermine generally accepted values about maleness, femaleness, and sexual love. To understand how he accomplishes this feat, some knowledge of *Maṇimēkalai* and its milieu is necessary.

The Text and Its Context

In *Maṇimēkalai,* Cāttaṉār uses didactically structured narrative to persuade his audience of the validity and value of the Buddhist world-view, as I have argued elsewhere.[9] Although scholars disagree about both the date of *Maṇimēkalai* and the specific historical circumstances that led to a growth of Buddhism in Tamil country,[10] it seems likely that Cāttaṉār's text was probably written ca. the sixth century C.E.[11] and sheds some light on Buddhist developments during this period. As the only extant Buddhist text written in Tamil, *Maṇimēkalai* provides a unique source for the study of South Indian Buddhism.[12]

In addition to Cāttaṉār's grounding in Buddhist thought, he also has a familiarity with the literary culture of Tamil tradition. The foundation of that literary culture is a corpus of Tamil compositions called *Caṅkam* poetry, the majority of whose poems are dated ca. first century to fifth century. This classical Tamil poetry consists of a set of anthologies and self-contained longer poems concerned with two topics: the private world of love (called *akam* or *inner* poems) and the public world of the court and the battlefield (called *puṟam* or *outer* poems).[13]

The audience that Cāttaṉār addresses—at least in the parts of *Maṇimēkalai* analyzed in this chapter[14]—is composed of connoisseurs of those classical Tamil love poems. In addressing such an audience, he can take for granted their knowledge of the conventional language used to describe love between a man and a woman. In telling of Maṇimēkalai's relationship with Prince Utayakumaraṉ, Cāttaṉār draws on the fund of literary conventions associated with love (*akam*) poetry, but uses those conventions to portray an "antilove" story. Although the telling of such a story might challenge and disconcert his audience, the familiar language with which Cāttaṉār tells the story enables his audience to grasp its meaning.

Cāttaṉār also builds on the previous literary experience of his audience by linking *Maṇimēkalai* to an earlier Tamil narrative. That narrative, *Cilappatikāram,* is the earliest example of Tamil *kāppiyam,* "extended and ornate literary narrative" (sometimes labeled *epic* in histories of Tamil literature).[15] *Cilappatikāram* (dated ca. 450 C.E.), tells the story of an affair between a married man named Kōvalaṉ and Mātavi, a courtesan. Their daughter is Maṇimēkalai. In *Cilappatikāram,* Maṇimēkalai plays a minor role, appearing only in the last two chapters.[16] In *Maṇimēkalai,* however, she has become the heroine whose progress on the Buddhist path provides the text with its direction. Once again, Cāttaṉār provides continuity for his audience—this time through his choice of main character—even though the content of his message presents a discontinuity.

In terms of the role gender plays in the narrative, Cāttaṉār's account of his heroine in *Maṇimēkalai* falls into two sections of unequal length. The first three-quarters of the text deals with Maṇimēkalai's efforts to be free of Utayakumaraṉ, culminating with the violent murder of the prince. In this section, conceptions about what it means to be male or female in Tamil culture shape the narrative in significant ways. The final quarter of the text, however, portrays Maṇimēkalai's study of the religious knowledge that will lead to *nirvāṇa,* the end of rebirth. Conceptions about gender have increasingly little place there. The majority of this paper, therefore, deals with the first three-quarters of the text. The summary that follows of the events in these two unequal sections will serve as the basis for the analysis of Cāttaṉār's use of culturally constructed notions of male and female behavior discussed in the remainder of this chapter.[17]

In the first few chapters (1–6) of the text, Cāttaṉār introduces Maṇimēkalai and explains how Prince Utayakumaraṉ comes to be infatuated with her. As the story opens, Mātavi (Maṇimēkalai's mother) learns that her former lover, by royal command, has been executed for a theft he did not commit. Taking his death as evidence of life's impermanence, Mātavi declares she no longer will perform as a dancer in the annual city festival. Instead, she will become a Buddhist, as will her daughter. When Maṇimēkalai learns of her father's death, the tears she sheds spoil the flowers she had been stringing into a garland. To fetch new ones, she goes to a nearby garden.

Hearing from a friend that the extraordinarily beautiful Maṇimēkalai has passed on her way to the garden, Prince Utayakumaraṉ follows her there, attempting to arrange an opportunity for sexual union. The prince's efforts fail because Maṇimēkalai flees to the protection of a glass pavilion in which she locks herself. The prince comes to the pavilion, sees Maṇimēkalai, and realizes she does not welcome his advances. After he departs, Maṇimēkalai confesses that, inexplicably, she feels strongly drawn to him. These first chapters of Maṇimēkalai, then, lay out the problematical relationship between Utayakumaraṉ and Maṇimēkalai.

The action in the next few chapters (7–14) takes place on Maṇipallavam Island, where Maṇimēkalai's religious quest begins to gain direction. Soon after Utayakumaraṉ leaves the garden, a goddess arrives and takes Maṇimēkalai to the island. There the girl awakens alone and experiences overwhelming anguish. In despair, she wanders through the island and comes upon a Dharma Seat[18] that, as she circumambulates it, reveals events in her past births. In addition to this vital knowledge, she receives a begging bowl, which when once filled with alms by a virtuous housewife, will never become empty. She is also given mantras enabling her to fly through the air, change her physical form, and rid herself of hunger. Most crucial to the narrative, the goddess reveals to her that Prince Utayakumaraṉ was her husband in her past birth.

When the goddess brings Maṇimēkalai back to the city, the prince persists in his efforts to win her sexual favors. In this section of the text (Chapters 15–20), Cāttaṉār simultaneously portrays her attempts to elude him and her efforts to feed the destitute with her inexhaustible begging bowl. As a result of these compassionate acts, she convinces the king to transform his prison into a place where the needy can receive food. The king's son, however, only intensifies his pursuit of her. To escape, Maṇimēkalai uses her mantra to take on the form of another woman. Unfortunately, the prince eventually recognizes her, despite her transformation, and continues to follow her about. When the husband of the woman whose form Maṇimēkalai has taken sees the prince with a woman he takes to be his wife, his jealousy is aroused. Later that night, the angry husband cuts the prince to pieces with his sword.

The final section of *Maṇimēkalai* (Chapters 21–26) deals with the aftermath of Utayakumaraṉ's death. When the queen learns of her son's murder, she determines to wreak vengeance upon Maṇimēkalai, holding her to be the agent of his demise. Although the queen tries in succession to have Maṇimēkalai drugged, raped, or suffocated, the heroine's mantras protect her from harm. When the queen beholds the failure of all her schemes, she comes to understand that the young renouncer is an extraordinary woman and begs for forgiveness. Maṇimēkalai then takes the opportunity to instruct the queen about life's impermanence.

After the prince's murder and Maṇimēkalai's sermon to the queen, Cāttaṉār abandons the "love" theme altogether, concentrating on the heroine's attainment of ever higher stages of religious understanding (Chapters 27–30). These stages begin when Maṇimēkalai surveys current non-Buddhist philosophies of significance during a visit to the city of Vañci.[19] Maṇimēkalai then goes to Kāñci to study with the great Buddhist sage Aṟavaṇa Aṭikaḷ. After teaching her the fundamentals of Buddhist logic,[20] the sage concentrates on explicating the principle of codependent origination, the four noble truths, and the three flaws. When she hears this discourse, Maṇimēkalai dedicates herself to avoiding rebirth. Thus, in the final section of *Maṇimēkalai*—with Utayakumaraṉ's attentions behind her—Cāttaṉār portrays Maṇimēkalai as wholeheartedly dedicated to the attainment of salvific knowledge.

Cāttaṉār's Portrayal of a Woman's Beauty

Conceptions of what constitutes ideal physical appearance vary from culture to culture. Consider, for example, the difference between the plumpness of the heroines in Tamil films who are so admired throughout South India and the slimness of European fashion models whom many Western teenagers seek to resemble. Beginning with the most ancient corpus of Tamil poetry, certain kinds of female physical features come to be highly regarded and often celebrated. A consistent pattern of gender differentiation occurs in these texts. Whereas descriptions of young women tend to focus upon their beauty, those of young men emphasize their valor, might, or lineage. In a parallel way, descriptions of female beauty most regularly occur in the context of one or another of the phases of sexual love (such as clandestine tryst, lovers' separation, lovers' quarrel), whereas descriptions of male appearance occur as often in the context of making war or ruling a kingdom. Because of the close relationship between female beauty and sexual love in ancient Tamil literary texts, Cāttaṉār uses and manipulates language about female beauty to undercut traditional assumptions about the validity of sexual desire.

In classical Tamil texts women appear for the most part in love poems, where poets devote a great deal of attention to describing their appearance. Not the particular physical characteristics of a specific heroine, but the generally acknowledged marks of female beauty are noted in such poetic descriptions. Familiar phrases like the following appear in poem after poem: eyes like carp, teeth like pearls, shoulders like plump bamboo, a mound of venus like a cobra's hood, hair filled with fragrant flowers, arms adorned with rows of bangles. Eyes shaped in the sinuous curve of a carp, teeth whose pearl-like gleam gives the heroine an entrancing smile, attractively sculpted shoulders, and a pubic mound as rounded as the hood of a cobra contribute to her sexual allure. Tamil conceptions of female beauty also shape the ways in which women stereotypically decorate their bodies. In Tamil poems, women decorate their glossy black tresses with garlands of flowers, fill their arms with bangles, and adorn their feet with cosmetic paste. Poets take for granted that women's physical features—both as they are and as they are enhanced by cosmetics or adorned with jewelry—serve both to make the heroine sexually attractive to the hero and to convey that sexual love is desirable.

To see the way perceptions of gender differences shape the portrayal of physical appearance in Tamil texts, let us consider the stereotyped ways in which poets describe male appearance. In *Maṇimēkalai* (as well as *Caṅkam* texts), men are not praised for the beauty of their eyes, waists, or fair feet. Descriptions of men refer largely to prowess, strength, or lineage rather than physical beauty. For example, Cāttaṉār describes Utayakumaraṉ's father as having strong arms—the better with which to hurl a spear or wield a sword in battle (19.127).[21] In other instances, when Cāttaṉār praises the flower garland of the prince, he is actually calling attention to the greatness of the kingly lineage, because the garland is composed of special flowers that are emblems of that lineage (P.68). Similarly, the praise of the warrior's anklets refers not to the beauty of the piece of jewelry nor to the enhancing effect it has on its wearer, but to the courage of a warrior in battle. In such poetry physical beauty and allure are not culturally accepted assets for a Tamil man in the way that they are for a Tamil woman.

In a seemingly puzzling manner, Cāttaṉār describes his heroine using conventional phrases about female beauty even though he is portraying a woman who renounces sexual involvement. *Cilappatikāram* reports that Maṇimēkalai underwent tonsure[22] but Cāttaṉār speaks repeatedly of her tresses adorned with flowers (for example 8.35–37, 26.62). On numerous occasions, characters in *Maṇimēkalai* note that our heroine has assumed the garb of an ascetic, yet Cāttaṉār continues to describe her tasteful jewelry and her bangle-covered wrists (for example 10.89, 13.2). Although she eschews sexual love, Cāttaṉār dwells on descriptions of her mound of venus (28.220) and the red lines in her eyes (21.45), traditionally signs of sexual attractiveness. In spite of his unconventional subject matter, thus, he utilizes the conventional ways of describing a woman.

Why does Cāttaṉār emphasize the physical loveliness of Maṇimēkalai, given that one of his goals in *Maṇimēkalai* is to demonstrate the value of a renouncer's life? Rather than attributing to carelessness or chance the fact that his descriptions are shaped by conventional notions of gender, one must consider the possibility that Cāttaṉār remains *unwilling* to relinquish those descriptions because he sees the didactic potential of that language. In fact, if one charts the development of Cāttaṉār's use of phrases about female beauty in the garden scene, the cremation ground scene, and the scene set in the public resting place respectively, one sees that these phrases become "tools in trade" for Cāttaṉār's agenda—to critique the everyday understanding of the meaning of women's beauty.

In the garden scene, Cāttaṉār sets out what appears to be the conventional relationship between phrases about female beauty and lover's union. As the scene opens Maṇimēkalai and Cutamati, her companion, arrive in the garden, only to hear the sound of Utayakumaraṉ's chariot at the gate. Usually, the heroine and her companion would welcome such a meeting with the hero. In this case, however, Cutamati urges Maṇimēkalai to avoid encountering the prince. After she departs, the prince approaches Cutamati and does what heroes usually do in love poems: He begins to praise the beauty of the heroine. He likens her teeth to a row of pearls and her long eyes to carp. By doing so, he hopes to indicate his desire for the heroine and to enlist Cutamati's aid in arranging for a lovers' tryst. Both the situation and the language are standard in *Caṅkam* poetry, where the heroine's girlfriend often facilitates a meeting between the heroine and the hero.

Because of Cāttaṉār's didactic goals in this scene, however, the prince's praise of Maṇimēkalai's beauty does not bring about a lovers' tryst.[23] Instead, the disgruntled prince leaves the garden in a huff after failing to achieve his desire. After he exits, Maṇimēkalai notes that she feels attracted to him. Surprisingly, she announces that she fervently hopes that her desire will disappear—rather than be fulfilled. Such an unusual outcome to a usual situation thwarts the expectations of Cāttaṉār's audience and confuses them. In what can be interpreted as a response to both Maṇimēkalai's ambivalent feelings toward the prince and to the audience's puzzlement over the heroine's departure from the expected behavior, Cāttaṉār then tells a story set in a cremation ground.

The cremation ground story, by undercutting culturally constructed preconceptions of physical beauty in a jarringly gruesome and morbid context, highlights the impermanence of sexual love. This story is narrated by a goddess, who arrives in the garden immediately after the departure of the prince. The tale relates how an innocent young lad wanders into a cremation ground by mistake. Upon entering, he is confronted with a ghastly sight: the dismembered corpse of a young woman, dressed for a tryst with her lover. Vultures and jackals gorge themselves upon pieces of the body, which Cāttaṉār describes in careful detail:

> There was the ceaseless, exultant howl of a jackal clutching in his jaws a [female] corpse's foot decorated with red cosmetic cream, a lump of wormy decaying flesh. Then he heard the drawn-out shriek of a vulture piercing and consuming a naked mound of venus, the unrestrained howl of an evil dog who had snatched and torn apart a severed arm stacked with bangles, and the crunch of the hungry kite seizing and eating beautiful, erect, young breasts adorned with sandalpaste. (6.110–117)

The dead woman's foot is covered with red cosmetic paste, believed to increase a woman's attractiveness. Bangles decorate her arms. Fragrant sandalpaste adorns her erect breasts. All these cosmetics and jewelry are thought to make a woman attractive and alluring.

In this situation, however, they can hardly create such an effect. In fact, they have no effect at all upon the female ghoul who approaches the corpse and begins to chomp on its head:[24]

> A female ghoul gleefully . . . grabbed a charred head. She did not ask herself, "What are these: Clouds or woman's tresses? Carp or eyes? Is this a *kumiḻ* flower or a nose? Are these lips or *kavir* flowers? Teeth or pearls?" She did not show any mercy. Instead, dancing with joy on her cloven feet, she gouged out the eyes of that head and ate them with insatiable glee. (6.119–126)

Here, among the other phrases, we find the same features praised by Utayakumaraṉ in the garden scene—the teeth like pearls and the eyes resembling carp. Normally, a poet compares a woman's teeth to pearls to indicate their extraordinarily beautiful shape and gleam, and her eyes to carp to compliment their alluring shape. Yet now Cāttaṉār uses the conventional phrases about female beauty only to mock them.

This cremation ground scene derives much of its didactic power from the fact that it appears immediately after Cāttaṉār has portrayed Utayakumaraṉ's attempt to seduce Maṇimēkalai in the garden. Utayakumaraṉ's speech to Cutamati, in which he praises Maṇimēkalai's teeth and eyes, is followed by the cremation ground story, in which a woman dressed to attend such a tryst is dismembered. In the garden the prince spoke of teeth and eyes in admiration, but in the cremation ground those same phrases become vehicles to convey the absolute indifference with which death destroys its victims. It seems likely that hearing the language of female beauty mocked—and mocked in such a gruesome setting—would be a disconcerting experience for Cāttaṉār's audience. Such an experience would force his readers to reconsider the assumptions of familiar classical love poetry.

By the time of the scene set in the public resting place, Utayakumaraṉ's desire for Maṇimēkalai has grown in intensity and, hence, Cāttaṉār uses conceptions of female beauty to submit sexual desire to an even more elaborate critique. This scene begins with a man praising Maṇimēkalai's beauty, using the conventional phrases discussed earlier. Soon afterwards Utayakumaraṉ approaches her, hoping to win her favors. In response, Maṇimēkalai calls his attention to an old hag once known for her great beauty.

By then systematically subjecting cultural assumptions about the value of female beauty to ridicule, Maṇimēkalai demonstrates that she has come to see the worthlessness of sexual longing, and that it is necessary for the prince to see it as well. She instructs him by contrasting—feature by feature, from head to toe—the loveliness of the crone in her youth with her current appearance. She notes that the once-black hair has become white, and eyebrows earlier like victorious bows presently resemble dried-up prawns. The old woman's eyes seemed like blue waterlilies in her youth, but now they are runny and swollen. Her teeth, like pearls in a row before, now resemble the uneven yellowed seeds in a bottle gourd. Maṇimēkalai drives the point home, describing everything from her drooping breasts, like empty bags, to the feet that resembled flower buds in her younger days, but now look like dried fruit (20.40–70). Once again the familiar phrases about, for example, teeth and eyes recur. Here they function to contrast appearance in youth and old age, enabling Maṇimēkalai to point out the transience of female physical beauty and of the sexual desire aroused by such beauty.

Significantly enough, soon after Maṇimēkalai's sermon to the prince, he is murdered because of his refusal to give up his pursuit of her. Before the heroine's sermon, Cāttaṉār reminded the reader of Maṇimēkalai's own beauty. Maṇimēkalai's sermon then indicates that when this old crone was young, she possessed the same kind of fresh beauty as Maṇimēkalai. Our young heroine's beauty too surely will fade over time, making her resemble this old woman. It is Utayakumaraṉ's inability to cultivate detachment from her beauty that leads to his death, only a few hours after Maṇimēkalai's sermon.

These three scenes indicate a developmental pattern in *Maṇimēkalai* with regard to praise of female beauty. In the garden scene, Maṇimēkali feels drawn to the prince, who speaks flattering phrases about her physical appearance. In the cremation ground scene, the goddess instructs the heroine about the nature of desire by undercutting the very same concepts expressed in the phrases. By the time of the scene set in the public resting place, Maṇimēkalai herself provides a critique of those phrases. In response to his sexual demands, couched in conventional language about female beauty, she attempts to instruct the prince. The outcome of this scene (Utayakumaraṉ's death) indicates that Cāttaṉār has used phrases about female beauty in service of his argument—that the failure to realize the impermanence of female beauty leads to suffering.

Analysis of these three scenes has shown how Cāttaṉār uses culturally constructed ideas about the difference between male and female physical appearance as a means by which he can critique conventional assumptions about the nature of reality. As a result of Cāttaṉār's self-conscious manipulation of the conventional phrases associated with the ideal of woman's beauty, even the modern reader begins to perceive how radically Cāttaṉār has undercut the assumptions of love poetry. Those members of his audience steeped in classical Tamil literary tradition and new to the tenets of Buddhism could hardly fail to experience something similar.

Cāttaṉār's Use of the Heroine's Anguish as a Motif

If Cāttaṉār's use of classical Tamil phrases of female beauty jars his audience, his use of the motif of separation has even more radical implications. Traditionally, *Caṅkam* poets wrote against the backdrop of the seashore landscape about the anguish of a heroine separated from her beloved. Cāttaṉār draws upon these same seashore elements for two key scenes in *Maṇimēkalai,* but he reverses the usual meanings of those elements. Cumulatively, these two scenes suggest that union of lovers—rather than separation—causes anguish. At the same time, they show a woman who leaves her home behind.

Although both men and women in traditional Tamil love poetry experience anguish due to separation from their beloved, the circumstances under which males and females are portrayed as experiencing this anguish differ. Among the reasons why lovers come to be separated one finds the heroine's mother's refusal to let them meet, the hero's journey to a faraway place to seek wealth or education, and the hero's responsibility to act as an emissary for the king. Whatever the reason for the separation of lovers, however, the woman always remains at home, while the man is away. For example, a number of poems describe the hero's longing for his beloved, who has stayed home while he crosses the barren and dangerous desert. In contrast, poems that depict the heroine's anguish describe her emotional upheaval as she steadfastly waits at home for the return of her lover. Many of the most beautiful poems about the heroine's anguish are set in the seashore landscape.

To see how Cāttaṉār uses and transforms the motif of the heroine's separation from the hero, we need to begin by examining the traditional depiction of the heroine in poems set at the seashore. In the *akam* genre, poets write of the situations of love against five landscapes, each one associated with a type of lovers' union or separation. Poets write about clandestine lovers' union against the backdrop of the mountainside, patient waiting for the hero's return as well as domestic happiness in a forest setting, the man's visit to courtesans (and the wife's subsequent sulking) in the countryside, separation mixed with danger amidst the desert, and anxious waiting for the hero's return by the seashore. Cāttaṉār chooses and manipulates images associated with the seashore to fulfill his didactic goals.

Tamil tradition labels this landscape *neytal*, the name for the dark lily that grows by the sea. Each landscape has associated with it, in addition to its emblematic flower name, a whole series of "native elements," whose presence clearly indicates to the reader the theme and setting of the poem.[25] Traditionally, *neytal* poems are set at nightfall and make references to elements of local geography and culture such as seagulls, fisherfolk, salt gatherers, laurel, screwpine, and the tigerclaw tree. Each poem need not contain all of these elements; as both poet and audience share a knowledge of these conventions, the poet can immediately evoke the mood of a lover's anxious waiting simply by including one or more elements associated with *neytal*, such as laurel or screwpine.

A look at a classical *neytal* poem will illustrate the way in which a poet uses particular native elements to intensify the mood of the poem. Consider, for example, *Aiṅkuṟunūṟu* 144 by Ammūvaṉār, in which the heroine tells of the feelings that separation from her lover have caused:

My body,
  young mango leaf,
  is now lovesick yellow

for that man
of the seashore

  where the stork sleeps alone
  in the flowering groves
  of tigerclaw trees.[26]

In this piece, the poet portrays the heroine speaking of her love for the hero. Lovesickness has lent her body a pallor that makes it resemble a tender mango leaf. The tigerclaw tree, mentioned at the end of the poem, is a native element of the *neytal* landscape. The scene of the lonely stork sleeping by the seashore is a way of referring to the lovesick heroine's own unhappiness because she cannot sleep with her lover. The poetic situation is anxious waiting; the native elements intensify the portrayal of the heroine's anguish.

If we turn to Cāttaṉār's borrowing of imagery from the *neytal* landscape to describe his heroine, we see *Caṅkam* imagery functioning for different ends. In portraying his heroine, Cāttaṉār weaves the imagery of *neytal* into an account of the arising of Maṇimēkalai's anguish, due to the bonds of love. Then, he depicts the ceasing of Maṇimēkalai's anguish, when those bonds are broken. The overall effect of Cāttaṉār's reversal of the meaning of *neytal* imagery is to suggest that women can separate themselves from both love and home. Cāttaṉār's transformation of the motif of separation is most evident in three scenes: the aftermath of the prince's departure from the garden, Maṇimēkalai's awakening on the island, and the deity's explanation of Utayakumaraṉ's death.

In the aftermath of the prince's departure from the garden, Cāttaṉār portrays Maṇimēkalai as experiencing anguish. Cāttaṉār describes her unhappiness by carefully employing imagery about her surroundings as night begins to fall (5.123–141). He begins by describing how a female swan, who accidentally entangled herself in a lotus flower, struggles to escape from its enclosing petals. Her mate rips apart the flower, picks her up, and carries her away—suggesting precisely what Utayakumaraṉ just sought to do. Then Cāttaṉār notes the chords of a lute playing the tune associated with the landscape of a man's visit to a courtesan as well as the tones of a flute sounding the song of domestic bliss. Both suggest the happiness of man and woman together. In contrast, such happiness is not for Maṇimēkalai. Cāttaṉār likens her to a widow, "who enters her family's house, after losing her husband on the battlefield" (5.137–141). In the following lines Cāttaṉār tells of how, at the moment of dusk, a lovesick pallor (*pacalai*) appears on Maṇimēkalai's body.

The conjunction of Maṇimēkalai's lovesickness and the falling of darkness suggests how the bonds of sexual love prevent Maṇimēkalai from attaining enlightenment. Conventionally, lovesickness is believed to intensify at dusk because that is the time when lovers usually meet. Even though Prince Utayakumaraṉ has just left the garden, Maṇimēkalai realizes she feels attached to him. The term *pacalai* specifically refers to the yellow appearance that Tamil poets attribute to a lovesick woman. (This same lovesick pallor was a major element in the *neytal* poem just analyzed.) Cāttaṉār links this *pacalai* conceptually with darkness, which in many South Asian religious texts, especially Buddhist ones, is a symbol for ignorance. Darkness is to be dispelled by light, which is identified with the Buddha or the wisdom he disseminated.[27] In this passage, then, Cāttaṉār connects Maṇimēkalai's attraction to Utayakumaraṉ—and the grief it causes her—to ignorance. In doing this for his audience, he links a new religious perspective to traditional Tamil imagery.

In the scene where Maṇimēkalai awakens on Maṇipallavam Island and her anguish intensifies, Cāttaṉār uses specific elements from the *neytal* landscape to describe her emotional situation in an evocative manner. Only a few hours after the dusk just described, a goddess arrives at the garden, tells Maṇimēkalai the instructive tale about the cremation ground, and then takes her to distant Maṇipallavam Island, in the midst of the vast sea. The lines describing the coast of this island suggest a great deal about Maṇimēkalai's situation, if we keep *neytal* poetic tradition in mind. At Maṇipallavam Island, Cāttaṉār tells us, the waves break on the sandy shore where pearls, bits of coral, and broken conches lie scattered. The tall stooping tigerclaw tree, the laurel with its curved stalks, and the flowering screwpine shade a lovely bed made of fragrant flowers (8.1–12). Here Maṇimēkalai awakens.

This description of the seashore lies squarely within *neytal* poetic tradition. Poets commonly include dashing waves, pearls, shells, coral washed ashore, and the rich dark sand in their poems about the *neytal* landscape. The tigerclaw tree, the laurel, the screwpine, and the lilies are all "native elements" of the landscape.[28] Appropriately enough, on this seashore the heroine feels terribly alone and unhappy. Her heart trembles, and she weeps. Cāttaṉār tells us that she feels "intense anguish."

In this passage, Cāttaṉār sets the scene for events to come by using the poetic resources available to him. His audience easily would recognize the evocation of the *neytal* landscape. Flora like laurel and screwpine would immediately evoke the scenario of love in separation. The anguish of the heroine would appear familiar to them, but one element remains significantly different: In this case the woman, not the man, has gone to a faraway place for the sake of education. On the island she learns many things about herself and the Buddhist path that enable her to pursue her spiritual goals with tenacity in the rest of the narrative. Because of Maṇimēkalai's commitment to a life of renunciation, her anguish also will be destroyed in a manner unlike that of the *neytal* heroine, who eagerly looks forward to reuniting with the hero.

The complete destruction of Maṇimēkalai's anguish is achieved when she is freed from sexual pursuit and comes to understand fully the reasons for Utayakumaraṉ's death as well as the path that she should follow in the future to attain Buddhist knowledge. After the prince dies, distraught Maṇimēkalai hears a voice, emanating from within the pillar of the nearby temple. She knows that the deity abiding in that pillar will speak no falsehood, so she does obeisance and entreats it to reveal the reason for Utayakumaraṉ's death. In the prince's previous birth, answers the deity, Utayakumaraṉ asked his cook to prepare a feast of rice for a wandering sage. While conducting his duties, the cook tripped and spilled the pot of rice. When Utayakumaraṉ saw the mishap, he flew into a rage and cut off the cook's head. The karma from that evil deed finally came to fruition. As a result, Utayakumaraṉ lost his head to an assailant who killed him in a similar fury. After revealing the reason for the prince's death, the deity culminates this discourse by foretelling the future events that will enable Maṇimēkalai to achieve her spiritual goals.

Through a key image Cāttaṉār next links the death of Utayakumaraṉ and the knowledge Maṇimēkalai has just received with spiritual progress. After Maṇimēkalai hears the deity's words, Cāttaṉār describes the result in this way: "Maṇimēkalai arose from the ocean of grief. . . . And just then, the sun with radiating rays awoke the whole world from its slumber" (21.185–190). Once again, Cāttaṉār connects Maṇimēkalai's state of mind with the setting around her, this time linking her moment of spiritual illumination with the rising sun: Her newly acquired understanding of her relationship to the prince as well as her understanding of her future as a female renunciant help rescue her from the ocean of grief.

Previously, on Maṇipallavam Island, the seashore imagery was both literal and metaphorical—it described the actual backdrop as well as Maṇimēkalai's state of mind. Now, however, the ocean to which Cāttaṉār refers is metaphorical. It is the ocean of endless rebirth from which human beings can be rescued through enlightenment. Buddhist writers identify Buddhist teaching as the raft that saves one from drowning in that sea.[29] As Cāttaṉār describes Maṇimēkalai arising from that sea, he also provides us with an image of ignorance disappearing—the rising sun. Here the pattern of imagery begun in Cāttaṉār's description of Maṇipallavam Island reaches its culmination. The anguish Maṇimēkalai felt is over—her bonds to Utayakumaraṉ have been severed, she has attained a state of separation from sexual pursuit, and her ignorance is being replaced by knowledge.

This analysis of the motif of separation in three scenes from *Maṇimēkalai* suggests how Cāttaṉār has taken the traditional portrayal of the anguished heroine and reversed certain aspects of it to achieve his didactic goals. According to the gender roles of classical Tamil poetry, the husband may go off to a distant land to further his education, for example, while the heroine waits at home for their reunion. Cāttaṉār takes up the situation of anxious waiting set by the seashore but uses it for his own purposes. Not the hero but the heroine goes off to a distant land, Maṇipallavam Island, to further her (spiritual) education. The heroine is not longing for union but permanent separation. And happiness is achieved not with the fulfillment of desire but with the cessation of that desire. Once again Cāttaṉār has taken traditional gender constructs—hero as traveler, heroine separated from her beloved and anxiously awaiting his return—only to transform them for the sake of persuasion.

Cāttaṉār's Depiction of Maternal Nurturing

Up to this point, we have examined the way in which Cāttaṉār used culturally constructed concepts about femaleness for the sake of critique. But things change radically when he focuses his energy on advocacy instead. Rather than undermining conventional assumptions, he now moves to emphasize the idea that one should give generously to aid all living beings. We saw him self-consciously manipulate, in a critical fashion, gender constructs such as "female beauty" and "the anguished heroine" to undercut the set of assumptions on which Tamil love poetry is based. In contrast, when Cāttaṉār turns to promoting the ideal of nurturance, he wholeheartedly accepts the gender construct of "maternal" behavior. But, he goes one radical step further, extending it as an ideal for both women and men. That is, he embraces a set of characteristics that Tamil society associates with females, but then indicates that they should be exemplary for both sexes.

Although he could draw on *akam* poetry to mount his attack on sexual love, those poems do not help him in his efforts to champion nurturing behavior.[30] Instead, he turns to the language of myth. Drawing upon a large body of mythic materials linking the cow with female nurturance, he argues for the acceptance of a particular kind of giving. O'Flaherty's wide-ranging survey of the motif of the cow indicates how Indian myth makers connect the good cow with unlimited generosity.[31] Beginning with the Vedic story of Pṛthu milking the earth cow and obtaining all that he desires, good cows in India are linked with a generosity not limited to their own biological offspring. O'Flaherty emphasizes the link between the cow and the good mother.[32] The cow remains a particularly apt image of such female generosity because she gives her nourishment not just to her own calves but to anyone who will milk her. The nature of the cow's generosity is crucial to understanding both the origins and meaning of Maṇimēkalai's ability to nurture all living creatures.

In the scene where Maṇimēkalai first receives her inexhaustible begging bowl, therefore, Cāttaṉār highlights links between the bowl and a cow's maternal nature. The very name of the bowl, *Amuta Curapi* has bovine resonances in myth. *Curapi* is the Tamil transliteration of Sanskrit *Surabhi,* the name of the celestial wish-granting cow whose udders give forth celestial ambrosia (Sanskrit *amṛta,* Tamil *amutam*).[33] After Maṇimēkalai receives the bowl, she envisions succoring the needy and that vision culminates with an image of her as a cow. She tells of how she longs to bestow on suffering people "the medicine of precious life" that pours forth from the hollow of her miraculous bowl, labeling it "that which gives what the heart desires."[34] This bowl, says the heroine, is like a cow's udder, from which sweet milk streams when the cow sees the face of her newly born calf and feels pity (11.114–118). In this telling passage, Maṇimēkalai articulates her recognition that her bowl is like the wish-granting cow (it "gives what the heart desires") after which it is named. When she sees the faces of hungry people and feels compassion, it enables her to feed others, as a cow does.

In the same scene, Cāttaṉār expressly links this maternal nurturance with Buddhism. First, the guardian of the island tells Maṇimēkalai that the inexhaustible begging bowl only emerges from the pond once a year—on the Buddha's birthday (11.42–45). Second, when the heroine receives the bowl, she expresses her gratitude by singing a hymn in praise of the Buddha. Third, the guardian of the island suggests that the eradication of hunger will further the progress of those who seek to escape rebirth. Because, as she puts it, extreme hunger can "destroy the great raft of learning onto which we grasp" (11.79),[35] eliminating hunger can advance the pursuit of spiritual knowledge. Maṇimēkalai can save people from desperate acts born from hunger, says the guardian: "Those who destroy the great hunger of destitute people personify the true path of life on this earth" (11.93–94). Her nurturing can enable them to hold fast to the "raft" of spiritual learning.

Because of the bowl's unique ability to help Maṇimēkalai feed destitute creatures, she desires to know its history. Her Buddhist mentor, Aṟavaṇa Aṭikaḷ, tells the story of its first owner—a story filled with bovine themes. In the story of the origin of the bowl, Cāttaṉār makes explicit the link between the begging bowl, the cow, and Buddhism. Specific maternal characteristics of the cow are highlighted: her ability to nurture in an unlimited way and her willingness to give milk to all that seek it, not just her own calves.

According to the story of the bowl's origins, Āputtiraṉ, the bowl's first owner, survived cruel abandonment as an infant because a compassionate cow suckled him, even though he was not her own offspring. Āputtiraṉ's brahmin mother had conceived the boy illegitimately and then forsaken him in a nearby garden. When a cow found the helpless infant, she nursed it with sweet milk and protected it until it was taken home by a brahmin family.

As a result of the cow's nurturance, Āputtiraṉ grew into a champion of cows, saving one from slaughter and making a speech to cruel brahmins about the admirable qualities of a cow. The story tells us that in his youth, Āputtiraṉ entered a house where priests were preparing for the sacrifice of a cow.[36] His heart went out to the frightened animal, and under cover of darkness, he stole it and set out for the forest. When the cow-thief was caught, he defended himself by arguing that such a noble creature should not be sacrificed: "The cow eats only the grass which grows on the land set aside for grazing. With a virtuous heart, she graciously feeds excellent sweet milk to all people in this wide land, beginning from the day they are born" (13.51–54). Here Āputtiraṉ articulated Cāttaṉār's own criteria for compassionate action toward living creatures—it should be generous and aimed at all, not just one's own children.

Āputtiraṉ himself then went on to model his own behavior after that of the cow for the rest of his life. When he was hounded out of the brahmin community for disturbing the planned cow sacrifice, he moved to Madurai, where he became known as the refuge of the hungry. Every day he collected alms to feed the blind, deaf, lame, and sick people, as well as orphans and widows.

Āputtiraṉ became the owner of an inexhaustible begging bowl as a result of a sitution in which his limited resources were not adequate to feed the hungry. Late one night some starving travelers arrived at his doorstep. As Āputtiraṉ had already distributed all his alms, he could not aid them. Because he was so distressed at not being able to feed them, the goddess Sarasvatī appeared in the nearby temple to bestow the inexhaustible bowl on him. From that moment on, he nurtured all the people around him, as the cow who saved his life had done. At the moment of his death, Āputtiraṉ threw his bowl into a pond called *Cow's Mouth* (*kōmuki*), commanding it to remain there until a person came along who would use it properly to nurture living creatures. Maṇimēkalai was that person.

The story highlights how the maternal actions of the cow were self-consciously adopted by Āputtiraṉ. He wandered through Tamilnadu with his bowl, the multiform of a cow's udder, feeding the hungry. For this Cāttaṉār labels him "one who always has a cow in his heart" (15.17–18). The Tamil scholar David Shulman was quick to note this point, labeling Āputtiraṉ *maternal.*[37] This portrayal of Āputtiraṉ demonstrates that what are conceived of in Tamil culture as maternal, cowlike, mothering characteristics can be adopted both by men like Āputtiraṉ and women like Maṇimēkalai. Those who understand the true nature of reality seek to imitate the cow (unlike the cow-sacrificing brahmins in the tale) and nurture generously, with compassion, all living creatures in need.

Cāttaṉār portrays this particular kind of nurturing in a pivotal scene toward the end of *Maṇimēkalai.* It occurs during Maṇimēkalai's journey to Kāñci, where she has gone to end the starvation due to a drought. She and the king of the city oversee the construction of a Buddha seat in the midst of groves and a pond they named *Kōmuki* (cow's mouth)[38]—all built to resemble those on Maṇipallavam Island, at the spot where she received her inexhaustible begging bowl. Then Maṇimēkalai places her bowl on the Buddha seat and calls all living creatures to come and eat. According to Cāttaṉār's narrative, people speaking the eighteen different languages[39] flock to the spot, along with animals and all other living creatures. Cāttaṉār carefully singles out certain kinds of human beings for special mention: the blind, the deaf, the lame, orphans, people with diseases, and those without clothing. All are included in this act of nurturance, even those who do not fit into traditional social communities or are considered polluting.

This scene culminates with the beginning of Maṇimēkalai's serious religious instruction under the tutelage of her mentor. As the many starving creatures eat the food bestowed by the bowl, the great sage Aṟavaṇa Aṭikaḷ enters the garden. After prostrating herself and washing his feet, Maṇimēkalai serves him food. When he finishes his meal, she voices her hope that she might receive that which she has long sought (28.239–244). And so she does. As recorded in *Maṇimēkalai's* final two chapters, Aṟavaṇa Aṭikaḷ teaches the heroine the nature of religious argumentation and then instructs her in the main tenets of Buddhism. Chapter 29 of *Maṇimēkalai* narrates Aṟavaṇa Aṭikaḷ's systematic and detailed discourse on ways to discern faulty reasoning in syllogisms. The text's final chapter contains the sage's succinct and comprehensive account of key Buddhist formulations (such as the four noble truths and the twelve *nidānas*). In sum, then, the final chapters of *Maṇimēkalai* link nurturance with gaining salvific religious knowledge.

In these three scenes from *Maṇimēkalai*—the acquisition of the bowl, the history of the bowl, and the installation of the bowl on the Buddha seat—Cāttaṉār depicts ideal nurturing behavior, always linking it to the qualities of the cow. Like the cow in pan-Indian myth who endlessly nurtures people, both Āputtiraṉ and Maṇimēkalai feed without limit a number of people, none of whom are their biological children. In addition to ending starvation, such nurturance is seen as fostering knowledge. When hunger is sated, human beings can turn their thoughts to religious matters. The act of feeding hungry people also bears fruit for Maṇimēkalai, as it culminates in her acquisition of knowledge that will enable her to cut off the bonds of rebirth.

In portraying the acquisition, history, and installation of the inexhaustible bowl, then, Cāttaṉār, uses a culturally constructed notion of femaleness, that of "the maternal nurturer." Once again, however, he is not content to accept the concept as it is. Instead, he extends the notion of motherhood by conceptualizing it not in terms of a human mother suckling her offspring, but in terms of a cow. The cow gives unlimited milk day after day and bestows it upon anyone who milks her. The ideal nurturer, according to Cāttaṉār, does something similar. That person gives and continues to give; such a person gives food to all human beings—not just members of the family or caste (*jāti*).[40] Such giving is motivated by compassion of the type that a cow is believed to feel for her hungry calf. Most surprising of all, such "maternal nurturance," as it is not necessarily linked to biological motherhood, can be a model for both females and males. By promoting such an ideal, Cāttaṉār once again shows his ability to use gender constructs, rather than be limited by them.

Conclusions

To describe the process by which a courtesan's daughter becomes a Buddhist nun, Cāttaṉār draws upon a variety of culturally constructed concepts of maleness and femaleness. In particular, he uses formulaic language of praise for female beauty, conventional portrayals of the heroine separated from her lover, and mythically shaped notions of the nurturing mother. Although he adopts traditional phrases lauding the physical beauty of women, he juxtaposes those phrases with situations that undercut the entire concept of sexual love. With similarly disquieting effects, he reverses the logic of the lovesick heroine's experience, implying that lovers' union—rather than separation—causes anguish and, therefore, that she should leave the hero behind. Finally, he extends biological motherhood into universal motherhood with mythic bovine resonances, as a way of affirming the behavior of compassionate nurturing for all living beings.

In employing these three rhetorical strategies of undercutting, reversal, and universalizing, Cāttaṉār demonstrates his ability to perceive culturally constructed notions of the differences between males and females in a critical fashion and use them for his own ends. He employs these concepts, but self-consciously transforms them for the sake of persuasion. They constitute a body of assumptions that Cāttaṉār can use to manipulate the response of Tamil readers—to engage them, to challenge their everyday assumptions, and to suggest an alternate worldview. As a rhetorically sophisticated writer, Cāttaṉār has composed a persuasive text in which he uses gender constructs to achieve his own goals, rather than letting those constructs constrain him.

Does our examination of Cāttaṉār's portrayal of Maṇimēkalai shed any light on the general relationship between Buddhism and gender? If so, perhaps it helps to illuminate the process by which individuals renounce the world and commit themselves to a religious discipline. In the early stages of Maṇimēkalai's involvement with Buddhism, concepts of what it means to be female play a large role. And naturally so. In an existence mired in passion, all defining dichotomous concepts (female-male, old-young, beautiful-ugly) shape behavior and perceptions of behavior. The closer one moves to enlightenment, however, the less hold such concepts should have on an adept. For this reason, the very final chapters of *Maṇimēkalai* contain little reference to gender. *Nirvāṇa*, the goal that Maṇimēkalai seeks, is portrayed as transcending gender in Cāttaṉār's text.

Notes

I am grateful to Caroline Bynum, José Cabezón, Jan Cooper, Michael Fisher, Charles Hallisey, Frank Reynolds, and Jessica Buccarelli for their comments on previous drafts of this article. Funding for the research on which this article is based was provided by a Fulbright-Hays Doctoral Dissertation Abroad Fellowship and a National Endowment for the Humanities Summer Stipend.

1. See, for example, rules about the punishment for sexual misconduct in Charles S. Prebish, *Buddhist Monastic Discipline: The Sanskrit Prātimokṣa Sūtras*

of the Mahāsāṃghikas and Mūlasarvāstivādins, Institute for the Advanced Study of World Religions Series (University Park: Pennsylvania State University Press, 1975). For rules designed to keep female and male members of the monastic community separate, see Cullavagga X of the *Vinaya Piṭaka* as translated in I. B. Horner, *Book of Discipline (Vinaya-Piṭaka)* (London: Luzac and Company for the Pali Text Society, 1963), vol. 5, pp. 352–356.

2. See, for example, Nancy Auer Falk, "The Case of the Vanishing Nuns: The Fruits of Ambivalence in Ancient Buddhism," *Unspoken Worlds,* ed. Nancy Auer Falk and Rita Gross (San Franscisco: Harper and Row, 1980), pp. 207–224; and I. B. Horner, *Women under Primitive Buddhism: Laywomen and Almswomen* (London: Routledge and Kegan Paul, 1930; reprint ed., Delhi: Motilal Banarsidass, 1975).

3. Nonetheless, this process is the focus of many spiritual biographies of nuns. See, for example, the accounts in the *Manoratha Pūranī* as translated in Mabel Bode, "Women Leaders of the Buddhist Reformation," *Journal of the Royal Asiatic Society of Great Britain and Ireland* (1893): 517–566, 763–798.

4. Tamil terms are transliterated in this chapter according to the system used in the *Tamil Lexicon.*

5. The narrative structure of *Maṇimēkalai* is complex; it contains the main story of Maṇimēkalai, the heroine, and sixteen other branch stories. These branch stories illustrate the value of Buddhist ideas such as *dāna* (giving) and *ahiṃsā* (noninjury to living beings). In this chapter I am concerned only with *Maṇimēkalai's* main story. For an analysis of its branch stories, see Paula Richman, *Women, Branch Stories, and Religious Rhetoric in a Tamil Buddhist Text,* Foreign and Comparative Studies, South Asia Series (Syracuse, N.Y.: Maxwell School, Syracuse University, 1988), Chapter 3–7.

6. In cultural anthropology, for example, see Sherry B. Ortner and Harriet Whitehead, eds., *Sexual Meanings: The Cultural Construction of Gender and Sexuality* (Cambridge: Cambridge University Press, 1981). In psychology, for example, see Carol Gilligan, *In a Different Voice: Psychological Theory and Women's Development* (Cambridge, Mass: Harvard University Press, 1982).

7. Caroline Bynum, Stevan Harrell, and Paula Richman, eds., *Gender and Religion: On the Complexity of Symbols* (Boston: Beacon Press, 1986), pp. 8, 2. For a discussion of the way in which gender-marked symbols function as more than signifiers of known realities in the Hindu tradition, see Larry Shinn, "The Goddess: Theological Sign or Religious Symbol?" *Numen: International Review for the History of Religions* 31, no. 2 (1984): 175–184.

8. Cf. the perspective developed in Roy Wagner, *The Invention of Culture* (Chicago: University of Chicago Press, 1981).

9. Richman, *Women, Branch Stories, and Rhetoric,* p. 4.

10. See Mayilai Cīni Vēṅkaṭacāmi, *Pauttamum Tamiḻum* (Tinnevelly: South Indian Saiva Siddhanta Works Publishing Society; henceforth abbreviated as SISS, 1940); K. A. Nilakanta Sastri, "Buddhism in the Tamil Country," *March of India* 8, no. 12A (November 1956): 51–54; K. Indrapala, "Buddhism among the Tamils A.D. 1000–1500," in *Proceedings of the Fifth International Conference-Seminar on Tamil Studies*, vol. 2. (Madras: International Association of Tamil Studies, 1981), pp. 12/27–12/39; C. Minakshi, "Buddhism in South India" in *South Indian Studies—II*, ed. R. Nagaswamy (Madras: Society for Archaeological, Historical, and Epigraphical Research, 1978), pp. 83–131; A. Velu Pillai, *Epigraphical Evidences [sic] for Tamil Studies* (Madras: International Institute of Tamil Studies, 1980), pp. 86–116.

11. Scholarly dating of *Maṇimēkalai* varies from the second to the eighth century. For discussions favoring the earliest date, see Varatarāja Ayyar, *Tamiḻ Ilakkiya Varalāṟu* (Madras: Aṇṇamalai Palkalai Kaḻakam, 1957), p. 148; and S. Krishnaswami Aiyangar, *Manimekhalai in Its Historical Setting* (London: Luzac and Co., 1928), pp. 11–12. For a discussion of the latest dating see S. Vaiyāpuri Piḷḷai, *Kāviyakālam* (Madras: Tamiḻ Puttakālayam, 1962), pp. 33, 141. For dating discussion based on *Maṇimēkalai's* chapter on Buddhist logic, see S. Kuppuswami, "Problems of Identity in the Cultural History of Ancient India," *Journal of Oriental Reseach, Madras* 1, no. 2 (April 1927): 192; K. Nilakanta Sastri, *The Cōḻas* (Madras: University of Madras, 1955), pp. 55–56, 62, n.117; K. G. Sesha Aiyar, "The Date of Maṇimēkalai," *Journal of Oriental Research, Madras* 1, no. 4 (October 1927): 321–329. Both Kandaswamy and Zvelebil make convincing cases for dating *Maṇimēkalai* ca. the sixth century, and this date is becoming generally accepted. See S. N. Kandaswamy, *Buddhism as Expounded in Maṇimēkalai* (Annamalainagar: Annamalai University, 1978), pp. 5–74 and Kamil Zvelebil, *Tamil Literature*, vol. 2 of *Handbuch Der Orientalistik*, general ed. Jan Gonda (Leiden: E. J. Brill, 1975), pp. 114–116.

12. At least two other Tamil Buddhist texts did exist at one time. Camaya Tivākara Vāmaṉa Muṉivar's commentary on *Nīlakēci* cites a few lines from *Pimpicārakatai*, a Tamil epic concerning Bimbisāra, king of Rājagṛha during the time of the Buddha. The story of another Tamil Buddhist text, *Kuṇṭalakēci*, has also been preserved in the commentary on *Nīlakēci* 176. See Kamil Zvelebil, *Tamil Literature*, vol. 10, of *A History of Indian Literature* (Wiesbaden: Otto Harrassowitz, 1974), p. 142.

13. The reader who seeks an introduction to Tamil literary convention in general, rather than an introduction to the Tamil literary conventions used by Cāttaṉār in *Maṇimēkalai*, should consult the following works: A. K. Ramanujan, *The Interior Landscape: Love Poems from a Classical Tamil Anthology* (Bloomington: Indiana University Press, 1967; Midland Books, 1975), pp. 97–115; Kamil Zvelebil, *The Smile of Murugan: On Tamil Literature of South India* (Leiden: E. J. Brill, 1973), pp. 45–118; M. Varadarajan, *The Treatment of Nature in Sangam Literature* (Tinnevelly: SISS, 1969); Rm. Periakaruppan, *Tradition and Talent in Cankam Poetry* (Madurai: Madurai Publishing House, 1976).

14. See Richman, *Women, Branch Stories, and Rhetoric*, p. 9, for a discussion of Cāttaṉār's audience.

15. For two perspectives on the definition and nature of this genre of Tamil literature, see Kamil Zvelebil, *Tamil Literature*, vol. 10 of *A History of Indian Literature*, pp. 130–131; and David Shulman, *The King and the Clown in South Indian Myth and Poetry* (Princeton, N.J.: Princeton University Press, 1985), p. 11.

16. Na. Mu. Vēṅkaṭacāmi Nāṭṭār, com., *Cilappatikāram Uraiyutaṉ* (Tinnevelly: SISS, 1968), Chapters 29 and 30.

17. This synopsis primarily highlights elements of the plot relevant to the analysis in this chapter. For a fuller synopsis, see Chapter 2 of Richman, *Women, Branch Stories, and Rhetoric.*

18. This unusual seat is called the *taruma* (Tamil transliteration of Sanskrit *dharma*) *pīṭikai*, "seat" or "throne." In *Maṇimēkalai*, the seat reveals the events that transpired in one's past births. Scholars believe this throne is the same one described in the *Mahāvaṃśa*. According to the story recorded there, two kinsmen were fighting over the possession of the throne. The Buddha, out of compassion for them, took his almsbowl and went to the scene of the battle. Hovering above the battlefield, he caused darkness to descend and then allowed light to appear once more. This miracle convinced the two kinsmen to stop fighting. Then the Buddha sat on the throne, and hence it is called the *dharma* throne. See Wilhelm Geiger and Mabel Haynes Bode, trans., *The Mahāvaṃśa or The Great Chronicle of Ceylon* (London: Published for the Pali Text Society by Henry Frowde, Oxford University Press, 1912), p. 507. An extremely condensed version of the story appears in *Maṇimēkalai*, Chapter 8, lines 44–63.

19. The viewpoints represented in this section include several varieties of Hindu sectarian philosophy as well as Ājīvika, Sāṃkhya, and Vaiśeṣika systems of thought. For a fuller summary of this material, see Paula Richman, "Indian Philosophy as Presented in *Maṇimēkalai*, a Tamil Buddhist Text," s.v. *Encyclopedia of Indian Philosophy*, vol. 13 (Princeton, N.J.: Princeton University Press, forthcoming).

20. For an analysis of the discussion of Buddhist logic presented in Chapter 29, see the references on Buddhist logic cited in note 11 as well as Kandaswamy, *Buddhism as Expounded*, pp. 253–312.

21. All references to *Maṇimēkalai* are based on the following edition: Na. Mu. Vēṅkaṭacāmi Nāṭṭār and Auvai Cu. Turaicāmi Piḷḷai, coms. *Maṇimēkalai* (Tinnevelly: SISS, 1946). The Tamil verse numbers are placed in parentheses after the English translation. *P* stands for the prologue (*patikam*) to the text.

22. For the passage in *Cilappatikāram*, see Vēṅkaṭacāmi Nāṭṭār, *Cilappatikāram*, pp. 431–432.

23. For a detailed analysis of the rhetorical strategies Cāttaṉār used in constructing this scene, see Paula Richman, "The Portrayal of a Female Renouncer in a Tamil Buddhist Text," in *Gender and Religion*, ed. Caroline Bynum et al., pp. 143–165.

24. It is noteworthy that the voracious flesh-eating ghoul is female. Such a gender-marked portrayal is typical of ancient and medieval Tamil texts.

25. For discussions of the concept of *karupporuḷ*, "native element," see Ramanujan, *The Interior Landscape*, p. 105; Somasundaram Pillai, *A History of Tamil Literature with Texts and Translations* (Annamalainagar: Author, 1968), p. 55; Zvelebil, *The Smile of Murugan*, p. 68.

26. A. K. Ramanujan, *Poems of Love and War from the Eight Anthologies and the Ten Long Poems of Classical Tamil* (New York: Columbia University Press, 1985), p. 40.

27. At least as early as the *gāyatri* mantra, light and knowledge have been linked in Indian religious texts. In Buddhist texts, there are many examples of a link between the two. See, for instance, John Ross Carter and Mahinda Palihawadana, eds., *The Dhammapada* (New York: Oxford University Press, 1987), verses 146, 382, and 387 and their commentaries on pp. 214, 390, and 394–395, respectively.

28. Nāṟkavirāca Nampi, *Akapporuḷ Viḷakkam* (Tinnevelly: SISS, 1979), p. 24A.

29. Michael Pye, *Skilful Means: A Concept in Mahayana Buddhism* (London: Gerald Duckworth and Co., 1978), pp. 136–137.

30. Among *akam* poems, those set in the *mullai* (forest) landscape deal somewhat with concepts of maternal behavior, but such poems do not contain the same universal resonances that Cāttaṉār gains from his use of bovine materials. For *Caṅkam* poetry dealing with maternal themes, see Ramanujan, *Poems of Love and War*, pp. 84–85, 180–185.

31. Wendy Doniger O'Flaherty, *The Origins of Evil in Hindu Mythology* (Berkeley: University of California Press, 1976), pp. 321–348.

32. Ibid.

33. Vettam Mani, *Purāṇic Encyclopedia* (Delhi: Motilal Banarsidass, 1979), pp. 379–381.

34. Significantly, *curai*, the word I have translated as "hollow" here also means "udder."

35. This is a particularly skillful incorporation of Tamil material. It is a quote from the *Tirukkuṟaḷ*, but has been interpreted within the Buddhist framework of the raft that crosses the ocean of rebirth. See couplet 1046 in Parimēlaḻakar, com., *Tirukkuṟaḷ* (Tinnevelly: SISS, 1979), p. 514.

36. For Vedic sacrifice of cows, see Wendy Doniger O'Flaherty, ''Sacred Cows and Profane Mares in Indian Mythology,'' *History of Religions* 19, no. 1 (August 1979): 16; and Romila Thapar, *Ancient Indian Social History: Some Interpretations* (New Delhi: Orient Longman, 1978), p. 54.

37. Shulman, *The King and the Clown*, p. 64.

38. Cf. O'Flaherty's discussion of the ''mare's mouth'' in ''Sacred Cows and Profane Mares,'' p. 15.

39. A formulaic way of describing people from different regions.

40. Note the difference between sexual love and the kind of nurturing affection linked with the cow. Sexual love is exclusive in nature, channeling one's emotions and affections toward just one other person. Such a bond leads to obsession, according to Cāttaṉār's portrayal. Bovine maternal affection, in contrast, is inclusive in nature; nurturance is available to all in need.

6

Lin-chi (Rinzai) Ch'an and Gender: The Rhetoric of Equality and the Rhetoric of Heroism

Miriam L. Levering

Chinese Ch'an Buddhism (the tradition that the Japanese inherited and called Zen) has been characterized at least from the time of the disciples of Ma-tsu Tao-i (709–788) by a rhetoric of equality. Whether one is rich or poor, noble or base, old or young is irrelevant to the question of whether one can attain enlightenment. This egalitarian rhetoric is based on the strong belief, emphasized in the Perfection of Wisdom (*Prajñāpāramitā*) tradition, that distinguishing characteristics or "marks" (in Sanskrit, *lakṣaṇa*; in Chinese, *hsiang*) belong only to the relative, temporal realm and are empty of any substantial existence.[1] Ch'an teachers such as Huang-p'o Hsi-yun (?–849)[2] insisted that focusing on them leads only to attachment to distinctions, which in itself prevents leaving behind the student's deluded habits of mind. The egalitarian rhetoric is also based on the equally strong Chinese Ch'an conviction that all persons have an "originally enlightened mind"; one has to do nothing to attain or perfect it, as it is already given.[3]

In extant texts dating from before 1005 CE, rhetorical passages whose theme is equality only rarely mention the irrelevance of distinctions of gender to the project of attaining enlightenment.[4] We find in extant sources frequent mention of the irrelevancy of gender distinctions to enlightenment only when we come to the records of two prominent Sung dynasty Ch'an teachers, both of whom are deservedly well remembered in the tradition: Ta-hui Tsung-kao (1089–1163) and Hung-chih Cheng-chüeh (1091–1157). Ta-hui was a dharma heir of Yüan-wu K'o-ch'in (1063–1135) of the Lin-chi lineage, famous for his final layer of commentary in the *Blue Cliff Record* (*Pi-yen lu*).[5] Ta-hui himself was most famous for his forceful advocacy of the *hua-t'ou* or "critical phrase" method for attaining enlightenment that came to characterize the Lin-chi school; Hung-chih was Ta-hui's rival and friend from the Ts'ao-tung lineage, famous for his teaching of the practice of "silent illumination" (*mo-chao*).[6]

This sudden appearance of the topic with some frequency in the records of these men, after centuries of silence or extremely scattered reference in extant sources, may be misleading, an artifact of the sources. Or it may indicate that, whereas it is likely that nuns were never excluded from the earlier Ch'an teaching lineages and communities, the numbers of nuns and laywomen drawn to Ch'an may have increased in the late northern and early southern Sung, and their significance to the maintenance of the community may also have increased. Hung-chih and Ta-hui both taught female disciples, as had Yüan-wu; Ta-hui and Yüan-wu both had female dharma heirs. In Ta-hui's case, the one I have studied most closely, twenty-four women students are mentioned by name in his records, and five nuns and one laywoman are among a list of fifty-four dharma heirs; indeed, Ta-hui's first dharma heir was a woman who became a successful teacher, the nun Ting-kuang. The monastic institutions and teaching activities of both Yüan-wu and Ta-hui were supported financially by women donors, including lay and clerical students. Ta-hui on many occasions gave his hearers details about his student-teacher relationships with a number of women disciples.[7] The extension of the rhetoric of equality to gender that we find more often than before in the records of Ta-hui and Hung-chih clearly must be understood in the context of the existence of an audience, the women students themselves, who elicited from these masters an affirmation of their equal potential for enlightenment.

Let us take a closer look at some samples of this emerging rhetoric of gender equality taken from the records of Ta-hui and Hung-chih. Even though he had women students and donors, Yüan-wu did not leave any record of explicit extensions of the rhetoric of equality to gender.[8]

The Rhetoric of Equality

The records of Ta-hui have quite a number of passages in which gender equality in relation to enlightenment is stated explicitly. Not only that, they contain extended sermons in which gender equality in the pursuit of enlightenment is the theme, something we do not find in the records of Yüan-wu and Hung-chih. (Nor, as far as I know, elsewhere in the records of Sung Ch'an.)[9] Let us first examine the rhetoric of his statements about gender equality:

1. To the Yung-ning Commandery Mistress[10] Ta-hui says: "This matter [that is, enlightenment] does not depend on being a man or a woman, a monk or nun or a lay person. If on hearing one word from a teacher one suddenly breaks off [the chain of deluded thought], that is complete realization."[11]

2. To another woman student Ta-hui says: "In this matter one does not need to consider [whether one is] a man or a woman, noble or of low degree, adult or child. It is equal and the same for all. How do we know? Because the World-Honored One (that is, Śākyamuni Buddha) in the Lotus assembly only ferried one person, a girl, to the achievement of Buddhahood; in the *Nirvāṇa* assembly he only ferried one person, the butcher Kuang-ku, to the achievement of Buddhahood.[12] You should understand that these two when they achieved Buddhahood had not made any other kind of effort, they simply trusted enough and had no other thought. . . . Although you are a woman, your determination is no less than that of the girl who became a Buddha."[13]

3. Another passage concerning a woman student conveys the same message: "Can you say that she is a woman, and that women have no share [in enlightenment]? You must believe that this Matter has nothing to do with one's being male or female, old or young. Ours is an egalitarian Dharma gate that has only one flavor."[14]

4. Finally, in another example Ta-hui makes the point with a vivid image: "For mastering the truth, it does not matter whether one is male or female, noble or base. One moment of insight and one is shoulder to shoulder with the Buddha."[15]

Ta-hui's Ts'ao-tung lineage contemporary, Hung-chih, also brings up the point explicitly. Talking about the continuing cycle of birth and death, with its births in heavens and hells, that awaits those who have not had a moment of enlightenment, Hung-chih says:

> If you have not arrived at such a moment, then you will enter the samsaric cycle of life and death, the hells and the heavens: when does it ever rest? This is only because you have never become a Buddha or a patriarch. If you had ever once been a Buddha or a patriarch, [*saṃsāra*] would not be able to turn you around and around. . . . In both the male and the female body there is the "mark" (*hsiang*) of becoming a Buddha and a patriarch.[16]

This rhetoric of equality of access is undergirded by these teachers' understanding of what enlightenment, as both men and women experience it, reveals about the nature of reality. As the following passages from the recorded sayings of Hung-chih make clear, for Sung

Ch'an teachers, as for later teachers in the tradition, enlightenment is the realization of a total transcendence of gender distinctions, which are revealed as phenomenal appearances that are ultimately irrelevant.

1. For example, Hung-chih describes the moment when one becomes free of all impediments, and discovers the reality, which is that

> The real mark is the mark of no mark,
> The real mind is the mind of no mind.
> The real attainment is the no-attaining attaining,
> The real activity is the no-activity activity.

> In that condition, each and every existent phenomenon (*dharma*) is within my power; if all marks appear in my person, all marks are beautiful. At such a moment, one does not see that there are such distinguishing marks as rich and poor, male and female, right and wrong, gain and loss. It is only because there are marks that you accept and marks that you reject that you are not able to join yourself to emptiness and experience equality with the Dharma realm [of ultimate reality].[17]

2. In another passage Hung-chih makes the same point: "Is it not that in this moment [of enlightenment] that a monk or nun receives the complete and sufficient activity [of the Buddha-nature]? It is where you act, and where I act, and where all the Buddhas and patriarchs are at work; how could distinctions of monastic and lay, male and female, matter then?"[18]

3. Again referring to the moment when one sees truly, Hung-chih says: "Everyone has this complete in himself or herself. At this moment there is no male or female or other distinction of mark (*hsiang*). Only a pure, single marvelous clarity, which is called the true mark, and in which all is included."[19]

Thus, beginning with the Sung, women students of Ch'an are given what seems to be an unambiguous message that this is a path of practice and enlightenment open to them. The message is that the Ch'an tradition is clear on the overall doctrinal question of whether maleness and femaleness are relevant to the project of becoming enlightened, and also clear on the point that in the experience of enlightenment, maleness and femaleness are completely transcended. Yet if we go beyond this doctrinal rhetoric and look at a different dimension of Ch'an rhetoric in the Sung, namely at gender-linked terms that refer to qualities needed for enlightenment, a more complex picture emerges. It becomes necessary to ask whether a second message is not also given: that only an exceptional woman can expect to attain enlightenment.

Lin-chi Ch'an, Women, and the Rhetoric of Heroism

If one examines the sermons and recorded sayings of these same Sung Ch'an masters for descriptions of qualities needed by the successful Ch'an student, one finds in the records of Yüan-wu and Ta-hui, prominent representatives of the Lin-chi Ch'an lineage of their time, an oft repeated theme that only someone who can act like a "great hero" (*ta-chang-fu*), or a brave, tough, determined, unstoppable fellow (*ta-chang-fu-han*), can expect to attain awakening. The following are some samples of this kind of statement.

1. A poem quoted by Ta-hui:

> A great hero (*ta-chang-fu*) of great roots and great abilities—
> Within the space of a single thought he finishes the "great affair"
> [of enlightenment]
> All the Buddhas of the three worlds are inferior to him[20]
> This person is good enough to be a servant of the Buddha.[21]

2. An excerpt from a sermon by Ta-hui: "Generally speaking, to take up the burden of this affair, you must be a ferocious hero (*meng-lieh ta-chang-fu*). For this reason the Capital Teacher Su-chen said: 'I'd rather ferry a hundred [man-eating] Rakṣa demons [to Buddhahood] than one deluded heretic.' For example, Old Śākyamuni preached the *Hua-yen Sūtra* about obtaining Buddhahood in one lifetime, and only ferried one youth, Sudhana; he preached the *Lotus Sūtra* and only ferried one dragon [king] Sagara's daughter. When he preached the *Great Compendium Sūtra*[22] he only ferried one demon king; when he preached the *Nirvāṇa Sūtra*, he only ferried one butcher Kuang-ku. As it is said, 'One who can kill a man without blinking can instantly become a Buddha; one who becomes a Buddha can kill without blinking.' "

Here Ta-hui tells the story of the Butcher Kuang-ku's enlightenment. He concludes: "You can be sure that a ferocious fellow (*meng-lieh ta-chang-fu*) is ferocious when he does evil and ferocious when he does good deeds; he is noble only in that his last thought corresponds exactly to this affair."

Ta-hui continues the sermon by telling an excerpt from the story of Sudhana in the *Gaṇḍhavyūha*.[23] He narrates how Sudhana, when he asks a teacher about the bodhisattva practice and the bodhisattva way, is instructed to climb a mountain of swords and throw himself into a lake of fire. He doubts and hesitates, thinking that the teacher might be a demon whose intention is to cause him to lose his hard-won human form and thus obstruct his progress. Guardian-kings appear to reassure him, and he repents, and hurls himself off the mountain of swords into the fire. Whereupon he attains *samādhis*, and finds the fire cool and delightful. Ta-hui concludes: "Know that the five desires and the dusts and toils of this world [like Sudhana's fire] are originally clear and cool.[24] When one is in the midst of the [mundane world of] dusts and toils suddenly to correspond with [enlightened mind] in a single instant of thought—that is that person's attaining of Buddhahood in one lifetime. Is this not the act of a ferocious hero (*meng-lieh ta-chang-fu*)?"[25]

What is a *ta-chang-fu* or a *ta-chang-fu han* like? Taken together, the passages in which the term is used in the *Recorded Sayings of Yüan-wu* supply the following picture of the kind of person and the kind of activity associated with the term. First of all, a *ta-chang-fu* has great courage;[26] if in a dangerous situation he hesitates or retreats, he is not a *ta-chang-fu*.[27] He is fearless, and regards any feat of daring anyone else can accomplish as something he should be able to do also.[28] He does not look up to anyone else, nor is he afraid of anyone else. He is independent, and carves out his own way.[29]

Speaking more directly about the qualities of a *ta-chang-fu* as they pertain to the project of attaining enlightenment, Yüan-wu says that a *ta-chang-fu* is able to reach enlightenment directly, paying no attention to arguments and mutual accusations and such distractions.[30] He does not get caught up in words, in pursuing intellectual understanding, in useless efforts to be smart.[31] He "wields the sword of wisdom, breaks into pieces all false thoughts, steps on the livers of demons."[32] Firmness of will and determination are his chief characteristics. He "has a strong, burning will and a heroic spirit. He is able to ignore all outward conditions and pays no attention to what happens inside his mind. He doesn't look up to the sage nor down on the ordinary person. He can break through the city of illusion, and directly attain the real inheritance [enlightenment]."[33]

Ta-hui, Yüan-wu's disciple and heir within the Lin-chi teaching lineage, also uses the term frequently. He says that a *ta-chang-fu* is one who has great karmic preparation for enlightenment and great capacities.[34] He can break through to enlightenment at a single stroke.[35] He is unstoppable, undistractable, goes straight to the heart of the matter.[36] He is the kind of person who, if he comes across a snake while walking in a forest, seizes it and breaks it in two.[37] Someone who investigates everything carefully, looks but doesn't leap, half doubts and half believes, is not a *ta-chang-fu*.[38]

Great heroes (*ta-chang-fu*) are bodhisattvas. Ta-hui writes of a layman: "If you have already reached this realm of enlightenment, then by means of this Dharma gate you must give rise to the mind of great compassion. Whether things are going for you or against you, wade into the mire. Caring nothing for your own life, have no fear of 'mouth karma' [incurring bad karmic effects through speech], but save all in order to repay the grace of the Buddhas. This alone is worthy of being called the behavior of a *ta-chang-fu*."[39] Most important, a *ta-chang-fu* brings to a rapid conclusion "this business" of enlightenment. A successful student, one who has had a thoroughly liberating experience of the ultimate, is thus a *ta-chang-fu*, as the following excerpt from a verse by Ta-hui for a lay official indicates:

> [Layman Chuang] had cut off the root of defilements,
> As a fierce fire burns dry grass.
> The foundation of his mind was already peaceful;
> How could demonic illusions disturb it?
> "You are often noisy and distressed,
> "I am always quiet and clear. . . ."
> At death he manifested a real returning [home] (*chen-kuei*)
> Just as though he were throwing off a worn-out cloth jacket.
> He crossed his legs and entered Ch'an *samādhi*
> Like a bright moon close to a clear pond.
> Passing through the barrier of life-and-death
> He shattered into bits the valueless jewels.
> A diamond-hard, [plumbline] true *ta-chang-fu*,
> Completing this One Thing, he completed all.[40]

History of the Terms Chang-fu and Ta-chang-fu in Ch'an and pre-Ch'an Discourse

There is no doubt that in this Ch'an discourse, which in the Lin-chi lineage in the Sung dwells with such persuasive effect on the need for courage, strength of will, and determination for successful practice toward enlightenment, the rhetoric employed is gender linked. In particular, the metaphor of *ta-chang-fu* or *ta-chang-fu-han* is inescapably masculine. The term *ta-chang-fu* had a long history in Chinese classics and other literature, beginning with the *Mencius*. From the first its root meaning seems to have been "a great and powerful man." Confucian moralists seem to have attempted to transform its meaning from physical strength and power of will alone to moral greatness, but they also specifically underlined the term's meaning of "manliness" as opposed to "womanliness." The *locus classicus* in the *Mencius* states:

> Ching ch'un said to Mencius: "Are not Kung-sun Yen and Chang I really great men (*ta-chang-fu*)? Let them once be angry, and all the princes are afraid. Let them live quietly, and the flames of trouble are extinguished throughout the kingdom." Mencius said, "How can such be great men (*ta-chang-fu*)? Have you not read the Ritual *Usages*?—'At the capping of a young man, his father admonishes him. At the marrying away of a young woman, her mother admonishes her, accompanying her to the door on her leaving, and cautioning her with these words, "You are going to your home. You must be respectful; you must be careful. Do not disobey your husband." ' Thus, to look upon compliance as their correct course is the rule for women. To dwell in the wide house of the world, to stand in the correct seat of the world, and to walk in the great path of the world; when he obtains his desire *for office,* to practice his principles for the good of the people; and when that desire is disappointed, to practice them alone; and to be above the power of riches and honor to make dissipated, of poverty and mean condition to make swerve from principle, and of power and force to make bend—these characteristics constitute the great man (*ta-chang-fu*)."[41]

A later text, the *Hou Han-shu*, also links the very meaning of the term to the gender distinction: "A great man (*ta-chang-fu*) should be able to fly like a male, not submit like a female; he should be able to sweep the empire clean of disorder and unite it in peace. If he does not eat the food of a feudal lord in his lifetime, then he should prefer to die and eat the meat of sacrifices."[42]

When the term appears in Chinese translations of Buddhist writings, and in Chinese commentaries, it also retains the strong gender marking. *Chang-fu* means man, particularly a manly man. However, there are indications that Buddhist authors recognized the problem with using a gender-linked term to point to a universal ideal. They "solve" the problem by saying that the terms *man* or *chang-fu* include women when women manifest the ideal. For example, the Te-i edition of the *Platform Scripture of the Sixth Patriarch*[43] contains the following passage attributed to the Fifth Patriarch: "If you do not know your original mind, studying the Dharma is of no use. If you know your original mind, and see your original nature, then you are called a *chang-fu*, a teacher of *devas* and humans, a Buddha." In his commentary on this passage, Ting Fu-pao at first refrains from bringing up the matter of the gender link: "A *chang-fu* is a brave and strong person (*jen*). It is what one who courageously cultivates the true way, and never turns aside from or gives up the practice is called."[44] But then he continues by raising the gender issue explicitly:

> Again, "*chang-fu*" refers to the title "master charioteer (lit. the man who drives the chariot skillfully)," which is one of ten [standard epithets or] titles of the Buddha. In the *Ta-chih-tu-lun* [*Mahāprajñāpāramitāśāstra, chüan*] 2, we find the following: Someone asked [concerning this title]: "The Buddha also caused women to attain the Way. Why does [this term] only speak of 'man' (*chang-fu*)?" The reply was: "Because men are of high status and women are of low status. Because women obey men. Because men are the rulers of affairs (*shih-yeh*). And furthermore, women have the 'five hindrances': They cannot become a Cakravartin king, or a Brahma, or Mara, king of the demon heaven [one of the six desire realms], or the heavenly king Śakra [Indra], or a Buddha. The Buddha for this reason did not proclaim [a feminine as well as a masculine title]. And furthermore, if one said that the Buddha were a female charioteer, that would be lacking in respect. If one says '*chang-fu*,' all [that is, the other gender] is included with it, in the same way that a king, for example, does not come by himself when he comes, but certainly has attendants who follow him."

Another example is found in a text by the T'ang T'ien-t'ai scholastic master Chan-jan called the *Chih-kuan pu-hsing ch'uan hung chüeh*. Commenting on the same term, Chan-jan says:

> *Chang-fu* refers to the best among men; only the best among men can be called *chang-fu*. The *Pai-hu-t'ung*[45] said: " '*Fu*' [as in *chang-fu*] means '*fu*' [to help, aid, assist, support]. Therefore it means to meet others with assistance by means of the Way." The present meaning is similar. Only if one aids by means of Principle is he called "*chang-fu*." Only if he has seen the Principle of the Buddha-nature is he called "*chang-fu*." Therefore the *Nirvāṇa Sūtra* says: One who has seen the Buddha-nature, even if she be a woman, is also called 'man (*nan-tzu*).' " " 'Man' is equivalent to '*chang-fu*'."[46]

Gender-linked Rhetoric for Courage, Strength of Will, and Determination: Some Questions about the Tradition

If *chang-fu*, *ta-chang-fu*, and *ta-chang-fu-han* as metaphors are strongly gender linked, indeed defined in their classical uses precisely as referring to that which in men is a virtue and in women is either non-existent or not a virtue and if these terms dominate the Sung Lin-chi Ch'an rhetoric concerning courage and determination, might this rhetoric not raise questions in the minds of hearers about whether women in fact had the requisite qualities for successful practice and enlightenment? This would be even more likely given the fact that

Chinese tradition generally and Sung classicists (= "Confucians") in particular put great stress on the "universal natural law of *yin* and *yang* hierarchical complementarity" as the source of the "natural" *yin-yang* hierarchical complementarity in the relationship of men and women. If men, as *yang*, are and should be full of determination and courage, then women, as *yin*, typically are and should be characterized by meekness and compliance. Yet in the Sung, precisely at the time that *yin* and *yang* hierarchy as a natural law theory was being emphasized more outside Buddhist circles, more women than ever before were studying Ch'an and becoming enlightened. How did women students and their teachers cope with this contradiction between, on the one hand, rhetoric and cultural assumptions and, on the other hand, the observable fact that women displayed the courage and determination of the *ta-chang-fu*?

It seems that there are two obvious options. First, as Buddhists, and particularly in the light of their egalitarian doctrine grounded in their unequivocally transcendent enlightenment experiences, Ch'an teachers might feel free to take the rhetoric of gender in the Mahāyāna Buddhist tradition prior to that time, and the rhetoric of gender of the Chinese tradition of *yin-yang* status and power hierarchies and quality complementarities, and invoke them in such a fashion as to reverse or contradict them, suggesting the transcendence and universality of the liberation they proclaimed. They might thus apply the gender-linked metaphor of *ta-chang-fu* to women students sincerely to celebrate the freedom of humans from limiting category distinctions.

A second possibility is that they might apply the gender-linked metaphor of *ta-chang-fu* to women students with unconscious condescension. They would continue to use the masculine metaphor, but allow it to apply to women when women manifested the ideal. That rhetorical strategy itself implies rarity: if women were manifesting the ideal as often as men, would not one change the metaphor? Thus their use of the metaphor would convey the message that some women did merit the appellation, but that only extraordinary women could expect to do so, and then only at a discount. In the face of this message, most women might hesitate to claim for themselves the real independence and fearless accomplishment of a *ta-chang-fu*.

Does either of these two obvious possibilities fit the case? In what follows I offer a summary of a sermon by Ta-hui honoring the Lady Ch'in-kuo, mother of his patron Chang Chün, with verbatim translations of the relevant passages.[47] In this sermon we can see most clearly what happens in Ta-hui's case when the rhetoric of gender equality meets the rhetoric of masculine heroism.

Ta-hui's Sermon Honoring Lady Ch'in-kuo

[Ta-hui begins the sermon as he often does by mentioning the particular circumstances of the sponsor's acquaintanceship with him and the sponsor's intention in sponsoring the sermon. In this case Ta-hui dwells on this theme far more than usual. He begins by giving his hearers information about Lady Ch'in-kuo.]

Today is the morning of the birthday of Lady Ch'in-juo, née Chi, [Dharma name] Fa-chen.[48] She diligently donated this pure wealth, and from a distance came to this mountain to practice by offering a pure fragrant vegetarian feast to the Ch'an assembly. Further, she ordered me (lit., this mountain rustic) to ascend this seat and preach generally to the assembly, raising and spreading *prajñā,* in the hope that all would advance in the Way without demonic [hindrances], and that their form bodies would be at peace (that is, in good health). This was the intention of Lady Ch'in-kuo.

How this old woman (*p'o-tzu*) ordinarily conducts herself is something every Szechwan monk knows; only the stupid monks (or, the monks who are sons of Lu)[49] do not yet know. Today, because of the vegetarian feast and celebration I want to praise her and hold up [her example] to the great assembly.

I understand that this old woman was around thirty when the late Grand Preceptor (that is, her husband Chang Han) died, and her two sons, Hui-yu and the Minister, were still young. She established her household in a way that put her head and shoulders above the rest,[50] and her manner was so awe inspiring[51] that no one dared to offend against her.[52] The neighbors to the east and west saw her deportment and knew to respect her. She went to great lengths to teach her two sons to study. In her handling of affairs she enforced family rules. Ordinarily Hui-yu and the Minister attended her, standing on her left and her right. If she did not tell them to sit down, they did not dare to sit. Such was her strictness. The Minister often says: "That I am an official today is due to my mother's daily training.[53] Except for daily food expenses, all the salary she received was given to feed the monks. She used this to pray for the long life of our emperor. She often regretted that she received a salary even though she made no contribution [to the state]. I have heard that when my late teacher [Yüan-wu K'o-ch'in] returned to Shu (that is, Szechwan), he received quite a bit of support from her."

The only thing missing was that she still did not know how to practice Ch'an. Hui-yu and the Minister however both had realized something at the place of my late teacher (Yüan-wu). Recently the

Ch'an teacher [Tao-]ch'ien was staying in their home. Hui-yu and the Minister personally said to [Tao-]ch'ien:

> Our mother has practiced for forty years, but she still lacks this one thing. You have attended the Ching-shan monk [Ta-hui] for a long time, and have heard and seen much. Please let us detain you so that morning and evening you can keep [our mother] company and talk [with her]. Probably we brothers, due to our relationship of son to mother, find it difficult to make suggestions to her [about how to practice to attain enlightenment].

I hear that she got together with [Tao-]ch'ien every day, and they did nothing but talk about this matter. One day she asked [Tao-]ch'ien, "What does the Ching-shan monk [Ta-hui] ordinarily do?" [Tao-]ch'ien said:

> The [Ching-shan] monk only instructs people to investigate the critical phrase (*hua*[*-t'ou*]) "Does a dog have the Buddha-nature? No (*wu*)," or the "Bamboo stick" critical phrase.[54] The only thing is, you must not comment on it,[55] you must not consider it,[56] you must not try to understand it with regard to the context in which it is raised [by the current teacher], nor should you take it on with regard to the circumstances in which it was first spoken [by the teacher in the story]. "Does the puppy have the Buddha-nature or not?" "No" (*Wu*). He instructed people to look at it just as it is.

She firmly believed him. Day and night she immersed herself in trying to understand it with her whole self (*t'i-chiu*). She often loved to read *sūtras* and worship the Buddha. [Tao-]ch'ien said:

> The monk [that is, Ta-hui] ordinarily says that if you want to take care of this matter, you must drop [all other Buddhist practices] such as reading *sūtras*, bowing to the Buddha, reciting *dharaṇīs*, and the like. You must stop your mind and plumb (*ts'an-chiu*) [the *hua-t'ou*]. Do not let your efforts be interrupted. If as of old you hold onto reading *sūtras* and bowing to the Buddhas in the hope of seeking merits, that will obstruct the Way. Wait until you, in a single thought, correspond to [the enlightened insight]. [At that point] if you read *sūtras* and bow to the Buddhas as you did before, then each stick of incense, each flower, each glance, each bow, all the various kinds of activities will all not be in vain. They will all be the Buddha's marvelous activity. This also is to practice by grasping the fundamental. Only listen to me and believe this, I absolutely am not deceiving you.

On hearing Tao-ch'ein's words, she dropped everything and concentrated on sitting meditation, investigating that *hua-t'ou*, "The Dog has no Buddha-nature." I hear that suddenly one night last winter she woke up startled; taking advantage of her excitement, she got up, sat in meditation, and raised the *hua-t'ou* [in her mind]. Suddenly she attained a great happiness (*huan-hsi ch'u*; used in Ta-hui's sermons to refer to a moment of enlightenment). Recently Tao-ch'ien has come back [from Szechwan].[57] Lady Ch'in-kuo [sent with him] a personal letter, and wrote several poems [telling about this new attainment] to present to me. Among them one poem says:

Day by day I read *sūtra* literature
It is like meeting someone I used to know.
Do not tell me that there are many obstacles [to understanding the words],
Everytime I pick up [a *sūtra*] I understand something new.

I often say to the brothers, "When you have finished investigating Ch'an, all of your reading of the words in *sūtras* will be like leaving your own house to go for a walk, or like meeting an old acquaintance from the past." Lady Ch'in-kuo's verse without any prior knowledge matches my words exactly![58] When you look at her you see a woman, but this is like the actions of a man (*chang-fu*), and she is able to complete the affairs of a great hero (*ta-chang-fu*).

[The sermon continues. Woven in among other examples, but in sufficient numbers to be unusual are several examples from *sūtras*, as well as earlier Ch'an literature, in which women figure. For example, Ta-hui brings up the story of the nameless woman whom the great earlier Ch'an master Chao-chou and his students encounter on the road to Mt. Wu-t'ai.[59] He also brings up the *kung-an* (Jap. *kōan*) about Mañjuśrī's inability to rouse a woman out of *samādhi*.[60] In the course of telling these and other stories he challenges his hearers to take them as koans. Finally he makes the question of women's enlightenment itself into a koan. Ta-hui says: "Think about it and give me an answer: in terms of fundamental endowment, is there anyone who is not a great hero (*ta-chang-fu*)?" At the very end of the sermon he offers the following poem (*gāthā*)]:

Among womankind there is a great hero.
Revealed in her present form, she transforms her kind.
By means of precepts, *samādhi* and wisdom, the liberating *dharmas*,
She suppresses greed, hatred, and delusion.
Wherever she may be in their midst she does Buddha deeds
As wind blows through the empty sky, depending on nothing.
The various buddhas and bodhisattvas, numerous as the sands of the Ganges,
With different mouths but the same refrain they utter this speech:
Excellent, extraordinary, rarely to be found in the world!
Her mind is clean and pure, without distress or joy,

She does not even think of being without distress or joy.
Encountering a stage she puts on a play, suiting the worldly conditions
But not becoming attached to any worldly conditions.
In the sixth month clouds of fire burn the blue sky; the sound of thunder suddenly shakes the 3000 worlds.
The hot and vexatious are refined away, obtaining the cool and pure.[61]
This is that great hero's birthday celebration.
I compose this poem to add to its brilliance,
And present it as a gift to all the women in the universe.

This sermon celebrating the enlightenment of Lady Ch'in-kuo does seem to convey a double message, to achieve at best a somewhat ambiguous tone. On the one hand, Lady Ch'in-juo has done something important, worthy of emulation. And Ta-jui's instructions for *hua-t'ou* inspection have worked: Her accomplishment gives Ta-hui an opportunity to celebrate a teaching method so powerful, and a vision of human nature so transcendent, that they make ultimately irrelevant to the project of enlightenment the merely phenomenal distinction between men and women. The details of the story of Lady Ch'in-kuo's efforts give specific meaning to the claim that courage, determination, perseverance, and trust (faith) are needed to break through to enlightenment through *hua-t'ou* practice. Ta-hui does seem sincere in his claim and in his demonstration through this story that there are among women those who do have courage, strength of will, and determination and are capable of being fully liberated and empowered in enlightenment.

Yet, perhaps despite Ta-hui's intention, there is a somewhat condescending tone to his praise of the extraordinary woman. This problematic tone, I would suggest, results at least in part from the conjunction of the rhetoric of equality with the rhetoric of masculine heroism. Ta-hui seems to go "too far" in his praise of Lady Ch'in-kuo.[62] Yet perhaps it would not seem excessive in the same way or to the same degree if the person being praised were a man. When the rhetoric is masculine, and when the model of the spiritual path is presented in imagery with such a strong masculine ring to it, it seems to "fit" naturally with our expectations for men. There is the implication, in associating a "masculine" ideal through gender-linked qualifiers to a feminine subject like Lady Ch'in-kuo, that one cannot possibly be sincere.

Furthermore, clearly for Ta-hui and his implied audience, the meaninglessness of gender distinctions on the ultimate level does not unsettle their faith in the significance of the distinction on the phenomenal level. It is their belief in the "reality" and "significance" of the distinction on the phenomenal level that allows them to continue to use the gender-linked metaphor. As in the case of "our father who art in Heaven," we obtain our understanding of the ultimate, in this case of Buddhahood or bodhisattvahood (the original *ta-chang-fu*), through metaphors taken from our experience on the mundane or phenomenal level. Our understanding of the ultimate, even one understood to transcend all distinctions, and of the attainment of the realization of that ultimate inevitably will be colored by the distinctions that inform these metaphors. The rhetoric of equality cannot stand up against the rhetoric of masculine heroism, when the latter is supported by gender distinctions so "real" to the culture and remain unambiguous. In this sermon Ta-hui says, "You see her as a woman, but she is a *ta-chang-fu*, a great hero." This is as unambiguous a statement of equality as this rhetoric can yield. But it is not so different from the formulation several times repeated elsewhere in Ta-hui's records, "Even though you are a woman, you have the will of a *ta-chang-fu*," a formulation that shows the androcentric character of Chinese Buddhism in general and of Ch'an in particular. Chinese Buddhism remained shaped by men as the primary participants, by their imagination and their language. It never allowed women's experience and language to have anything like an equal influence on its expressive forms. Thus, it never could become "androgynous"—a religion in which the imaginations and experiences of men *and* women, which might be expected to differ, could both enrich the tradition.[63] Within the Ch'an lineages some men, such as Ta-hui, willing to teach women and influenced no doubt by women's interest and success, embraced a vision and a rhetoric of equality. To have done so of course was a considerable achievement. But whatever the vision may have been, within the rhetoric, the tension between androcentric social and cultural norms and perceptions and the religious vision whose expression cannot fully escape from them is never resolved, as this sermon shows.

Appendix: Yüan-wu K'o-ch'in's Implicit Invocations of Gender Equality in Two Cases

In the first case, in a "Dharma instruction" (*Fa-yü*) to a nun,[64] Yüan-wu tells part of the story of the monk Kuan-ch'i's challenge to the nun Mo-shan Liao-jan, a classic story also recorded in the *Ching-te ch'uan-teng lu*.[65] After losing his first sparring of Ch'an wits with Mo-shan, Kuan-ch'i asks her: "What is the person who lives on this mountain (that is, you) like?'' The nun replies: ''She has neither the male distinguishing mark nor the female distinguishing mark.'' Kuan-ch'i presses the question: ''[If she is so enlightened,] why doesn't she [use her power as a bodhisattva to] transform herself [into a masculine form]?'' The nun Mo-shan Liao-jan replies: ''She's not a goddess, she is not a ghost—what should she become?'' Mo-shan wins this exchange and demonstrates that she is truly enlightened by showing that she understands that male and female form are irrelevant to buddhahood.[66]

In the second case, Yüan-wu brings up the famous story of the eight-year-old daughter of the dragon king, who demonstrates to Śāriputra in the *Lotus Sūtra* that she has perfect wisdom and is ready for full buddhahood, despite being female, an eight-year-old, and a *naga*-divinity rather than a human being.[67] This is the story to which the exchange between Mo-shan Liao-jan and Kuan-ch'i most likely refers, since in this story the girl demonstrates her enlightenment by changing her female body into a male body and attaining full buddhahood in that body. But the story also is used in Ch'an literature to make the point that enlightenment is ''sudden,'' ''abrupt'' in the sense that any sentient being can attain it ''in an instant of thought'' despite an apparent lack of perfect karmic qualifications.

Notes

1. For the consequences of the emptiness insight for the early Mahāyāna view of women, see Ku Cheng-mei, ''The Mahāyāna View of Women: A Doctrinal Study'' (Ph.D. dissertation, University of Wisconsin, 1984).

2. In the *Essentials of the Transmission of Mind* (*Ch'uan-hsin fa-yao*); I am indebted to John McRae for the realization that this is one of the best sources we have for the teachings of the early Ma-tsu, or Hung-chou, school.

3. An idea found in the influential *Ta-sheng ch'i-hsin lun* (*Awakening of Mahayana Faith*) attributed to Aśvaghoṣa.

4. I have surveyed many early Ch'an texts, traced the appearance of this rhetoric as applied to gender, and provided a more detailed discussion in my ''The Dragon Girl and the Abbess of Mo-shan: Gender and Status in the Ch'an Buddhist Tradition,'' *Journal of the International Association of Buddhist Studies,* 5, no. 1 (1982): 19–35.

5. In the Sung dynasty there were five lineages or ''houses'' of Ch'an. The Lin-chi lineage traced its teaching style to Lin-chi I-hsüan (?–866). This lineage continued in Japan, where it is known as the Rinzai school. *The Blue Cliff Record* is available in a recent translation by Thomas Cleary and J.C. Cleary

published by Prajna Press, 1978. The Ts'ao-tung lineage traces its teaching style to Tung-shan Liang-chieh (807–869) and Ts'ao-shan Pen-chi (840–901), and continued in Japan as the Sōtō school.

6. The rhetoric of gender equality that suddenly appears in the records of Yüan-wu, Ta-hui and Hung-chih corresponds to the sudden appearance of women teachers and their students in the "Transmission of the Lamp" genre of geneological histories of Ch'an. Out of a total of seven women who have individual entries in the "lamp" histories (including Mo-shan Liao-jan), one was a dharma heir of Yüan-wu, and three were dharma heirs of Ta-hui. Cf. the *Lien-teng hui-yao, Dainihon zokuzōkyō* 2, 10, 1, pp. 77cd, 108a, 118a, 136a–b; and the *Wu-teng hui-yüan, Dainihon zokuzōkyō* 2, 11, 4, pp. 385c, 401a–b.

7. For more detailed discussion of these aspects of Ta-hui's records and for full references, see my forthcoming book on Ta-hui.

8. Yüan-wu's records have passages that give an implicit message of gender equality: he quotes, and in at least one case to a woman student, stories from the tradition in which gender equality is one of the major points. However in these passages Yüan-wu does not spell out his interest in that particular point as a moral to be drawn from the story. See the appendix to this chapter.

9. The only other extended sermon or essay of this kind that I know of in roughly contemporaneous Ch'an-Zen records is the thirteenth century Japanese teacher Dōgen's "Raihaitokuzui" chapter in his *Shōbōgenzō*.

10. Yung-ning Chün-fu-jen's surname was Ts'ao and her name (unclear what kind of name) was Shan-yin. She became the nun Tzu-ting. Cf. *Chia-t'ai p'u-teng lu, chüan* 18, p. 136c.

11. *Ta-hui P'u-chüeh Ch'an-shih yü-lu, Taishō shinshū daizōkyō* 47, pp. 903c–904a (hereafter cited as *Ta-hui yü-lu*).

12. The first reference is to the story of the Dragon King Sagara's daughter recorded in the *Lotus Sūtra*. The second reference is to a story recorded in the *Nirvāṇa Sūtra,* in which a butcher "puts down his knife and straightaway attains Buddhahood," which the bad karma accrued in his life as a butcher should have made impossible.

13. Ibid., p. 909.

14. *Ta-hui Chüeh Ch'an-shih p'u-shuo* (in four *chüan*), *Dainihon zokuzōkyō* 2, 31, 5, p. 455a; hereafter cited as *P'u-shuo.*

15. Ibid., p. 433b.

16. *Hung-chih Ch'an-shih kuang-lu, Taishō shinshū daizōkyō* 48, p. 67c.

17. Ibid., p. 64.

18. Ibid., p. 65c.

19. Ibid., p. 67c.

20. The text has *li-hsia-feng*, to stand in an inferior position. The meaning of *an inferior position* for *hsia-feng* is attested very early, in the *Tso chuan*. Cf. Morohashi, *Daikanwa jiten*, (Tokyo: Taishūkan shoten, 1955) vol. 1, p. 232c (14.521), under *hsia feng*, where a passage is quoted that seems very parallel to Ta-hui's usage, in that ministers (*ch'en*) occupy the inferior position (*hsia feng*).

21. *Ta-hui yü-lu*, p. 845c. Ta-hui goes on to comment on the paradox that someone who is superior to the Buddhas is fit to be their servant.

22. *Ta-chi-ching*.

23. The *Gaṇḍhavyūha* has recently been translated into English in full by Thomas Cleary as *Entry into the Realm of Reality* (Boston and Shaftesbury: Shambala, 1989).

24. Reading *ching*, "pure," as a mistake for *liang*, "cool," as in the preceeding phrase.

25. *P'u-shuo*, pp. 401d–402b.

26. *Yüan-wu Fo-kuo Ch'an-shih yü-lu, Taishō shinshū daizōkyō* 47, p. 776c, also p. 795a; hereafter cited as *Yüan-wu yü-lu*.

27. Ibid., p. 771c.

28. Ibid., p. 784ab.

29. Ibid., p. 773c; also p. 757a.

30. Ibid., p. 749a.

31. Ibid., p. 786c and 749a.

32. Ibid., p. 755c.

33. Ibid., p. 749a.

34. *Ta-hui yü-lu*, p. 845c.

35. Ibid.; also *P'u-shuo*, p. 434a.

36. *P'u-shuo*, p. 428c.

37. Ibid., p. 434cd.

38. Ibid.

39. *Ta-hui yü-lu*, p. 925c.

40. Ibid., p. 856bc.

41. *Mencius* 3B2, in James Legge's translation, *The Works of Mencius* (New York: Dover Publications, 1970), pp. 264–265.

42. Quoted in Morohashi, *Daikanwa jiten*, vol. 3, p. 459, no. 5831–2507.

43. Edited in 1291; also known as the Ming canon version. Cf. Charle Luk's translation, "The Dharma Treasure of the Altar Sutra," in his *Ch'an and Zen Teaching*, Series 3 (London: Rider and Co., 1962).

44. Ting Fu-pao, *Liu-tzu t'an-ching chu-chieh*, the title given on the cover to a text entitled "Liu-tzu t'an-ching ch'an-chu" (Taiwan: Ch'ing-fang shu-chü, 1961), p. 14.

45. *Discourses of the White Tiger Hall*, a Han dynasty non-Buddhist text.

46. *Taishō shinshū daizōkyō*, 46, p. 196a (*chüan* 2, section 2).

47. Lady Ch'in-kuo is very interesting as a window through which we can learn about female patronage and participation in Sung Buddhism. In another essay prepared for the University of Illinois Project on the T'ang-Sung Transition I discuss all extant Buddhist and non-Buddhist sources concerning Lady Ch'in-kuo in detail.

48. Her title, T'ai-fu-jen, indicates that her status is derived from being the mother of an important person. Another title, Fu-jen, indicates that one is the wife of an important person. The sermon was probably given when Ta-hui was fifty-one years old, in 1140, when Chang Chün was an important political figure.

49. Chinese (C.) *Lu tzu seng*; I have not been able to trace the meaning of this; if it were *Lu seng* it might mean "monks from the state of Lu (modern Shantung)." One meaning of "*lu*" is "dull, stupid, uncomprehending."

50. Taking *chuo-chuo* in the sense in which it is used in a famous allusion from the *Shih-shuo hsin-yü*, in which someone is said to stand *chuo-chuo* above the rest like a crane among chickens; cf. Morohashi, *Daikanwa jiten*, vol. 2, p. 558c (2741.58).

51. C. *lin-jan*, stern, severe; it is interesting that both *chuo-chuo* and *lin-jan* are used to describe Confucius. Is their use to describe a woman perhaps rare?

52. By treating her insultingly or taking advantage of her, as they might well have done, given that she was a defenseless widow.

53. On the desireability of a widow managing her family affairs herself, because of the difficulty of relying on the willingness, honesty and competence of her husband's male relatives or her own, and on the relative rarity of "wise and worthy women" able to manage their own affairs and avoid bankruptcy, see the excerpt from Yuan Tsai's contemporaneous *Rules for Social Life* quoted in Patricia Ebrey, "Women in the Kinship system of the Southern Song Upper Class," *Historical Reflections*, 8:113–128 (1981), pp. 115–116.

54. "If you call this a bamboo stick, then you touch it; if you do not call it a bamboo stick, then you turn your back on it."

55. *Hsia-yü*, "pronounce a judgment."

56. *Ssu-liang*, "weigh it."

57. The text is unclear as to where Tao-ch'ien came back to or from and where Lady Ch'in-kuo is at the moment of speaking. What I offer here is only one possible reading.

58. C. *an-ho Sun-Wu*, an allusion to one Shan Tao, who without ever studying the military writers Sun-tzu and Wu-tzu, devised strategies that fit their teachings as though he knew them (*an yu-chih ho*); cf. Morohashi, *Daikanwa jiten*, vol. 3, p. 863 (6987.114).

59. Cf. Tao-yüan, ed., *Ching-te ch'uan-teng lu, chüan* 10 (Taipei, Taiwan: Chen-shan mei ch'u-pan-she, reprint edition of 1967), pp. 178–179.

60. Cf. *Wu-men-kuan* (Jap. *Mumonkan*), *kung-an* number 42. The story is originally found in the *Chu-fo-yao-chi-ching*, part two, translated by Dharmarakṣa.

61. "The cool and pure" is a Buddhist technical term. But the poem becomes more interesting if one realizes, as Stephen Bokenkamp has pointed out to me, that in T'ang poems women are normally compared to cool mists and gentle rain-bearing clouds. Is the implication that the great hero, who can transform herself at will, in her enlightenment moment also now manifests fully her female form?

62. On the other hand, in the way Ta-hui tells her story he presents her through cultural tropes—the chaste, upright widow, the virtuous mother who produces grateful, filial, and well-educated sons (cf. Mencius's mother) that honor her yet keep her invisible in that they prevent us from imagining the reality of this woman's character, experience, and accomplishments as they would have appeared to her. In this sense he does not go "far enough" in praising Lady Ch'in-kuo.

63. I am grateful to Rita M. Gross, whose writings and personal conversations about Buddhism as an androcentric tradition that has the potential to become an androgenous tradition in this century have helped me to understand this point.

64. *Yüan-wu yü-lu*, p. 779.

65. *Chüan* 11; *Taishō shinshū daizōkyō*, 51, p. 289a.1ff; Yüan-wu's version is similar enough to suggest that this was his source.

66. For a full discussion of the role of this story in Ch'an literature, see Levering, "The Dragon Girl."

67. *Yüan-wu yü-lu*, p. 771b; on this story, see Levering, ibid.

IV

Gender and Buddhist Symbols

7

The Gender Symbolism of Kuan-yin Bodhisattva

Barbara E. Reed

All living beings are distressed
And bear unlimited pains;
Kuan-yin's profound wisdom and power
Can save the world from pain.
—from the *Lotus Sūtra*[1]

Somehow during the assimilation into Chinese culture Kuan-yin Bodhisattva underwent a sexual transformation. The male bodhisattva from India, Avalokiteśvara, became a beautiful white-robed Chinese woman. In addition to the sex change, the female symbolism of the bodhisattva was expanded further by the addition of *yin* symbols (for example, moon, water, vase) from the *yin-yang* polarity of Chinese thought. In a Chinese culture dominated by Confucian social values, Chinese women saw this female symbol as particularly relevant to their problems as women. Not only was Kuan-yin an object of devotion for Chinese women, she also was a popular subject for women artists from at least the Ming dynasty (1368–1644).

This essay examines whether the female symbol of Kuan-yin Bodhisattva helped Chinese women transcend the restrictions of a Confucian-defined, male-dominated society or whether the symbol tended to reinforce those restrictions. This essay suggests that women saw the symbol of Kuan-yin Bodhisattva as clearly liberating them from the physiological suffering particular to the female *sex* (that is, those problems due to menstruation and childbirth). But the liberating symbolism of Kuan-yin is more complex in the ways it alleviates women's suffering due to culturally defined *gender* restrictions. This essay considers the ways Kuan-yin Bodhisattva has both liberated women from culturally defined roles in family and marriage and also accommodated women to those roles by alleviating some of their suffering.

The Development of Kuan-yin Bodhisattva

The earliest Buddhist texts mentioned only male buddhas and bodhisattvas; female bodhisattvas were first introduced around the late fourth century.[2] Avalokiteśvara, a male bodhisattva in India, became known as Kuan-yin in China and was viewed as female more often than male from the Sung dynasty (960–1127) to the present. Sinologists and buddhologists have produced several theories about the strange transformations of Avalokiteśvara in China: the translation of the Sanskrit name Avalokiteśvara ("the lord who looks down") into the Chinese Kuan-yin ("one who observes the sounds") and the metamorphosis of the bodhisattva into female form. Causes cited for the sexual transformation include the growing popularity of Tārā, the female consort of Avalokiteśvara; the amalgamation of Kuan-yin with Taoist goddesses such as Hsi Wang-mu, Queen Mother of the West; and the Chinese tendency to associate compassion with women because of the nature of the Chinese family.[3] I am concerned in this chapter not with the process by which Kuan-yin became female, but rather with the symbolism of the evolved female figure of Kuan-yin and her impact on the spiritual and worldly aspirations of Chinese women.

Kuan-yin's popularity grew with that of the scriptures in which her compassion was described. As the *Lotus Sūtra* became more widely read and preached, especially in Kumarajīva's translation of 406 CE, Kuan-yin became known as the salvific being of Chapter 25. According to this scripture, Kuan-yin can appear in thirty-three forms, seven of them female: nun, Buddhist laywoman, elder's wife, householder's wife, officer's wife, a Brahman woman, and a young girl.[4] Kuan-yin promises to manifest herself in whatever form is effective to save all beings in distress—from fires, robbers, drowning, and more. And she promises to grant the wishes of her worshipers: for women Kuan-yin's assent to requests for bearing good sons or daughters is especially significant. Kuan-yin as a savior from physical disaster or childlessness is portrayed vividly in the Buddhist art of China.

As the Pure Land *sūtras* gained popularity after the sixth century, Kuan-yin also became popularly known as the compassionate assistant to A-mi-t'o (Amitābha) Buddha, who created a pure buddhaland in the west in which his followers could be reborn after death. In China Kuan-yin served to link the popular, but divergent, traditions of the Pure Land *sūtras* and the *Lotus Sūtra.* At Tun-huang Kuan-yin appears as the savior of the *Lotus Sūtra* in one painting, whereas in a nearby painting from the same period she appears as the assistant of A-mi-t'o Buddha, leading people to the pure buddhaland. It is Kuan-yin who unites these artistic images and the devotional traditions which they represent.[5]

The *Hua-yen (Avataṃsaka) Sūtra* enjoyed a contemporaneous popularity with the *Lotus Sūtra* during the middle of the T'ang dynasty (618–907). In the chapter of the *Avataṃsaka Sūtra* entitled "Entering the Dharmafield" *(Ru fa-chie p'in),* Kuan-yin appears as a bodhisattva residing on top of Mount P'u-t'o (Potala), which the Chinese located as an island off the coast of Chekiang. In this form Kuan-yin was associated with the Taoist Niang-niang goddesses who act as guardians of the ocean, and she became known as the guardian of the Southern Sea.[6]

Both the male representation of Kuan-yin and his female consort Tārā became popular among the Chinese through the dissemination of tantric texts and *dharaṇī.* In the eighth century the introduction of a tantric scripture about a white-robed female Kuan-yin inspired artists and popular religious devotion. Folk religion accepted and promulgated Kuan-yin devotion with legends about her Chinese manifestations and the magical powers of her images. Some of the legends about her may have originated from Taoist or folk traditions in China; if so, they were later linked to the popular bodhisattva imported from India. In the T'ang dynasty (618–907) Kuan-yin began appearing often in female form; by the Sung (960–1127) the bodhisattva's female representations were more common than the male images. The legends and visual images made Kuan-yin both more Chinese and more female in the Sung dynasty.

By the Ming dynasty (1368–1644), innumerable forms of Kuan-yin had appeared in legends, paintings, and sculptures. The promise of the *Lotus Sūtra,* that she would appear to living beings in whatever form could best save them, engendered acceptance and enthusiasm for the diversity of images. She appeared in radically different forms, such as the Chinese princess Miao-shan, a common fisherwoman, a goddess springing from a clam, and thousand-armed and thousand-eyed deity whose multiple arms and eyes symbolize the infinite powers of her saving compassion.

Women as Disseminators of Kuan-yin Symbolism

Chinese Buddhism in its elite form was adopted and transmitted primarily by the men who had access to education and property. The scriptures that helped spread devotion to Kuan-yin Bodhisattva were probably written and transmitted by an almost exclusively male group. What roles, then, did women play in the development of Kuan-yin as the most popular bodhisattva?

Certainly the most important roles women had in transmitting devotion to Kuan-yin Bodhisattva was through their activities as nuns and through their education of young children as mothers, servants, and relatives. In these roles they related stories and taught devotional rituals related to the bodhisattva. Beyond the family sphere wealthy laywomen have served as patrons of Buddhism and donors for Buddhist temples and art. Although they often had less freedom of movement than common women, who could at least meet in the evenings to do their washing, some women of wealthy families occasionally were able to gain an education or build a power base that enabled them to have an influence on the transmission of religion outside the family.[7] For example, the Buddhist paintings from the T'ang and Northern Sung dynasties in the caves at Tun-huang include several depictions of laywomen donors.[8]

Because so much religious art is painted anonymously, it is difficult to estimate the degree to which women contributed to the development of Kuan-yin images as artists. If the special exhibition of Kuan-yin paintings presented by the National Palace Museum (Taipei, Taiwan) during fall 1985 is representative, then the contribution of women was significant.[9] Out of the total twenty-six paintings, six were by women artists, twelve were by men, and the rest were painted anonymously. The proportion of paintings by women artists compared to other segments of this imperial collection seems quite high. I would assume that women's role in creating less artistic images of Kuan-yin for personal religious use was even greater.

Two of the artists represented in the National Palace Museum Collection, women of the Ming dynasty, are known because they are closely related to famous male artists. The woman who is recorded only as Tu-ling nei-shih (late sixteenth century) was the daughter of painter Ch'in Ying, whose two paintings of Kuan-yin also appear in this exhibit. Tu-ling nei-shih painted Kuan-yin in her manifestation as white-robed Kuan-yin *(pai-yi Kuan-yin)* on a huge white lotus blossom. Kuan-yin here appears as a beautiful women who, because she is painted in color on a monochromatic background, seems to rise from the paper. Her luminous image is similar to the description of her in the Ming dynasty novel *Journey to the West:*

> A mind perfected in the four virtues,
> A golden body filled with wisdom,
> Fringes of dangling pearls and jade,
> Scented bracelets set with lustrous treasures,
> Dark hair piled smoothly in a coiled-dragon bun,
> And elegant sashes lightly fluttering as phoenix quills.

Her green jade buttons
And white silk robe
Bathed in holy light;
Her velvet skirt and golden cords
Wrapped by hallowed air.
With brows of new moon shape
And eyes like two bright stars,
Her jadelike face beams natural joy,
And her ruddy lips seem a flash of red.
Her immaculate vase overflows with nectar from year to year,
Holding sprigs of weeping willow green from age to age.[10]

Hsing Ts'u-ching, another woman of the Ming dynasty and the sister of Hsing T'ung, painted a series of thirty-two gold-on-black paintings of Kuan-yin, four of which appeared in the 1985 exhibition. The thirty-two (or thirty-three) manifestations of Kuan-yin had already become a popular subject for devotion and religious art, inspired by (but not restricted to the images of) the thirty-three forms in Kumarajīva's translation of the *Lotus Sūtra.* In one painting Kuan-yin is seated on a lotus blossom accompanied by her young male attendant Shan-ts'ai t'ung-tzu. Another shows Kuan-yin holding a lotus blossom while standing in a net of pearls and gold. In Hsing Ts'u-ching's third painting in the exhibit Kuan-yin Bodhisattva rides a dragon while holding her water vase containing the dew of compassion. Her fourth painting here belongs to the category of *shui-yüeh* (water-moon) Kuan-yin: she sits on a rock comtemplating the reflection of the moon in the water.[11]

The third woman artist represented in the exhibition, Ch'en Shu (1660–1736), painted "Kuan-yin Emerging from the Sea" when she was fifty-three years old. By then she had established herself through her ties to her son, Ch'ien Ch'en-ch'u, who was a high official under Ch'ing emperor Ch'ien-lung. Through her son she had high status and was given an honorary title. In her representation Kuan-yin, having just surfaced from the ocean depths, appears seated on a boulder.

As women who lived during the Ming and Ch'ing dynasties, these three women painted Kuan-yin in the form that had become most popular—obviously female. In these women's paintings, Kuan-yin is shown with female face and form. Moreover, she is shown surrounded by other female symbols that were also used in the more asexual representations of the bodhisattva: lotus blossoms, vases, willow branches, water, and the moon. The association of the lotus blossom with the female sexual organ is derived from tantric Buddhism, but the female symbolism of the other objects is as much Taoist as it is

Buddhist. The womblike qualities of an empty vessel or vase are extolled in the *Tao te ching:*

> The Way is like an empty vessel
> That yet may be drawn from
> Without ever needing to be filled.
> It is bottomless; the progenitor of all things in the world.[12]

The dew inside Kuan-yin's vase symbolizes her compassion and her healing power. The use of water to symbolize compassion is found in both the *Lotus Sūtra* and the *Tao te ching.* The *Lotus Sūtra* states: "Just as that great cloud rains down on all grasses and trees, shrubs and forests, and medicinal herbs, and just as they all, in accord with their nature and kind, derive full benefit of the moisture, each gaining in growth, just so is the Dharma preached by the Thus Come One."[13] In the *Tao te ching,* water symbolizes the highest good not only because it benefits all living things, but also because it takes the lowest position.[14] Both the empty vessel and water are *yin:* the passive and yielding side of the Chinese *yin-yang* polarity. As such they are both Taoist symbols for the power of the passive and yielding Tao. The moon is also a *yin* element. Some Taoists practiced "moonbathing" in order to absorb the *yin* element as part of their quest for immortality.[15] Willow branches have also been used to symbolize the female, specifically feminine beauty, in Chinese poetry and painting since the T'ang dynasty.

In Buddhist scriptures Kuan-yin transcends sexuality, as do all advanced bodhisattvas. However, Buddhists "see" the meaning of Buddhism at least as much in the visual symbols as in their written texts and spoken teachings. The Chinese since the Sung dynasty have "seen" Buddhist compassion as female: female figures surrounded by female symbols. I would assume that the visual reinforcement of the femininity of this bodhisattva has made her seem directly relevant to Chinese women, especially to the problems they have simply because they are women.

Symbol of Liberation from Women's Suffering

According to Pure Land Buddhist scriptures, Kuan-yin liberates living beings from the six realms of suffering by leading them after death to the Pure Land of A-mi-t'o Buddha, where they are assured of eventual enlightenment.[16] She also liberates them from specific sufferings within each of the realms. The sufferings from which she liberates in this world are listed in the *Lotus Sūtra;* they include incineration, imprisonment, drowning, and victimization by wild animals and robbers. These can either be interpreted objectively (literally), as in folk religion, or subjectively (psychologically), the case with Buddhist philosophical schools. The lion symbolizes pride, fire is anger, robbers are wrong views, and so on.[17]

Kuan-yin offers liberation for all suffering beings, even if they do not deserve it. As Wolfram Eberhard has shown in his study of sin and guilt in traditional China, the Chinese have maintained in their popular religious views a tension between the idea of destiny and that of individual responsibility.[18] The divine salvation represented by Kuan-yin and others breaks through both fate and karma by allowing for the possibility of liberation through the compassionate actions of an external entity. Kuan-yin can intervene to prevent suffering for which one is destined or that one creates by sinning.

Women are in special need of salvation because of the impurities and inferiority of their female forms. According to popular Chinese beliefs, the blood of both menstruation and childbirth is spiritually polluting. Kuan-yin responds compassionately to the suffering to which women are doomed merely because of their sex. In a popular tale associated with P'u-t'o Island, Kuan-yin rescues a menstruating girl in need. She and her sister-in-law had been looking forward to making a pilgrimage to P'u-t'o Island for years. After overcoming numerous difficulties the two were about to dock when the girl began menstruating. Because she was in such impure state, she had to stay alone on the boat while everyone else went ashore. When she was stranded unexpectedly on the boat because of high tides and began suffering from thirst and hunger, a beautiful woman walked across the waters to present her with food. As in most Kuan-yin tales of rescue the identity of the woman is not clear until later: the sister-in-law finally returns and reports that the bottom of the robes of the Kuan-yin statue in the temple were dripping wet.[19]

Childbirth, although providing a Chinese woman status and some hope for eventual power in her husband's family, is also an act of extreme pollution according to moralistic texts. Giving birth is a sin for which women are tortured in hell, being placed in a pond of bloody birth fluids, and it is said that through the act of giving birth women pollute even Heaven and Earth. According to some Chinese, women who die in childbirth are pitiful souls in hell, pinned down by a heavy stone:

> The soul groans, yes, cries out in agony. As its eyes anxiously dart all around it sees only blood. It eats only blood clots; it drinks only

> bloody fluid. It is not the fresh blood of animals—which in its raw state is already an abomination for the people of Tsinghai—but inevitably foul vaginal blood and fluid. The soul cannot rest in the dreadful torment that it endures. Incessantly it groans and cries, but no friendly spirit approaches to help it. All good spirits shun the soul of a woman who has died in childbed.[20]

Kuan-yin saves suffering beings in all the Buddhist realms of existence, including these women in hell. In some versions of the Princess Miao-shan legend Kuan-yin descends to hell and disrupts it completely by her powerful compassion. Kuan-yin Bodhisattva saves women from their terrible suffering, whether it arises from childlessness or childbearing.

Liberation from Marriage

In several traditional legends Kuan-yin escapes marriage or helps another woman escape. Chinese women often considered marriage as one form of suffering in the human realm. A woman who married as an adult found herself in a house of strangers—married to a man she had never met and dominated by a resentful mother-in-law. In an alternative (and probably more painful) form of marriage popular in Taiwan until the early twentieth century, infant daughters were adopted by families to become the eventual wives of their sons. A woman often found the sexual demands of marriage to a man she viewed as a brother impossible to bear.[21] Moreover, marriage provided little security because a man could take a second wife or concubine. A woman's only hope was to bear a son and hope for his loyalty and generosity.

Biographies of virtuous women have been a popular means of teaching morality to Chinese women. Some were used to inculcate Confucian virtues, such as *Lieh nü chuan,* written by Liu Hsiang,[22] which was influential into the early Ming Dynasty. Other biographies have served to spread Buddhist morality and the popular devotion to Kuan-yin. These are biographies of those to whom she appears and of those women in whose form she manifests herself. The values taught in these stories differ greatly from those Confucian biographies extolling the Confucian virtues of *li* (propriety) and *hsiao* (filial piety). In the Buddhist biographies parents are to be honored, but only in a higher way. Parents may be spiritually liberated by their children, but after perhaps blatant rejection of their parents' stated worldly desires.

The most important biographical tale about Kuan-yin Bodhisattva is the legend of Princess Miao-shan, which provides her with a Chinese origin. There are several versions of this legend, but the most popular is the twelfth century one attributed to Pu-ming.[23] Miao-shan was the youngest of three daughters of King Miao-chuang. As the monarch had no sons the marriage of his daughters was crucial for his kingdom. Miao-shan, in un-Confucian manner, defied her parents and refused to marry. She wanted to devote herself to following the Buddhist path. One version of the story says that after she became a Buddhist nun her father took his revenge on her and her sister nuns by trying to burn them alive: His rage left little doubt about the relative values he attached to female Buddhist devotion and Confucian filial piety. Miao-shan devoted herself to Buddhist teachings, underwent various adventures with human and supernatural characters, and eventually retired to P'u-t'o Island in meditation. This Chinese princess thus became the compassionate bodhisattva of the *Lotus Sūtra* and the bodhisattva of Mount Potala (P'u-t'o) of the *Hua-yen Sūtra*.

In the legend of Miao-shan, the princess rejected her parents' plan to follow what she saw as the higher path, that of the Buddha. But in the end she saved her father, both physically and spiritually, by choosing the higher Buddhist path. She saves him physically by cutting off her own arm to use as a magical medicine to cure his blindness. She saved him and her mother spiritually by preaching the *Dharma* to them once she had become a bodhisattva. Although counter to Confucian teaching about family relationships, this story accommodates the Confucian virtue of respect for parents by showing that it can be fulfilled only in Buddhism. This is similar to the story of Buddha's disciple Mu-lien (Maudgalyāyana) who asked permission to descend to lower realms to teach his greedy mother the saving truth of Buddhism.[24] She too opposed her child's religious commitment, but in the end was saved from suffering in hell by hearing Buddhism preached by her loving son, Mu-lien. Chinese Buddhists valued this scriptural account of the life of Mu-lien because it helped counter Confucian criticism that Buddhism was unfilial. The tension between filial piety and Buddhist devotion is common to the Miao-shan and Mu-lien legends and is resolved in such a way as to produce a rather satisfying and ingenious synthesis.

Rejection of marriage is the core of another legend of Kuan-yin's appearances in this world. The story of Mrs. Ma tells of a devout young woman who promised to marry the man who could recite the Kuan-yin chapter of the *Lotus Sūtra* by the next day.[25] On the following day twenty men succeeded in reciting this for her, so she increased the number of Buddhist verses to be memorized until at last only a Mr. Ma was left. He recited the scripture and they were wed. However, on their wedding night the devout bride died, leaving behind the firm belief that she was indeed a manifestation of Kuan-yin. It is striking that there is little display of supernatural power in this legend except for the woman's ability to die at her chosen moment and then have her corpse disappear. Her great act of compassion and salvation was merely to demand that men equal her, a humble fisherwoman, in devotion to the Buddhist path.

In a related legend Kuan-yin manifested herself as Ling Chao, a plain fisherwoman who was the daughter of a Ch'an believer.[26] This legend serves as the basis of some of the simplest and most realistic paintings of Kuan-yin. In the National Palace Museum collection, there is a large painting of Kuan-yin with a fishing basket done by Chao Meng-fu (1254–1322). She appears as a large plain woman with bags under her eyes, a strong common woman with character. Her appearance is extraordinary only because she has the long ear lobes symbolizing the perfect wisdom of the Buddha. Another representation of Kuan-yin with a fishing basket is that by Wu Pin of the Ming dynasty—also of a large, handsome fisherwoman but this time accompanied by Kuan-yin's attendant Shan-ts'ai, who appears small in comparison to Kuan-yin. Kuan-yin with a fishing basket and Kuan-yin as Mrs. Ma are often merged into a single personality because they both appear as common women.

Kuan-yin's miraculous powers not only save women from marriage (along with childbearing and often difficult sexual relations), they also save women from sexual attacks that bring physical, emotional, and social suffering. A good example of this kind of tale is from *T'ai-shang pao-fa t'u-shuo,* one of the popular morality texts used to teach values to common people:

> When a woman sacrificed in a temple, the judge-deity smiled and visited her at night, expressing the wish for sexual relations. Refusing, she ran away, finally flew and landed on top of a pagoda. When she went down, she came into a bedroom where she met the judge. Now she could not refuse him and lived with him. During the day, he went out and did his job of meting out punishment to sinners; at night he returned with food for her. In a conversation with him she learned that a person can improve his fate by reciting the Kuan-yin sutra. This she did, with the result that the judge-deity became unable to have sexual relations with her. She was miraculously returned to her own house and bed. It was found out that only her soul, not her body, had had sexual relations with the deity.[27]

Many representations and legends of Kuan-yin come straight out of Indian art and scriptures—the miracles of the *Lotus Sūtra,* the stories of the Pure Land *sūtras,* and the descriptions of tantric texts. But the legends previously described are concretely Chinese. Although some are indirectly inspired by Indian Buddhist texts, they all firmly tie Kuan-yin to Chinese people and places.

The legends of Kuan-yin, especially in her form as Miao-shan, provide an alternative path for women by giving them a model for resisting parental marriage arrangements, thereby escaping the pain of marriage and the pollution of childbirth. Because Miao-shan entered a Buddhist convent, her role as a model for Chinese women who sought to become nuns is obvious. Kuan-yin also served as a model for less traditional marriage resistance by laywomen. Marjorie Topley's study, "Marriage Resistance in Rural Kwangtung," is evidence of this function of Kuan-yin devotion from the early nineteenth to early twentieth century.[28] Financially independent young women in the silk industry banded together and formed sisterhoods to avoid marriage. Women interviewed said that they had wanted to avoid the loneliness and oppression of marriage, the lack of financial independence, or the pain and punishment of childbirth. They also valued the lay vegetarian houses of these sisterhoods because they provided freedom from marriage without the restrictions implied by being a nun.[29]

Kuan-yin served as both a model and patron goddess for these women. The women often cited the story of Kuan-yin's manifestation as the stubbornly celibate Miao-shan as a justification for their own rejection of marriage. Because most of the vegetarian houses had one room dedicated to Kuan-yin and A-mi-t'o Buddha, Kuan-yin's presence was always visible to these women. By seeing Kuan-yin Bodhisattva daily they experienced an affirmation of their own lives and choices. In one house girls joined the sisterhood by signing a statement of their commitment and burning it in front of their role model and protector, Kuan-yin.[30]

A Symbol of Coping

The most commonly observed Kuan-yin devotion by women is aimed not at escaping marriage but coping with it. The gift of a male child by Kuan-yin, promised in the *Lotus Sūtra,* was the hope of many female worshipers. In Chinese society the highest moral value was filial piety and according to Confucian tradition the worst violation of filial piety was the failure to have male descendents. [31] C.K. Yang, in his *Religion in Chinese Society*, identifies the social function of the Kuan-yin cult as the promotion of fertility for the continuation of the lineage.[32] In his survey of eight localities, he locates most Kuan-yin temples in the category of temples that serve the "integration and well-being of social organizations," specifically by supporting the kinship group through their promotion of fertility. Some Kuan-yin temples are listed as primarily serving the "general public and personal welfare" by bestowing general blessings, but these are found mainly in the north where Taoist temples dedicated to the Taoist child-giving goddesses Nai-nai or Niang-niang served the fertility function.[33]

The birth of a son to a Chinese family ensured the continuation of the male lineage by providing male descendents to carry on the family name and the ancestral rituals. For a woman the birth of a son gave her the opportunity to build a small power base for herself in a perhaps hostile family whose ideology was based on perpetuating the male lineage. Margery Wolf has identified this power base as the uterine family—the children who are tied to their mother through bonds of affection and obligation.[34] A husband provided no definite security, but if a woman could emotionally bind her son to her for life she would have comfort and peace in her later years. The patriarchal structure of the lineage or the male family gave women no power, although it needed them for its own perpetuation. But the uterine family gave women both emotional fulfillment and the hope for some power. As Yang's study shows, devotion to Kuan-yin for bearing sons perpetuated the values of the male family. However, it was also the means by which women survived in the family. It was their means of coping with the male family by creating the shelter and strength of their own uterine family.

Contemporary Symbolism: Liberation and Coping

Legends about Kuan-yin appearing as Princess Miao-shan and others continue to be transmitted and expanded in contemporary Taiwan. Anthologies of these legends, called her *biographies* (*chuan*), are printed and distributed as acts of devotion and to show gratitude for her help. The *Kuan-shih-yin p'u-sa chuan*, widely circulated in Taiwanese temples, contains both traditional legends and modern advice.[35]

On the first page of the *Biography* is what claims to be a "true image" *(chen hsiang)* of Kuan-yin Bodhisattva that is printed in many devotional texts and sold separately in shops throughout Taiwan. It looks somewhat like a blurry black and white photograph of white-robed Kuan-yin hovering above the ocean on what appears to be a dragon's back. The traditional emphasis on seeing Kuan-yin Bodhisattva has been updated here. Whereas in legends and novels, Emperor T'ai-tsung ordered an artist to capture the "true form" of Kuan-yin after she appeared to him,[36] today we have photographers capturing the visions of the bodhisattva.

Most of this devotional book is dedicated to retelling the traditional legends. These are based on older collections such as the twelfth century version attributed to Pu-ming. They include the stories of Princess Miao-shan and Mrs. Ma, recounted earlier, and many more. One traditional tale is striking in its ties to a Chinese historical figure: T'ang Emperor Wen-ts'ung meets Kuan-yin Bodhisattva in a legend that is meant to explain his sudden devotion to her.[37] While eating clams the emperor found one that refused to open. The Emperor responded by praying and the clam shell suddenly transformed itself into a humanlike being. A monk later explained that it was an appearance of Kuan-yin Bodhisattva. According to this legend, this vision of Emperor Wen-ts'ung is the reason for his having built Kuan-yin images and temples throughout China.

The last forty pages of the *Biography* deal with contemporary family and emotional problems. This section, "The Way of Happiness" *(Hsing fu),* discusses ways to transform one's own attitudes and environment to bring about happiness. It begins by pointing out that people who see specific external objects as their problem cannot find true happiness. Neither money nor health is the answer. The author cites Helen Keller and a woman artist from Osaka who lost both arms in an accident as examples of happy people who transcended their physical difficulties. The author heard Helen Keller give a lecture through a Japanese interpreter and quotes her as saying "although my eyes cannot see, my ears cannot hear and my mouth cannot speak, I believe I am the world's single happiest person."[38]

The role models used are women, and the advice given is aimed at women within the family whose happiness seems so tied to their family relationships. At one point the author defines happiness as "a life full of joy," then more specifically as a complete family whose members all happily pass their days.[39] After meditating, chanting scriptures, and writing out the *Heart Sūtra,* the author found the Buddha's path to be summarized in a simple prescription for domestic happiness:

> If throughout the day, you do not get angry,
> And throughout the day, you do not say evil words,
> Then throughout the day the family will find peace and quiet.[40]

Each person must take responsibility for herself and not look to others for happiness. In this essay of advice to women, the author points out that often a husband will get up in a bad mood and when the wife sees this she begins feeling anxiety or other negative feelings. But she should take responsibility for her own attitude regardless of him and be happy.[41]

There is much emphasis on the power of words in this essay. A Chinese saying summarizes this for the author: "Burning incense attracts ghosts" *(Shao hsiang yin kuei)*.[42] The author glosses this to mean that "if you speak of the bad, bad things will arrive." The author argues that this is not superstition and gives a psychological explanation based on the power of negative and positive thoughts to change people's perceptions of their situations. Because good speech is as powerful as bad speech, the author has a simple formula for integrating the power of words into one's life. Two phrases are singled out as having the most importance—"thank you very much" *(tuo hsieh)* and "very good" *(hen hao)*.[43] These common expressions are like Buddhist chants or scriptures—they are perceived as having the power to move the human personality or situations toward states of greater happiness. This essay on happiness is aimed at women devoted to Kuan-yin Bodhisattva. Like the symbol of Kuan-yin herself, the essay expresses two different messages to women. The advice can be empowering: A woman should take responsibility for herself and create her own happiness through positive words and thoughts. Or the advice can be understood as calling for accommodation to an oppressive situation: She should not demand changes in her family situation but should learn to cope with it. It is easy to see reflected in this latter bit of advice the traditional interests of the male lineage.

The essay ends with a section on gratitude and charity. One should give thanks to nature and to all people. We are dependent on sun, water, and air for our own existence and we depend on people for the clothes we wear and the food we eat.[44] We should show our gratitude with acts of charity, beginning with those closest to us—spouses, children, and siblings (in that order and, surprisingly, with no mention of parents).[45] Both monetary and nonmonetary charity is important, but monetary charity can be useless or even harmful if the manner of its dispensation is not given careful consideration. This section on gratitude and charity adds a dimension of Buddhist morality to an essay primarily concerned with a woman's personal happiness.

The basic elements of this contemporary Buddhist essay on positive thinking and the responsibility that one has for one's own happiness could apply to anyone in any culture. In this instance, however, these elements are applied to a Chinese family that no longer is the traditional family based on an arranged marriage where a son's obligations to his parents is central. This is a family where the husband-wife relationship is much more important than relationships with parents and in-laws. The husband still has greater power and the wife has responsibility for the emotional well-being of the family.[46]

Thus, the *Biography of Kuan-shih-yin Bodhisattva* as a whole combines the two opposing roles of this religious symbol for women. The traditional legends provide a model of an independent woman and the contemporary essay provides advice for women coping in a new, but still male-dominated, family.

Another popular religious tract in Taiwan and one that has reappeared in temples in the People's Republic of China is the *Sacred Chant of the White-Robed Great Sage Kuan-yin (Kuan-yin ta-shih pai-yi shen-chi).* A Taiwan version printed in February 1985 is much more than a book of chants; it is a small handbook on all aspects of Kuan-yin devotion.[47]

In the brief introductory description of Kuan-yin in the *Sacred Chant* the issue of the Bodhisattva's sex is raised in simple terms: "Is Kuan-yin Bodhisattva after all male or female?" This question has been discussed by Japanese and Western scholars; it continues to be a topic of lively discussion among Chinese temple worshipers.

The answer given in the *Sacred Chant* is that theoretically only men can become sages as the result of karma, but that bodhisattvas whose existence depends on compassion rather than karma are neither truly male nor female. This introduction also notes that Buddhist texts mention thirty-two different forms of Kuan-yin but that almost all the images and appearances today are of Kuan-yin as a woman. It further explains that Kuan-yin appears in whatever form is appropriate for the person in need but does not explain why most Chinese have needed female forms since the Sung dynasty.

The *Sacred Chant* itself contains some of the most common visual images of Kuan-yin as a woman. It has two pictures of a white-robed Kuan-yin holding a willow branch in one hand and the vase with the dew of compassion in the other (see Figure 1). There are two other outline drawings of white-robed Kuan-yin and the popular pseudo-photograph of her "true form" hovering over the ocean. In addition to these five traditional female Kuan-yin, there is also the female Sung-tzu Kuan-yin, the Kuan-yin who bestows male or female children according to the wishes of the worshiper. Again the verbal message is that the bodhisattva transcends gender categories, but the visual images are those of Kuan-yin, and therefore compassion, as female.

Figure 1

White-robed Kuan-yin bodhisattva, from a devotional text distributed in contemporary Taiwan. From the *Kuan-yin ta-shih pai-yi shen-chi* [The Sacred Chant of the White-robed Sage Kuan-yin] (Taipei, 1985), p. 4.

Two other images of Kuan-yin in the *Sacred Chant* are usually depicted as male or at least androgynous. First, there is Kuan-yin as part of the Pure Land triad with A-mi-t'o Buddha and Ta-shih (Mahāsthāmaprāpta) Bodhisattva, but even here the picture of Kuan-yin is quite feminine. Second, there is the eleven-headed, thousand-armed Kuan-yin who looks appropriately asexual. This is apparently one image even the Chinese find difficult to transform into a realistic looking woman, so they leave it close to its original form.

Beyond the pictures and explanations of Kuan-yin, the *Sacred Chant* contains all the basic information for Kuan-yin devotion. Of course, there is the "Sacred Chant of White-Robed Great Sage Kuan-yin." Also included are two other chants: the "Dharaṇī of the thousand-armed, thousand-eyed Kuan-yin of Unlimited Compassion" and the *Heart Sūtra* (in which Kuan-yin Bodhisattva also appears). Readers also are given advice on the essentials of chanting, phonetic symbols for the difficult characters used to transliterate the Sanskrit, and a convenient page of 500 empty circles with the instructions that after each 20 repetitions of the sacred chant you should fill in one circle with a red pen. When all circles are filled, 1000 chants will have been completed and your petition to Kuan-yin will be answered. This religious tract also gives a schedule of Kuan-yin–related festival days and a chart showing the best possible ways to arrange incense sticks in Buddhist rituals to bring about family happiness.[48] Each arrangement results in specific good or evil consequences for one's health, fortune, social life, and so forth. The symbol of Kuan-yin Bodhisattva unites various practices of popular religion in contemporary Taiwan just as it united various popular Buddhist traditions in China since the T'ang dynasty.

Lest the reader doubt the power of devotion to the bodhisattva, the last few pages of the *Sacred Chant* contain descriptions of eleven cases in Taipei alone of people who have seen Kuan-yin in dreams and had their prayers answered after reciting the chants.[49] Each case gives the person's full name, a detailed address, a description of the problem and the miraculous solution. Almost all the cases focus on women—women who are sick, who have problems with childbirth or who are concerned with the well-being of family members. Only one fits the traditional stereotype of a woman praying for a male child: she was thirty-one years old and after Kuan-yin appeared to her in a dream she became pregnant and had a son. These are modern Taipei women worrying about their health and their families. One woman, along with her husband who was a teacher, hoped that by devotion to Kuan-yin their son could pass the exams for admission into medical school. At the time of the report, the son was said to be a second-year medical student in Taipei.

Conclusion

From the Sung dynasty to the present, the Chinese have chosen to create and worship a female form of their most popular bodhisattva, Kuan-yin. For women this has meant a symbol of someone who would serve as their savior from all suffering, but especially from the suffering arising out of their female birth: arranged marriages, sexual attacks, the pain and stigma of both menstruation and childbirth, and the powerlessness of childlessness in a patriarchal society. A Buddhist savior from suffering, Kuan-yin sometimes is also a role model in her manifestations as women. In many traditional legends that still are propagated she serves as a model of piety and independence from family restrictions. In other traditions, particularly the image of the Kuan-yin who delivers children (Sung-tzu Kuan-yin), the symbol of the bodhisattva offers a means of coping with the pressures of a patriarchal family and thus remaining within it. These legends continue to be popular but are combined with modern advice for family life and recent testimonials to Kuan-yin's compassionate power to heal the body and support the modern family.

Although the stories of her miracles have been updated for the 1980s, her images remain virtually unchanged since the Ming dynasty. One Kuan-yin image dominates contemporary devotion: the white-robed Chinese woman holding willow branch and vase. In Taiwan this representation of Kuan-yin appears in temples, domestic altars, protective charms, operas, and even in film and television adaptations of *The Journey to the West.* She is virtually independent of the traditional schools and scriptures of elite Buddhism. She is not primarily the bodhisattva who assists A-mi-t'o Buddha of the Pure Land scriptures, the thousand-armed deity of tantric traditions, or even the saving bodhisattva of the *Lotus Sūtra.* Kuan-yin is a Chinese female bodhisattva known primarily through Chinese legends, art, novels, plays, and recent miracles. The woman who is saved in contemporary legends is a modern Chinese woman, but the woman who saves is from that indistinct and confused past of the T'ang-Ming often used as the setting for movies and television series. Two contemporary role models of devotional literature, Helen Keller and a handicapped Japanese artist, follow the traditions associated with Kuan-yin as a role model: they are extraordinary women with no apparent family obligations. Kuan-yin devotion continues to symbolically reconcile the conflicting values in women's lives: the value of independence from social demands to allow for spiritual growth and the value of nurturing the family relationships to which many women look for meaning and happiness.

Individual women may not be able to realize both values due to the way gender roles have been defined by traditional and contemporary society, but the tension between the values is resolved in the images and stories of Kuan-yin, a figure who upholds both.

Notes

An earlier version of this paper was presented at the 1986 Midwest Conference on Asian Studies. The author would like to thank Ann Waltner for her comments on that earlier version and Gary M. Davison for comments on later drafts. All Chinese terms in this essay are given in Wade-Giles transliteration.

1. Translation by Diana Y. Paul, *Women in Buddhism: Images of the Feminine in Mahÿāna Tradition* (Berkeley, Calif.: Asian Humanities Press, 1979), p. 263; Kumarajīva's version of the *Lotus Sūtra* has been translated in its entirety by Leon Hurvitz, *Scripture of the Lotus Blossom of the Fine Dharma* (New York: Columbia University Press, 1976).

2. Edward Conze, *Thirty Years of Buddhist Studies: Selected Essays,* (Columbia: University of South Carolina, 1968), p. 81.

3. Various theories about these names are discussed by Marie-Thérèse de Mallman, *L'Introduction à l'étude d'Avalokiteçvara* (Paris: Presses Universitaires de France, 1967); and by C.N. Tay, "Kuan-yin: The Cult of Half Asia," *History of Religions* 16, no. 2 (1976): 147–177. For theories about the sexual transformation of Kuan-yin see Paul, *Women in Buddhism,* 250–252; and John Chamberlayne, "The Development of Kuan Yin, the Goddess of Mercy," *Numen,* 9 (January 1962): 45–52.

4. Hurvitz, *Scripture of the Lotus Blossom,* 25–26, and Paul, ibid., p. 259; Tay discusses the concept of Kuan-yin in the *Lotus Sūtra* (and the *Sūraṃgama* and *Thousand-hand Dharaṇī Sūtras)* in "Kuan-yin."

5. Leroy Davidson, *The Lotus Sutra in Chinese Art* (New Haven, Conn.: Yale University Press, 1954), p.71.

6. See Davidson, ibid., p. 85; and Michibata Ryōshū, "Chūgoku ni okeru minkan shinkō to Kannon," *Indogaku Bukkyōgaku kenkyū* 3, no. 1 (September 1954): 337–340, as cited by Alicia Matsunga, *The Buddhist Philosophy of Assimilation,* (Tokyu: Charles E. Tuttle, 1969), p. 137.

7. For a study of Chinese women's communities and women's power through their uterine families, see Margery Wolf, *Women and the Family in Rural Taiwan* (Stanford, Calif.: Stanford University Press, 1972); Wolf also did research in China in 1985 and comments on the fate of these structures in *Revolution*

Postponed: Women in Contemporary China (Stanford, Calif.: Stanford University Press, 1985).

8. A survey of the Buddhist paintings at Tun-huang illustrates the occasional power of women as patrons of religious art; their images are among those painted on the cave walls. On the east wall in cave 329 is a simple portrait of a young woman donor in a posture of devotion holding a lotus flower. A more extravagant portrait of a female donor is the Northern Sung painting of Princess Li of Khotan, who married Ts'ao Yen-lu of the ruling Ts'ao family of Kua-chou and Sha-chou. She appears in cave 61 on the east wall with her attendants and is adorned with an elaborate headdress, jewelry, and makeup. According to a colophon on the mural, Princess Li of Khotan commissioned the paintings on the east wall. Another indication of the support of royal women for Buddhist art is the T'ang dynasty painting of two women of a royal family undergoing the tonsure ceremony (cave 445). See *The Art Treasures of Dunhuang,* compiled by the Dunhuang Institute for Cultural Relics (New York: Lee Publishers Group, 1981), pp.227, 235, 229.

9. The following information on Kuan-yin paintings is based on my own observations at a special exhibit at the National Palace Museum (Taipei, Taiwan) in 1985 and museum notes accompanying the collection.

10. *Hsi yu chi,* translation by Anthony C. Yu, *The Journey to the West,* 1 (Chicago: University of Chicago Press, 1977), p. 185.

11. For a study of water-moon Kuan-yin paintings, see Cornelius P. Chang, "Kuan-yin Paintings from Tun-huang: Water-moon Kuan-yin," *Journal of Oriental Studies* 15, no. 2 (1977): 140–160.

12. *Tao te ching* IV; translation by Arthur Waley, *The Way and Its Power: A Study of the Tao Te Ching and Its Place in Chinese Thought* (New York: Grove Press, 1958), p. 146.

13. Hurvitz, *Scripture of the Lotus Blossom,* p. 102.

14. *Tao te ching* VII; Waley, *The Way and Its Power,* p. 151.

15. For example, according to a Taoist text of the third or fourth century, *The Classic of the Five Talismans,* one could absorb the *yin* element by "moonbathing." See Anna Seidel, "Taoism," *Encyclopedia Britannica.* vol. 17, pp. 1034–1044.

16. Chih-yi described the six forms of Kuan-yin in the realms of hell beings, hungry ghosts, animals, *ausras,* humans, and deities in his *Chih-kuan* [T. 46, p. 156]; see Matsunaga, *Buddhist Philosophy,* p. 122.

17. For a good example of a psychological interpretation of physical dangers in Pure Land Buddhism, see Shan-tao's "Parable of the White Path" in *Kuan-ching shu (Taishō daizōkyō,* 37: pp. 272–273); a partial translation can be found

in Wm. Theodore de Bary, ed., *The Buddhist Tradition in India, China and Japan* (New York: Modern Library, 1969), pp. 204–207.

18. Wolfram Eberhard, *Sin and Guilt in Traditional China* (Berkeley: University of California Press, 1967).

19. Ju Gong-wen, ed., *Puto shan* (Beijing: China Travel Publishing Society, 1982), pp. 27–28. Chun-fang Yu documented pilgrimages to P'u-t'o Island and the Upper T'ien-chu Monastery in Hangchow in honor of Kuan-yin's birthday during 1987 in a film, *Kuan-yin Pilgrimage,* distributed by R. G. Video.

20. Johannes Frick, "Mutter und Kind bei Chinesen in Tsinghai, I: Die Sozial-religiose Unreinheit der Frau," *Anthropos* 50 (1955): 341–342, as cited by Emily Ahern in her excellent study, "The Power and Pollution of Chinese Women," *Women in Chinese Society* (Stanford, Calif.: Stanford University Press, 1975), p. 214.

21. Margery Wolf studied the relationship between marriage and suicide for Chinese women in "Women and Suicide in China," in *Women in Chinese Society,* pp. 111–142. Arthur Wolf discusses the sexual aversion and lower fertility rates of the marriages of sons and adopted daughters in "The Women of Hai-shan: A Demographic Portrait," ibid., pp. 89–110.

22. Joanna Handlin, "Lü K'un's New Audience: The Influence of Women's Literacy on Sixteenth Century Thought," ibid., p. 16.

23. *Kuan-shih-yin p'u-sa chuan* [Biography of Kuan-shih-yin Bodhisattva], author unknown (Taichung, 1985) is the popular version today and the source for the stories cited here; for an English translation of the Miao-shan story, see Glen Dudbridge, *The Legend of Miao-shan* (London: Ithica Press, 1978).

24. For a translation of a Tun-huang manuscript of this story, see Arthur Waley, *Ballads and Stories from Tun-huang* (London: George Allen & Unwin, 1960), pp. 216–235.

25. *Kuan-shih-yin p'u-sa chuan,* pp. 150–155; for an English summary of this legend see Henry Dore, *Researches into Chinese Superstitions,* vol. 6, (Taipei: Chengwen Publishing Co., 1966), pp. 213–214.

26. See Matsunaga, *Buddhist Philosophy,* p. 131.

27. Eberhard, *Sin and Guilt,* p. 114.

28. Marjorie Topley, "Marriage Resistance in Rural Kwangtung, " *Women in Chinese Society,* pp. 67–88.

29. Ibid., p. 79.

30. Marjorie Topley, "Women's Vegetarian Houses in Singapore," *Journal of the Malayan Branch of the Royal Asiatic Society* 27, no. 1 (1954): 51–67; references are found on pp. 59 and 62.

31. According to Mencius, "There are three things which are unfilial, and to have no posterity is the greatest of them." See *Mencius* 4A:26; trans. James Legge, *The Four Books: Confucian Analects, The Great learning, The Doctrine of the Mean, and The Works of Mencius* (New York, 1966), p. 725.

32. C. K. Yang, *Religion in Chinese Society* (Berkeley: University of California, 1961), pp. 6–11.

33. Ibid., pp. 7–11.

34. Margery Wolf, *Women and the Family in Rural Taiwan* (Stanford, Calif.: Stanford University Press, 1972).

35. *Kuan-shih-yin p'u-sa chuan* [Biography of Kuan-shih-yin Bodhisattva], author unknown (Tai-chung, 1985).

36. This is described in *Hsi yu chi;* see Yu, *Journey to the West,* p. 278.

37. *Kuan-shih-yin p'u-sa chuan,* pp. 156–161; summarized by Matsunaga, *Buddhist Philosophy,* p. 133.

38. *"Hsing fu,"* pp. 1–3, in *Kuan-shih-yin p'u-sa chuan.*

39. Ibid., p. 5.

40. Ibid., p. 6.

41. Ibid., p. 8–14.

42. Ibid., p. 20.

43. Ibid., p. 22.

44. Ibid., p. 37.

45. Ibid., p. 38.

46. For a discussion of changes in the Chinese family in Taiwan, see Chun-kit Joseph Wong, *The Changing Chinese Family Pattern in Taiwan* (Taipei: Southern Materials Center, 1981).

47. *Kuan-yin ta-shih pai-yi shen-chi* [The Sacred Chant of the White-Robed Sage Kuan-yin], author unknown (Taipei, 1985).

48. Ibid., P. 11.

49. Ibid., pp. 12–13.

8

Mother Wisdom, Father Love: Gender-based Imagery in Mahāyāna Buddhist Thought

José Ignacio Cabezón

Much of feminist critique in the area of religious studies has been devoted to the question of gender-based religious imagery. In patriarchal societies, where culture as a whole has been male dominated, it is not surprising that, in the religious sphere, symbols both created by and relevant to men have been propagated as the norm and the ideal. In this sense, Buddhism is no exception to the rule; and yet, even though patriarchal cultures (those in which Buddhism arose and to which it spread among them) tend to employ a good deal of masculine symbolism, imagery involving the feminine is not unknown. However, the presence of female symbolism, in and of itself, is no guarantee of enlightened attitudes toward women. It is clear that, in the hands of men, female images have been, and are still, used effectively to further patriarchal ends. This chapter is not an exercise in feminist critique. Only tangentially, as it impinges on other issues, does it seek to explore the patriarchal basis for, and the ends served by, the kind of gender-based religious imagery found in Buddhist texts. Nonetheless, it is my hope that in its primary task the chapter does not lose sight of the fact that such imagery developed in, and was directed at, a predominantly male religious culture. It would be more than misleading to suggest that the Mahāyāna Buddhist philosophers and yogis who were the wielders of such symbols had as their goal providing female religious imagery, either for the woman adept or for Buddhist society as whole.[1] With this in mind we proceed to our main task, that of exploring the nature of gender-based imagery in Buddhist texts.

A Historical Preamble

Gender-based religious imagery, that is, the use of the categories of male and female to symbolize religious concepts, in the Indian context, is as old as the earliest known civilization, that of the Indus Valley culture.[2] The large numbers of seals, depicting primarily male figures and animals associated with masculine qualities, on the one hand, and the equally large numbers of votive figurines of female "deities" suggests gender differentiation as a vehicle for religious meaning.[3] The details and the exact use of such symbols, however, due to lack of textual corroboration, are extremely difficult to determine. In recent years some headway has been made in the interpretation of the significance of the cultic scenes depicted on the seals and with this of the meaning of the gender-based imagery. By comparison to the religion of the Elamite culture, whose practices are described in Sumerian texts, scholars are beginning to draw some tentative conclusions concerning the nature of the religion of the Indus Valley civilization.[4] In this regard, one of the most interesting areas of investigation concerns the use of male-female symbology. For example, Wolkstein and Kramer[5] describe a cultic practice associated with the moon goddess Inanna[6] in which men dress half their bodies in womens' clothing and women do the same with mens' garments. Despite the very fascinating nature of the comparative studies between the pre-Āryan Indian and the Elamite cultures, much of the work is still highly speculative. To date we can say little more than that there was widespread use of gender-based imagery in Indus Valley civilization. If, as current theories would have it, Buddhism and the other śramaṇic movements contemporary with it were the inheritors of many of the elements of Indus Valley culture, one might expect that Buddhism also might have been heir to some of this gender-related symbolism that seems to have been so important a part of Harappan religion. Still, as things stand now, the discipline is far from able to make definitive claims in this regard.

The Vedic period is far more one sided as regards gender-related imagery. "Male domination in the Ṛg Veda," to use an expression of Wendy Donniger's[7] is but a reflection of the preoccupation with the masculine that is endemic to Āryan culture as a whole.[8]

Though influenced by many Brahmaṇic ideas, Buddhism, as mentioned, also was heir to pre-Vedic religious concepts. Even though much of Buddhist doctrine is not Vedic in origin, and hence potentially free from the rigidly male-dominant symbolism of Āryan religious culture, we find in early Buddhism little by way of gender-based imagery.[9] There is one interesting exception. In a passage from the *Dhammapada,*[10] the saying "father and mother are to be killed" is ascribed to the Buddha. It is considered the quintessential example of a passage that is of provisional meaning (*neyārtha*), one that cannot be taken literally. The tradition glosses it to mean that *karma* and *kleśas* (symbolized here as father and mother) are to be eliminated. In the *Visuddhimagga,* a post canonical Pali work, there are several lines that may be related to this scriptural passage: "ignorance etc. are the basis for this body, as is the mother for the child; karma is the begetter, as is the father of the son."[11] Nonetheless, symbolism of this sort is relatively rare in the early Buddhist tradition.

In the Mahāyāna the contrary is true. In the "greater vehicle" gender-related religious imagery abounds, both in the *sūtras* (the primary scriptures considered to be the buddha Śākyamuni's word) and in the *tantras* (the esoteric literature). In what follows we shall examine the use of gender categories (female and male) as symbols for the two most important concepts of Mahāyāna Buddhism, wisdom (*prajñā*)-gnosis (*jñāna*) on the one hand, and method (*upāya*)-compassion (*karuṇā*) on the other. We find in the scriptures of the Mahāyāna several instances in which wisdom is identified as female, and more specifically as mother (*mātṛ*),[12] whereas the less analytic[13] and more emotive states that constitute "method," namely love (*maitrī*), compassion, altruism (*bodhicitta*), and so forth, are identified with the male or "father" (*pitṛ*).[14] By examining the meaning of some of these scriptural passages, we attempt to come to some understanding of the nature of this symbolism in its full complexity, examining both the conceptions of gender that condition it as well as the implications of this doctrine to the question of gender.

A Linguistic Note

Anyone familiar with Sanskrit grammar, in which nouns are feminine, neuter, or masculine in gender, cannot help but notice that many words associated with knowledge or wisdom—*prajñā, vidyā,* and *parijñā,* for example—are feminine, whereas many words associated with emotive states, such as compassion and love—*preman* and *sneha,* for example—are masculine. Is the gender-based imagery found in Buddhist religious and philosophical literature, then, motivated simply by the gender of nouns, and therefore indicative of nothing more than a grammatical peculiarity of the language?[15] I will show that it is not the case. Even if it were so, however, it would still leave unanswered the question of how analytic states came to be associated with the feminine and emotive ones with the masculine *in the first place*, that is, in the very process of determining the gender of nouns.

It is not the case, however, that epistemic-analytic terminology (words dealing with wisdom) are exclusively feminine and emotive terminology exclusively masculine. For nearly every feminine word related to "wisdom," we can find a masculine one (*jñāna, abhisamaya, adhigama, bodha*); likewise, for nearly every masculine word related to "compasssion" and "love" we can find a feminine one (*maitrī, karuṇā, kṛpā*). Hence, the charge that Buddhist philosophers fell into the gender imagery adventitiously, as it were, as an accident of language, is not supported by the linguistic evidence. It therefore must be seen as a conscious choice on their part and not as unconsciously motivated by the gendered structure of the language itself.[16]

On Methodology

My methodology in this study has two chief components. It is first of all textual, relying on primary sources, in attempting to come to an understanding of what the tradition itself considers the nature and implications of gender imagery. Second, consonant with a such a method, I am committed to a phenomenological approach to the nature of meaning that relies heavily on Wittgenstein's theory of family resemblances.[17] Although Wittgenstein himself develops a theory of "meaning as use" in the context of language, it seems to me that the implications of such a notion to the study of symbols is profound. Hence, my approach is to begin to come to an understanding of the meaning of a symbol, here a gender-based image, by examining its use within a scriptural tradition, here the Indo-Tibetan Buddhist Mahāyāna scholastic tradition. My claim is that to understand the nexus of multifarious interconnections between such point instances of use or, in Wittgenstein's terminology, to understand the "family resemblances," is to understand the meaning of a symbol. My approach, therefore, is consistent with a "polysemic" view of symbol, though not identical with either Victor Turner's treatment of symbolism nor with the way that Turner's views have been adapted most recently by Caroline Walker Bynum.[18] With this by way of preamble, let us turn to the task at hand, the examination of gender-based imagery in Mahāyāna Buddhism.

Wisdom as Mother: The Gestation of Enlightenment

The *Abhisamayālaṃkāra*, one of the most important treatises of the scholastic tradition of Mahāyāna Buddhism, begins with an homage to the perfection of wisdom (*prajñāpāramitā*) as the mother of the various types of spiritually accomplished beings: "I bow down to the Mother of the hosts of disciples (*śrāvakas*), bodhisattvas and buddhas."[19] Haribhadra, in commenting on this verse, glosses the word *mother* as the three types of knowledge (*mkhyen gsum*) that lead the different types of spiritual aspirants to their respective goals. He says that the Lord Maitreya, the author of the text, realizing that this perfection of wisdom "is the source of all good," begins his text with this verse to "arise in others the desire for the unsurpassable and infinite special qualities of the Noble Lady (*bhagavatī*)."[20] According to some Tibetan exegetes who comment on Haribhadra's text, the Mother being referred to here has three aspects (*rnam pa gsum*), her manifestation as scripture (here referring to the *Prajñāpāramitā Sūtras*),[21] as path (the series of mental states that lead to illumination), and as result (enlightenment itself). Sometimes a fourth aspect is added, as essence (*rang bzhin*). In this case, the "essential" *Prajñāpāramitā* is emptiness, the essence, or final nature, of all phenomena. Other interpreters opt for glossing "the three aspects" as the three primary *Prajñāpāramitā Sūtras* on which the *Abhisamayālaṃkāra* is based.[22] Be that as it may, whether viewed as scripture, spiritual state of mind, the goal of enlightenment, or emptiness, the perfection of wisdom is here being identified not only as feminine but as a mother.[23]

Wisdom is considered the mother of the different spiritual types because she is their cause. However, it is clear from other texts[24] that spiritual accomplishment has various causes. Why selectively choose wisdom, and why characterize it as the mother? Just as the mother is one of the two principal causes of a child, so too is wisdom one of the two chief causes of enlightenment. The other, of course, is method. To stress this fact, namely that wisdom is what nurtures the adept on the path, it is characterized as their "mother." Just as a mother must bear the child in her womb for ten (lunar) months, the traditional gestation period, so too does wisdom nurture the adept along the way through the ten *bhūmis*, the stages of the bodhisattva path. Hence, it is gestation in mother wisdom's womb that brings about the birth of enlightened beings.[25] In this sense it is interesting to note that the role of altruism is very similar to the father's role in procreation. Whereas the mother must continue to nurture the child in her womb until its birth, the father's actual role in procreation occurs at the beginning and, by comparison, is relatively short in duration. Likewise, in the exegetical literature we find a great deal of discussion of the systematic development of wisdom over the entire spiritual career of the adept but little mention of such development in the case of compassion or altruism, whose primary function comes at the outset, at the very beginning, of the Mahāyāna path.[26]

Emptiness qua Logical Negation as Mother

In a work of a completely different genre, a short yet fascinating text on meditation beloning to the dGe lugs pa school of Tibetan Buddhism, a text popularly known as *Recognizing One's Mother, The View*[27] (*A ma lta ba ngos 'dzin*), the work of the great lCang skya rol pa'i rdo rje (1717–1786), the analogy is taken even further. Here the state of ignorance is represented metaphorically by a small child, an insane child, who, though living next to its mother, reality (*chos nyid*), does not recognize her. The scenario, though taken to extremes at times (in one verse an elder brother, "Dependent Arising," appears on the scene), is quite touching, and it is clear that the author is using the emotions elicited by the tragedy of a child's separation from its mother to great rhetorical advantage. Be that as it may, in this case *reality*, that is emptiness, is identified as the mother *and not wisdom*. In so far as emptiness is the object of wisdom, however, in so far as reality is the thing that wisdom perceives, the identification of *it* as the mother is not surprising. Actually, even in the literature associated with *Abhisamayālaṃkāra* we will recall that of the four aspects of *Prajñāpāramitā*, of the Perfection of Wisdom, the essential one was emptiness itself. In the commentary to the present text, dKon mchog 'jigs med dbang po (1728–1791) states: "Here, it is utterly appropriate to call emptiness 'mother' because even in the *Prajñāpāramitā Sūtras* emptiness is spoken of in maternal epithets."[28] In the verses that follow, the metaphor is expanded further as new characters and ideas are introduced. The concept of dependent arising, a positive corollary and implicate of emptiness, is symbolized as an "older brother" (*jo jo*), reinforcing the notion that only emptiness, as the logical negation (*med dgag*) that it is, (or its cognition—wisdom) is feminine, whereas positive concepts, that is, logical affirmations (*sgrub pa*), such as dependent arising, are to be considered masculine.

Mother Wisdom, Father Love[29]

The final selection that we shall examine comes from the writings of the Tibetan sage Tsong kha pa (1357–1419).[30] In his monumental synthetic work on the practice of Mahāyāna Buddhism, *The Great Exposition of the Graded Stages of the Path* (*Lam rim chen mo*), we find several pages devoted to the present question. Tsong kha pa's work is most useful in explaining the precise *reason* for depicting wisdom as female and, more specifically, as mother, pitting it as he does against method (*upāya*) or the altruistic mind (*bodhicitta*), considered as father.[31]

Basing his interpretation on the fact that in ancient India and Tibet the ethnicity of a child was based on the ethnicity of the father, Tsong kha pa explains the metaphor in the following way. He says that wisdom is a spiritual quality shared by all spiritually accomplished individuals, be they followers of the Śrāvakayāna or of the Mahāyāna. Just as a mother can bear children of different castes or nationalities, depending the ethnicity of the various men who father them, so too can wisdom bring forth a variety of spiritually accomplished individuals: śrāvakas, pratyekabuddhas, and buddhas. Because the mother, wisdom, is the same in all of these cases, the father will determine the spiritual lineage of the adept. If the father, method, is particularly prominent (possessing the "prayer", "activity," and "dedication" of the *bodhisattvayāna*) then the child will be a buddha. If, on the other hand, the father is relatively impoverished in these qualities, the result will be the lesser enlightenments of the Hīnayāna (the states of śrāvaka and pratyekabuddhahood).

That this is not a particularly Tibetan conception but has its origins in India is witnessed by the fact that there exists a similar account related to the birth of Asaṅga and Vasubandhu. These two half-brothers were born of the same mother but of different fathers. Asaṅga's father was a *kṣatriya*, making him of the warrior caste by birth, whereas Vasubandhu's father, being a *brāhmaṇa*, meant that Vasubandhu was a member of the priestly caste.[32] Hence, that the ethnicity of a child is dependent on the father is a notion known to Buddhists from the very origins of the scholastic tradition. It is by analogy to the role that gender plays in society, then, that the metaphors of wisdom as mother and method as father come about. Of course, whether the social presuppositions concerning the role that gender plays in ethnicity is what actually motivated the creators of the symbol or whether reference to these societal norms are a de facto afterthought of scholastics attempting to understand and justify the use of gender polarity to symbolize philosophical concepts is impossible to say.[33]

It would appear that the use of woman (and more specifically of motherhood) as the symbol of a positive spiritual quality (wisdom) in the Mahāyāna, taken in isolation, is a great leap forward in the religious thought of India. Indeed, this point is made most eloquently by Joanna Macy in ''Perfection of Wisdom: Mother of All Buddhas.''[34] That the symbol carried with it positive elements can hardly be denied. When properly contextualized, however, aspersions begin to be cast upon the use of the symbol as an *unequivolcal* source of value for women. If we take into account all of the aspects of the symbol, we cannot overlook that at the root of the metaphor is an implicit assumption demeaning to the status of women, namely that a woman's ethnic heritage is of no consequence in determining the ethnic heritage of her children, that the man's ethnic background is the sole determinant of the child's ethnicity. Just as man is ''more important'' in determining the ethnicity of the child, so too is father-love in the spiritual realm.[35] When mother-wisdom is the progenitress of a variety of spiritually accomplished beings, ranging from the lowest śrāvaka arhant to the most perfected buddha, is not her position inferior to that of father-love's who is unique in determining the Mahāyānic ethnicity of the child?[36] Compassion and altruism are the principal trademarks of the Mahāyāna, and gender is used as such to affirm this—these qualities are after all masculine. What is more, in a culture where monogamy and female fidelity were considered so important, are not the implications of mother-wisdom's liasons with different men once more an implicit deprecation of the feminine? True, wisdom may be the mother of these different types of spiritual beings, but only at the expense of being (at least implicitly) implicated in acts of promiscuity.

Carolyn Walker Bynum[37] has argued that ''gender related symbols, in their full complexity, may refer to gender in ways that affirm or reverse it, support or question it.'' We have shown how the use of this particular gender-based symbol, wisdom as mother, might be derived from and how it affirms—at least in part—a patriarchal conception of gender. It is naive to think that the mere presence of a symbol of the feminine in a tradition is derived from a conception of gender that is affirming of the status of women or that the presence of such a symbol is sufficient to guarantee that a positive attitude toward the feminine is going to be conveyed to women, or more generally to society, through that symbol. Gender-related symbols, and indeed religious symbols in general, are simply too complex to allow for such linear-denotative models as viable theories concerning the function of symbolism. What this implies as well is that religious symbols are too complex to accept at face value, without contextualizing them historically and sociologically. Especially important in this regard is the determination of the audience and cast; that is, those for whom and by whom the symbols are to be played out and experienced, respectively. In the present context, the point might be made more succinctly by saying that much more dangerous than Greeks bearing gifts is the patriarchy bearing female symbols. The mere existence of female symbols in a religious tradition (Asian or Western) is simply no guarantee that truly universal religious aims are being met.[38]

Conclusion

Now that we have explored the use of gender-based imagery in several different contexts we can notice a pattern of family resemblances between these point instances of use. We find the image of mother, for example, used to symbolize wisdom, emptiness, analyticity, logical negation, and generative multiplicity. We find this in contradistinction to the father or male image that, as we have seen, comes to represent method, compassion, interdependence, the emotive states, logical affirmation, and generative specificity. The picture that emerges is a fascinating one, one very different from gender-based symbolism in the West, religious or otherwise. It is interesting that in both cultures, and here we must not lose sight of the fact that by examining the textual traditions we are for the most part examining culture as seen through the eyes *of men,* we find a dichotomy between the analytical and emotive aspects of human personality. That the dichotomy exists in both Asian and Western cultures and that both cultures use gender-related symbolism to bring out the tension, I believe, is significant. It is indicative of the fact that, at least from a male perspective, (1) there exists a fundamental human tension between analytical-cognitive states and emotions and that (2) this tension is in some way related to (at least to the point that it can be symbolized by) the tension (and distinctions) between genders.[39]

An obvious desideratum at this point would be to investigate texts written by women, examining them for whether this tension between analytical and emotional states (1) exists and (2) is symbolized by the tension between genders. Given the virtual absence of women's textual traditions in Buddhism, however, any conclusions in this regard must remain speculative. Still, if it is true that "women's mode of using symbols seems given to the muting of opposition," whereas "men's mode seems characterized by emphasis on opposition, contradiction, inversion and conversion,"[40] then we would expect that this difference between modes of thought might not be perceived as a tension and therefore might not be depicted at all, much less through the use of gender-based imagery. Only the continued scrutiny of what little we know of women's religious experience in the Buddhist tradition will bear this out, however.

Perhaps what is most fascinating about the situation in patriarchal cultures is neither that this tension exists in both societies (Buddhist and Western), nor that the tension is symbolized by means of gender distinctions, but that the association of specific genders with specific mental modes in the two cultures is exactly opposite. In the West qualities like wisdom and analyticity, in the stereotyping of sex-roles, have been identified as masculine qualities, whereas the emotive mental states have come to be associated with the feminine.[41] At least in the textual traditions that we have examined, exactly the opposite is the case. The reason for this is clear. The way that the gender-based symbols are used in the Buddhist texts we examined is more complex and circuitous than simply assigning to a mental state the gender of the group that most exemplifies that quality. Wisdom is not represented as female because women were considered to be more wise than men or more analytically capable. Indeed, a great deal of literature within the tradition is dedicated to showing that this is not the case. I have shown that if wisdom was considered feminine it was for more complex reasons and that the process was more metaphorical than linear. Wisdom is characterized as feminine (1) because of wisdom's inferiority in determining Mahāyānic ethnicity and (2) due to the Mahāyāna's preoccupation with the centrality of emotional states as *the* distinguishing characteristic (its uniqueness) as a tradition, therefore considering them as more important to Mahāyānic identity, and hence characterizing them as masculine. Clearly, neither of these two reasons for using gender-based symbols adds to the status either of wisdom or women.

We must reiterate that this entire discussion is based on texts written by men predominantly for men and that the tension between analytic and affective states, as well as the use of gender-based imagery to characterize it, might very well be peculiar to men's mode of perceiving the world. Although the existence of this tension and the use of gender-based imagery to elucidate it is something common to both (*patriarchal*) religious cultures (Asian and Western) and hence arguably universal, the association of specific modes of thought with specific genders seems to be culture specific.[42] Nonetheless, we have shown that the imagery in large part presumes and affirms the lower status of women. If Bynum's hypotheses concerning the use and experience of symbols by women is found to be true in a Buddhist context then we eventually might conclude that this symbology of tension is gender specific across cultures, found only in the writings and thought of men, and both presuming and affirming the inferiority of women.

Appendix: A Selection from Tsong kha pa's Lam rim chen mo *(Dharmasala: undated blockprint), folios 185b–186b.*

The unsurpassable altruistic mind, from among all of the different causes of the emergent seedling of buddhahood, is the uncommon cause, like the seed [that is, which is the chief cause], whereas wisdom, that is, the realization of emptiness, like water and fertilizer and so on, is a common cause [because many other kinds of seedlings also have these as a cause]. That is why [we find the following] passage in the *Uttaratantra*: "Faith in the highest vehicle is the seed while wisdom is the mother that breeds the buddha's qualities."[43] This is saying that the altruistic mind is like the father's seed, whereas the wisdom that is the realization of selflessness is like the mother. For example, if the father is Tibetan it is impossible for the child to be an Indian or a Tartar and so forth. Hence, the father determines the ethnicity (*rigs*) of the son. On the other hand, sons of various [ethnicities] can be born from a Tibetan mother. Hence, she becomes a cause that is in common [to a variety of sons of different ethnicities, depending on whether the father is Tibetan, Indian, and so forth].

The Protector Nāgārjuna also states: "The emancipatory path that is relied upon by buddhas, pratyekabuddhas and śrāvakas is but one [namely wisdom]. That is why beside you there is no other." Here he is praising the perfection of wisdom (*sher phyin*). Even śrāvakas must rely on it. Therefore, as the perfection of wisdom is called the *mother*, it is the mother of the children (*sras*) of both the greater and the lesser vehicle. Hence, the greater and the lesser vehicles are not distinguished on the basis of the wisdom that realizes emptiness [because such wisdom exists in both vehicles]. They are distinguished on the basis of the altruistic mind (*byang chub kyi sems*) and the tremendous activities (*spyod pa*) [of the bodhisattvas]. That is why the *Ratnāvalī* says: "Since the Śrāvakayāna does not explain such things as the bodhisattvas' prayer (*smon lam*), activity (*spyod pa*) and dedication (*yongs bsngo*) how can they [śrāvakas] become bodhisattvas?"[44] This is stating that [śrāvakas and bodhisattvas] are not distinguished on the basis of the view (*lta ba*), being instead distinguished on the basis of their activity.

In this way [we can see that] if the wisdom that realizes emptiness is not a special path of the Mahāyāna, what need is there to mention [that it exists in] paths other than that one? Therefore, it is clear that if, having been exposed to the doctrine of altruism, (p. 186b) one does not practice it, but instead, paying only occasional lip service to it, one vigorously applies oneself to the more subtle aspects of the path, there will be extremely little by way of spiritual attainment.

Just as, in general, both father and mother are required in giving birth to a child, just so, in completing the path, it is necessary to complete the aspects of both method and wisdom. In particular, two things are necessary: the chief form of method, the altruistic mind (*byang chub kyi sems*), and the chief form of wisdom, the realization (*rtogs pa*) of emptiness (*stong pa nyid*). What if one meditates only on one of them? Take the case of those who strive only for emancipation from *saṃsāra*. Granted that they must meditate on selflessness, that is, emptiness, without mistaking mental tranquility (*śamatha*) for insight (*vipaśyanā*). If one is considered a Mahāyānist, however, it is necessary to [also] train in the altruistic mind. Why? For the following reasons. As the Lord Maitreya says:

> By knowing (*shes pas*) one does not abide in existence (*srid pa*).
> By means of compassion one does not abide in peace (*zhi ba*).[45]

Wisdom (*shes rab*) stops one from falling into the extreme of *saṃsāra* and compassion is necessary in blocking one's fall into the extreme of peace [that is, into a Hīnayānist's *nirvāṇa*]. Hence, wisdom cannot stop one's falling into peace. [The altruistic mind is also important] because, even in the Hīnayāna, there are those who have not fallen into the extreme of peace whereas the chief thing to be avoided on the bodhisattva's path is falling into the extreme of peace.

That is why in the *Saṃdhinirmocana* the children of the conqueror [that is, the bodhisattvas] who have become trustworthy (*tshad mar gyur pa'i rgyal sras*) understand it to be an amazing thing and say, "if one generates this precious mind in one's mental continuum one has generated a most incredible path."

Notes

An earlier version of this paper was given before the Harvard Buddhist Studies Forum in October 1987. I would like to thank J. McRae and M. Nagatomi for their invitation, and all of the participants for their very helpful comments. For their very detailed criticism of several points in the paper I owe special thanks to M. Nagatomi, R. A. F. Thurman, J. Willis, Alan Sponberg, and Paula Richman.

1. For another perspective concerning this question, see Alison H. Black's excellent essay ''Gender and Cosmology in Chinese Correlative Thinking'' in *Gender and Religion: On the Complexity of Symbols*, ed. C. W. Bynum, S. Harrell, and P. Richman (Boston: Beacon Press, 1986).

2. It is interesting that Alex Wayman, in the context of discussing female symbolism in the Buddhist *tantras*, begins his essay, ''Female Energy and Symbolism in the Buddhist Tantras,'' with the following words: ''the worship of divinity under sexual emblems is very ancient in India, presumably as old as the Mohenjo-daro civilization.'' The same point, that the basis for a great deal of female imagery lies in pre-Āryan Dravidian civilization, also is made by Agehananda Bharati in *The Tantric Tradition* (New York: Doubleday Anchor, 1970), pp. 204–205.

3. For another interesting case of such gender-tension, characterized by Annemarie Shimony as ''complementarity,'' as a vehicle for expressing and experiencing religious meaning see her ''Women of Influence and Prestige among the Native American Iriquois,'' in N. Falk and R. Gross, eds., *Unspoken Worlds: Women's Religious Lives in Non-Western Cultures* (San Francisco: Harper and Row, 1980), p. 250.

4. For a summary of this work see T. J. Hopkins and A. Hiltebeitel, ''Indus Valley Religion,'' in the *Encyclopedia of Religion* (New York: Macmillan, 1987), pp. 215–223.

5. D. Wolkstein and N. Kramer, *Inanna: Queen of Heaven and Earth* (New York: Harper and Row, 1983), p. 99.

6. On an Indo-European moon goddess who becomes incorporated into Vedic lore, see W. D. O'Flaherty, *Women, Androgynes and Other Mythical Beasts* (Chicago: University of Chicago Press, 1980), p. 79.

7. Ibid.

8. Whether or not Vedic culture was a particularly positive period for women—see Katherine K. Young, ''Hinduism,'' in A. Sharma, ed., *Women in World Religions* (Albany: SUNY Press, 1987)—it remains clear that as regards symbols, the masculine predominates.

9. The *Jātaka* might be considered an exception.

10. The verse is found in *Dhammapada* (v. 294), ed. S. Sumangala Thera (London: Pali Text Society, 1914), where it reads *mātaraṃ pitaraṃ hantvā / rājāno dve ca khattiye / raṭṭham sānucaraṃ hantvā / anīgho yāti brāhmaṇo*. It is also cited in *Nettipakaraṇa*, a postcanonical work (London: Luzac and Co., 1961), p. 165. See also *Undānavarga*, (tib. *Thsoms*), Toh. no. 4099, mNgon pa *tu*, folio 31a; and Donald Lopez, *A Study of Svātantrika* (Ithaca, N.Y.: Snow Lion Press, 1987), p. 285.

11. As translated by H. C. Warren in *Buddhism in Translation* (New York: Atheneum, 1984; originally published in 1896). It might be argued, based on this passage and the discussion that follows concerning the Mahāyāna, that throughout Buddhism there exists a tendency to associate the masculine with the active and the feminine with the passive. Is it not the case, after all, that Early Buddhism associates activity (*karma*) with the masculine and the relatively more passive mental states (*kleśa*) with the feminine and that the Mahāyāna also has a strategy of associating method (a series of active practices such as giving) with the masculine and wisdom (the more passive mental equipoise on emptiness) with the feminine? I remain unconvinced, however, of the validity of the active-passive distinction (made much of by Agehananda Bharati in his discussion of "Polarity Symbolism" in *The Tantric Tradition*, pp. 119–227) in Buddhism. It might be argued that there is no reason to consider mental states any more passive than physical ones—certainly Buddhists never did. Although a case might be made for considering the distinction partially valid in the doctrinal context just discussed, Bharati's attempt to extend the present notion of "active-passive" to the sexual sphere I find to be totally unsubstantiated. He finds it paradoxical that though Tibetans consider the masculine to be active in the doctrinal context, that in the iconographic depictions of the sexual positions of deities the male should be passive (because the female sits on the male's lap). First of all, it remains to be seen that this constitutes sexual passivity. Even if the male were portrayed iconographically as passive (and I question this) it is not at all clear to me that this has any connection to (the still unsubstantiated) doctrinal passivity. Why should it be paradoxical that *upāya* be considered male and that the male partner in sexual union be passive? In short, Bharati's arguments seem to me problematic, as does the application of the distinction between active and passive, either to the Sūtrayāna or to the tantric traditions of Buddhism.

12. One of the most famous examples in the *sūtra* literature occurs in the *Prajñāpāramitā Ratnaguṇasaṃcayagāthā*, Conze's translation, in *The Perfection of Wisdom in Eight Thousand Lines and Its Verse Summary* (Berkeley, Calif.: Four Seasons Foundation, 1973), p. 31, reads:

If a mother with many sons had fallen ill,
They all, sad in mind, would busy themselves about her:
Just so also, the Buddhas in the world-systems in the ten directions
Bring to mind this perfection of wisdom as their mother.

The Saviours of the world who were in the past, and also those that are [just now] in the ten directions,
Have issued from her, and so will the future ones be.
She is the one who shows the world [for what it is], she is the genetrix, the mother of the Jinas,
And she reveals the thoughts and actions of other beings.

It is interesting that in the *Aṣṭasāhasrikā* (Conze trans., ibid., p. 173) *perfect wisdom* is portrayed as the teacher of the Buddhas who instructs them as to the nature (that is, the emptiness) of the world qua five aggregates, just as a mother instructs her children in the ways of the conventional world.

13. Although not all forms of wisdom are analytical (for example, the meditative equipoise of āryans on emptiness) and although analytical meditation is utilized in the generation of mental states other than wisdom, analytical activity is an essential prerequisite of all forms of wisdom. What is more, in the scholastic tradition, upon which we base this study, the forms of conceptual analyses that investigate the ultimate, the nature of things, are considered to themselves be forms of wisdom. Hence, the view of some scholars, that only the nonrational "mystical" forms of gnosis were associated with the feminine, is unfounded.

14. In one of the very few anthropomorphic metaphors concerning emotive states, in the *Bodhicaryāvatāra* (hereafter *BCA*) of Śāntideva (I, 13)—P. L. Vaidya edition (Darbhanga: Mithila Institute, 1960), p. 10—*bodhicitta*, the altruistic mind that seeks enlightenment for the benefit of others, is likened unto a great hero (*sura*) who can protect one from fear. In a perhaps more tenuous association of affective states with male images, both the *Aṣṭasāhasrikā* and *BCA* use the jewel (*ratna*) as a metaphor for compassion (see Conze, *Perfection of Wisdom*, p. 239, and *BCA*, p. 25). In this regard, more important than the fact that the word itself is masculine in gender is the fact that in tantric literature the jewel is the secret epithet for the male sexual organ. One of the most important canonical passages that uses the gender distinction as a way to differentiate between analytical and affective states is to be found in the *Vimalakīrtinirdeśa Sūtra*. See E. Lamotte, trans., *L'Enseignement de Vimalakīrti*, English translation by Sara Boin, *The Teaching of Vimalakīrti* (London: Pali Text Society, 1976), p. 130: "For pure Bodhisattvas their mother is the Perfection of Wisdom and their father is Skill in Means; of such parents as these are the Leaders born." Snellgrove, *Indo-Tibetan Buddhism* (Boston: Shambhala, 1987), points out that although Prajñāpāramitā is personified as a goddess in the later Mahāyāna "there is as yet no cult of her as a great goddess in Mahāyāna sūtras" (p. 150). In an interesting departure from this distinction, the *Guhyasamāja Tantra* states that the spiritual teacher is "the father of all us Buddhas, the mother of all us Buddhas" (Snellgrove, ibid., p. 177). Although such statements, that masculine and feminine exist as a balanced unity within all individuals, abound in literature related to the *tantras*, the association of wisdom with the feminine and method with the masculine is very much a part of the Buddhist tantric tradition. See Snellgrove, ibid., pp. 244, 280, and 299.

15. An affirmative answer to this question is offered by B. Bhattacharya when he states, "the word *Nirātmā*, it may be noted, is in the feminine; the *Nirātmā* [tantric consort] is therefore a *Devi*" (cited by A. Bharati in the *Tantric Tradition*, p. 206).

16. Even though the gendered structure of the language cannot be said to be the cause of gender-related bifurcation of mental states into male-affective and female-analytic, it might be the case that the previously acknowledged gender polarity at the level of symbols affects the choice of metaphors used by scholastics. For example, there is textual evidence to indicate that (whether consciously or not) Buddhist authors opted for male-gendered nouns to act as the metaphors, epithets, and symbols of affective states. For example, in the first chapter of the *Bodhicaryāvatāra* (Vaidya edition, pp. 1–21) all the major metaphors for *bodhicitta* are masculine: tree (*vṛkṣa*), elixir (*rasa*), hero (*sura*), and jewel (*ratna*). See note 14.

17. As presented, for example, in the L. Wittgenstein, *Philosophical Investigations*, trans. G. E. M. Anscombe, (Oxford: Basil Blackwell, 1953), pp. 31e–32e; also see his remarks in the *Blue and Brown Books* (Oxford: Basil Blackwell, 1960), pp. 17–18. For some interesting remarks on these passages see P. Feyerabend, ''Wittgenstein's *Philosophical Investigations*''; R. Brambough, ''Universals and Family Resemblances''; and H. Khatchadourian, ''Common Names and 'Family Resemblances','' all in G. Pitcher, ed., *Wittgenstein: The Philosophical Investigations* (Notre Dame, Ind.: University of Notre Dame Press, 1966).

18. See, for example, Victor Turner, *The Forest of Symbols: Aspects of Ndembu Ritual* (Ithaca, N.Y.: Cornell University Press, 1967); *The Ritual Process: Structure and Anti-Structure* (Ithaca, N.Y.: Cornell University Press, 1969), and the comments of Carolyn Walker Bynum in her introduction to *Gender and Religion*, pp. 2 passim. Bynum's insight is to modify Turner's views in light of French feminist criticism.

19. *Śrāvakabodhisattvagaṇino buddhasya mātre namaḥ / Abhisamayālaṃkāra* (I, 1d), ed. R. Tripathi (Sarnath: Central Institute for Higher Tibetan Studies, 1988), p. 4 (of the Sanskrit Edition).

20. See the *Sphuṭārtha* of Haribhadra, Tib. translation, *'Grel ba don gsal* (Sarnath: Pleasure of Elegant Sayings, 1978), p. 3.

21. Edward Conze (*Thirty Years of Buddhist Studies* [Columbia: University of South Carolina Press, 1968], p. 189) ''sees'' many ''feminine features'' in the *Prajñāpāramitā Sūtras*: their reliance on intuition, their scant attempts at reasoning that end up being ''far from conclusive'' or ''inconsequential,'' that they win one over by ''fascination and not by compulsion.'' That these are traits ascribed to the feminine by Western patriarchal cultures can hardly be denied. In what follows it should become clear that this certainly is not what the *Buddhist* tradition means by calling these *sūtras mother*.

22. The *Prajñāpāramitā Sūtras* in 100,000 lines, 25,000 lines, and 8,000 lines. For extensive discussions of this point see the *rTog dka'i snang ba* of mKhas grub dGe legs dpal bzang in the *gSung 'bum* edition (Dharmasala: 1981),

folio 3a; the *Khabs dang po'i spyi don* of Se ra rJe bstun pa (Bylakuppe: undated blockprint), folio 3a; the *Legs bshad gser phreng* of Tsong kha pa (Buxador: undated blockprint), folio 6b; Bu ston's *Lung gi snye ma* (Sarnath: Sakya Students' Union, 1982), p. 4; and rGyal tshab rje's *rNam bshad snying po'i rgyan* (Sarnath: Gelugpa Student Welfare Committee, 1974), p. 7.

23. It is interesting that in the dGe lugs pa tradition of Tibetan Buddhism, in the *Madhyamakāvatāra* (the major Indian textual source for the study of the Madhyamada school of Buddhist philosophy, the way the *Abhisamayālaṃkāra* is used in the study of the Prajñāpāramitā) the first set of verses is an homage to compassion, the correlative of wisdom, as the chief cause of all spiritual achievement. There, however, though considered the cause of these different states, compassion is not characterized as "Mother." See *Madhyamakāvatāra* (I, 1) of Candrakīrti, ed. Louis de la Vallée Poussin (Osnabruck: Biblio Verlag, 1970); see also Tsong kha pa's comments in *dBu ma dgongs pa rab gsal,* in *rJe'i gsung lta ba'i skor,* vol. 2 (Varansi: Pleasure of Elegant Sayings, 1975), p. 203. In my translation of bLo bzang rta dbyang's *One Hundred and Eight Verses in Praise of Great Compassion* (Mysore: Mysore Printing and Publishing, 1984), pp. 1–3, compassion is characterized as the "mother of all the conquerors." See also Guy Newland's *Compassion: A Tibetan Analysis* (London: Wisdom Publications, 1984), pp. 17 passim.

24. See the previous note.

25. It should be noted that in the rNying ma system of the Great Perfection, specifically in the *kLong chen snying thig,* "the womb of the mother-consort [Yeshey Tsogyal] is reality; it is the source of all Buddhas, the basis of all coming and going; the place of arising of all existents"—cited by A. Klein in "Primordial Purity and Everday Life: Exalted Female Symbols and the Women of Tibet" In *Immaculate and Powerful,* ed. C. W. Atkinson, C. H. Buchanan, and M. R. Miles (Boston: Beacon, 1985), p. 131. Klein (p. 132) implies that because both female and male deities in the *tantras* are associated with the qualities of emptiness, gender specificty of the symbolism is lost. I am not sure that this is the case, however. The existence of terms like *mother Tantra, father Tantra,* and the designation of the Tantric consorts by the term *Wisdom* (*vidyā*) implies to me that, in this particular instance, Klein's conclusion may be too broad.

26. Relevant to this, see Newland's *Compassion,* p. 66.

27. The root text, officially called *A Song on the View: Recognizing One's Mother,* is by lCang skya rol pa'i rdo rje, and the commentary, *A Lamp of Words: A Commentary to "A Song on the View"* is by dKon mchog 'jigs med dbang po. I have used the Madhyamaka Text Series edition, vol. 1 (New Delhi: Lha mkhar yongs 'dzin, 1972), pp. 581–611.

28. Ibid., p. 589.

29. It is worth noting that this same theme is extremely important in the tantric tradition of Buddhism. In an interesting variation, Tilopa, in *Dohas*, calls the mind "father" and emptiness "mother," their union, the equipoise of the mind on reality, being symbolized by sexual union. See E. Conze, *Thirty Years of Buddhist Studies*, p. 189.

30. This passage is translated as an appendix to this chapter.

31. I am indebted to Robert Thurman for pointing out to me that at the beginning of his *sNgag rim chen mo*, Tsong kha pa also discusses this same question in the context of the Buddhist tantric tradition. There he uses the symbolism of emptiness (or more specifically its cognition) as the mother to give legitimacy to all of the three Buddhist vehicles (*yānas*). He validates the efficacy of all three vehicles by pointing out that the enlightened beings of the three, Śrāvakayāna, Pāramitāyāna, and Vajrayāna, all spring from the same mother, the cognition of emptiness. See the Dalai Lama's comments on this passage in Jeffrey Hopkins, *Tantra in Tibet* (London: George Allen and Unwin, 1977), p. 43.

32. See Tāranātha's *Chos 'byung* (1946 Potala edition), folios 55a and 60a; D. Chattopadhyaya, *History of Buddhism in India* (Simla: Institute of Advanced Study, 1970), pp. 155, 167. The story is also mentioned in the *Blue Annals*.

33. In the former case, that is, if it actually is with this notion (of the role gender plays in determining ethnicity) in mind that the symbol was created, it contradicts Bharati's claim that it is arbitrary which was cast as male and which as female. Whether or not the assignation of genders was initially arbitrary, clearly from the time of the early scholastics on, it was no longer perceived to be so by the tradition.

34. *Anima*, 3, no. 1 (1977): 75–80.

35. In another interesting and relevant passage, Tsong kha pa (folios 187a passim) brings up the story of Atīśa (eleventh century) and his master Suvarṇadvīpin. Even though the latter had no understanding of the Madhyamaka's doctrine of emptiness (the tradition considers him a Yogācāra), it was nonetheless fitting that Atīśa (who *was* a Mādhyamika) study with him because Suvarṇadvīpin possessed *bodhicitta*, the key to the Mahāyāna. Just as woman is subservient to man in the world so must wisdom bow down to altruism in the spiritual realm. That other metaphors imply the equality of method and wisdom (that is, the two wings of the bird) does not argue against the present interpretation of *this particular* metaphor.

36. As mentioned earlier, we must not lose sight that there are positive aspects of this symbolism as well. From another point of view it might be argued that mother-wisdom is more supple than father-method in that she can nurture any one of a variety of spiritual adepts, whereas the father's role is specific to the lineage in question.

37. Bynum et al., *Gender and Religion*, pp. 2, 13, 16.

38. As Bynum points out, however, that religious symbols have sometimes been manipulated in ways detrimental to women and their status in society is not "the fault of the images," ibid., p. 16. I would add that coming to understand a gender-based image in its full complexity is the first step to divesting the image of those patriarchal accretions to which most human-made symbols are heir. See Klein, "Primordial Purity and Everyday Life," pp. 111–138.

39. For a discussion of other such dichotomies in the Christian religious tradition, see Rosemary Ruether's *Sexism and God-Talk* (Boston: Beacon Press, 1983). Conze, *Thirty Years of Buddhist Studies*, p. 188, has suggested that the tradition relies on the use of gender symbolism in this case to bring out the fact that this is a tension that must be relieved, as it is relieved in sexual union. This is more true in tantric Buddhism, however, than it is in the Pāramitāyāna.

40. See Bynum, *Gender and Religion*, p. 13, for a more complete discussion of this question. She goes on to say that "women's myths and rituals tend to explore a state of being; men's tend to build elaborate and discreet stages between self and other."

41. See Rosemary Radford Ruether, *New Woman, New Earth: Sexist Ideologies and Human Liberation* (Minneapolis: Seabury Press, 1975). There is in the West a tradition of considering wisdom (as *gnosis—sophia*) to be feminine and this cannot be overlooked. We might suggest that this represents a view of the feminine in the religious sphere that never truly penetrated the cotidian perceptions of women. The same claim might be made of the Buddhist case, however, namely that this religious distinction that associated wisdom with the feminine never had an impact on Buddhist society. See Michael A. Williams, "Uses of Gender Imagery in Ancient Gnostic Texts," in Bynum et al., eds., *Gender and Religion*, pp. 196–227.

42. It would be interesting to investigate, almost as a sequel to this study, how this tension is characterized (if at all) in other religious cultures, whether gender-based imagery is used to this end, and, if so, which gender is associated with which mental mode.

43. *Ratnagotravibhāga*, v. 34; see J. Takasaki, ed., *A Study of the Ratnagotravibhāga (Uttaratantra): Being a Treatise on the Tathāgatagarbha of Mahāyāna Buddhism* (Rome: IsMEO, 1966), p. 207.

44. *Ratnāvalī*, v. 390.

45. *Abhisamayālaṃkāra* (I, 11ab): *prajñayā na bhave sthānaṃ kṛpayā na śame sthitiḥ*; see ibid., ed. Tripathi, p. 7 (of the Sanskrit edition).

V

Buddhism and Homosexuality

9

Homosexuality As Seen in Indian Buddhist Texts

Leonard Zwilling

To examine the Indian Buddhist view of homosexuality may appear at first glance to be an anachronistic enterprise because the very term *homosexuality* as a category in a schema of sexual typology, as has often been pointed out, is of fairly recent provenance, and we, therefore, should not expect any term with the precise connotation of *homosexuality* to appear in Buddhist literature. However, homosexual behavior stemming from an apparent disposition to seek sexual gratification through relations with members of one's own sex in preference to the other did not go unnoticed and was discussed by Indian authors in a variety of contexts including ritual, medical, grammatical, lexicographic, erotic, and religious. The aim of this chapter is to survey the literature of one important religious-cultural movement, namely Buddhism, in the hope that we may increase our understanding of how sexual nonconformity was perceived by one of the major cultures of classical Asia.

The primary sources upon which this enquiry is based are the *Vinaya* or monastic law and *Abhidharma* or metaphysics of both the Pali and Sanskrit traditions together with their commentarial literature. In surveying this literature we shall attempt to answer a number of questions that include the following. How did Buddhism understand homosexuality? What ethical and psychological implications were associated with it? What was the position of publicly labeled sexual nonconformists as religious or lay followers of Buddhism? Lastly, homosexuality will be considered in the light of Buddhist sexual morality as a whole.

The first step in delineating the Buddhist understanding of homosexuality is to examine the terminology used in connection with this and related phenomena. The primary term employed in the literature is *paṇḍaka*, a word of obscure origin but that ultimately may be derived from *apa* + *aṇḍa* + *ka*, "without testicles."[1] However, we must not conclude from this that *paṇḍaka* is to be taken as meaning "eunuch" in a literal sense, as has been customary. In an earlier paper[2] I considered this at some length and concluded that the eunuch was virtually unknown in pre-Muslim India, and that the terms usually translated as such, for example, *klība, ṣaṇḍha, napuṃsaka,* and *tṛtīyāprakṛti* have been misconstrued from a variety of motives.[3] Rather, *paṇḍaka* and its synonyms[4] are to be interpreted metaphorically as we do in English when it is said of a weak or pusillanimous person that he (or even she) "has no balls."

This becomes obvious when we turn to the classification and discussion of the *paṇḍaka* as found in such works as Buddhaghosa's *Samantapāsādikā*, Asaṅga's *Abhidharmasamuccaya*, and Yaśomitra's commentary to the *Abhidharmakośa*. These three works contain nearly identical lists of five types of *paṇḍakas*, a list also to be found in the Sanskrit-Tibetan lexicon, the *Mahāvyutpatti*,[5] and that corresponds in part to lists in various brahmanical medical and legal treatises.[6] The five types of *paṇḍakas* are (first in Sanskrit, then in Pali):

1. *jāti, prakṛtip-; napuṃsakapaṇḍaka*
2. *īrṣyap-; usūyapaṇḍaka*
3. *pakṣap-; pakkhapaṇḍaka*
4. *āsekap-, āsecanap-, āsaktaprādurbhāvipaṇḍaka; āssittapaṇḍaka*
5. *āpatp-; opakkamikapaṇḍaka*

According to Buddhaghosa[7] the *napuṃsakapaṇḍaka* is one who is congenitally impotent;[8] the *usūyapaṇḍaka* is that individual who, out of frustration, satisfies his sexual desires by watching others engage in sexual relations, or as we would say, through voyeurism;[9] the *pakkhapaṇḍaka* is one who, owing to the "maturation" of nonvirtuous conduct, becomes temporarily impotent for fourteen "black days" of the month but regains his potency during the fourteen "white days," that is, from the new to the full moon;[10] the *āsittapaṇḍaka* is that person who satisfies his sexual desires by fellating another to ejaculation;[11] and finally, the *opakkamikapaṇḍaka* is that individual who attains ejaculation through some special effort or artifice.[12] The list of Yaśomitra[13] differs from those of Asaṅga and Buddhaghosa only in its inclusion of the castrate (*lūṇapaṇḍaka*)—I hesitate to use the word *eunuch* as it implies intentional castration as opposed to accidental castration[14]—in place of the *āpatp-; opakkamikapaṇḍaka*. From Buddhaghosa's explanations, which are in conformity to what we may call ancient-Indian *paṇḍaka*-lore, we may conclude that for the Buddhist commentarial tradition the term *paṇḍaka* did not signify eunuch because, with the exception of the congenitally impotent, the remaining types are capable of either erection, ejaculation, or the experience of sexual pleasure.[15]

It is evident, then, that we are dealing with a variety of sexual dysfunctions and variations categorized under the general rubric "*paṇḍaka*," and the reason for this is that they all share the common quality of being "*napuṃsaka*," "lacking maleness." That is, for one reason or another they fail to meet the normative sex role expectations for an adult male. In the *Vinaya* literature references to *paṇḍakas* are made almost invariably within the context of sexual, specifically homosexual, behavior, and we find in many societies a tendency to label a boy or man who participates in homosexual activity as not being a "real man."[16] Even as early as the period of the *Atharva Veda, paṇḍakas* were viewed as a distinct group, different from ordinary males and females, and apparently transvestite. The *Vinaya*, in fact, goes so far as to distinguish sexual activity between normative males from sexual relations between a socially normative male and a *paṇḍaka*.[17]

The *paṇḍaka* was also viewed as possessing a distinct psychological makeup. According to Buddhaghosa *paṇḍakas* are full of defiling passions (*ussanakilesa*); their lusts are unquenchable (*avūpasantapariḷāha*); and they are dominated by their libido (*pariḷāhavegābhibhūta*) and the desire for lovers just like prostitutes (*vesiyā*) and coarse young girls (*thulakumarikā*).[18] Thus the *paṇḍaka*, who is distinguished not by homosexual behavior per se, but by the failure to fulfill male role expectations, was considered in some degree to share the behavior and psychological characteristics of the stereotypical "bad" woman. For Vasubandhu, the psychological makeup of the *paṇḍaka* is such as to have significant ramifications for his ability to practice religion. On the one hand, *paṇḍakas* are incapable of religious discipline (*saṃvara*) because to an inordinate degree they possess the defiling passions of both sexes (*ubhayāśrayakleśādhimātratā*), and they lack the sense of modesty and shame (*hrīvyapatrāpya*) necessary to counteract them.[19] On the other hand, paradoxically, the *paṇḍakas* also is incapable of the unrestraint (*asaṃvara*) one must have the capacity to check if one is going to successfully lead the religious life. Ignored by his parents on account of his condition, the *paṇḍaka* does not develop the strong emotional ties to them which would make him capable of committing the "mortal sin" (*ānantarya*) of matricide or patricide.[20] Nor is he able to undermine the fundamental bases of ethical progress (*kuśalamūla*) because he is incapable of holding strong views.[21] I can only speculate that this view of the *paṇḍaka* as lascivious, shameless, unfilial, and vacillating is based on the social disabilities incurred by the *paṇḍaka* as a member of a stigmatized and outcasted group, such as is formed by their present-day counterparts, the *hiñjras*,[22] as well as on the inability or unwillingness of such offspring to bring satisfaction to their parents either in this life by producing children or in the afterlife owing to their disqualification from funerary and afterdeath rites.[23]

As for the etiology of the homosexual condition, Indian Buddhist tradition, at least as represented by Buddhaghosa, agrees for the most part with traditional Indian medical thought in seeing it as being essentially an organic disorder, although one with an important psychological component.[24]

Buddhaghosa[25] begins his analysis by pointing out that men and women obviously differ not only in what we call primary and secondary sexual characteristics, but in interests and inclinations as well. For example, girls like to play with dolls, baskets, and household implements, whereas boys play with farm tools and building dams. In addition, men and women differ in their ways of walking, eating, lying down and general deportment. All these differences may be ascribed to two "powers"; that is, the "power of femininity" (*itthindriya*) and the "power of masculinity" (*purisindriya*).[26] However, the possession of these "powers" has no inherent connection with the possession of a particular set of sexual organs; that is, although the "powers" are certainly the cause of masculine or feminine characteristics or interests, in the language of Buddhaghosa, they are not the "cause of the sexual organs (*byañjanakaraṇam*)." This he attempts to prove by an explanation of what he takes to be the phenomenon of hermaphroditism (*ubhatobyañjanatā*), but that, in fact, clearly is a description of bisexuality or homosexuality. Hermaphrodites, he argues, are actually endowed with only one "power"; that is, hermaphrodites may actually be divided into males and females. Now when owing to sexual craving (*rāgacitta*) a female hermaphrodite desires sexual relations with a woman, she manifests male sexual organs, retracting and concealing her own female sexual organs,[27] whereas the converse situation obtains for the male hermaphrodite. In fact, he goes on to say, the female hermaphrodite can both impregnate other women and be impregnated herself, although the male hermaphrodite can only impregnate others. This account, with its confusion of bisexuality, hermaphroditism, and homosexuality, is not at all peculiar to Buddhaghosa, and was common enough in much of the writing on homosexuality down to the present day, in the West as well as in the East.[28]

If we wish to determine to what extent homosexual behavior was negatively evaluated in the Indian Buddhist tradition, we should examine the moral and legal consequences of this behavior. Sexual misconduct (*kāmamithyācarā; kamesu micchacara*) is supposed to be avoided by the pious laity as well as the clergy. Buddhist tradition essentially conceives of sexual misconduct in terms of sexual relations with various types of prohibited women (*agamyā*) and the performance of nonprocreative sexual acts.[29] Among the commentators only Buddhaghosa and the anonymous author of the commentary to the *Abhidharmasamucaya* include men among forbidden sexual objects.[30] The *Vinaya* punishes all intentional sexual conduct by monks or nuns, providing a hierarchy of penalties depending upon the nature of the offense. Penetration with emission results in expulsion from the order, regardless of the gender or species of the partner or the orifice penetrated.[31] Other types of sexual contact, such as masturbation of one monk by another, although still a serious offense, does not require expulsion, and nonorgasmic contact such as touching another's genitals is a relatively minor offense.[32] As a rule, offenses committed with a *paṇḍaka* require less severe punishment than those involving a woman, although more than if they were committed with a socially normative man.[33] Mutual masturbation among nuns is also reckoned with, but is considered a relatively minor offense,[34] and there are far fewer explicit references to homosexuality in the *Bhikkhuṇīvinaya* (the monastic rules for nuns) than the *Bhikkhuvinaya* (that for monks).

Also, a number of rules laid down in monastic law are meant to minimize the occasions for homosexual activity inevitable in closed, same-sex communities; for example it is forbidden for two nuns to share the same bedcover[35] and it is not allowed for two novices to serve one monk; this rule having been promulgated after it was discovered that two novices had each committed a sexual offense with the other.[36]

As to the ordination of the sexually nonconformist male, it will certainly be no surprise to find ordination denied to such individuals and that such denial has solid canonical authority. As with all the rules in the system of Buddhist monastic law, this regulation purportedly arose in response to a specific set of circumstances that in the Pali tradition are recounted in the *Paṇḍakavatthu* section of the *Mahāvagga*.[37] The account is short enough, and of interest for the light it sheds on the perceived characteristics of *paṇḍakas*, that I give it here in its entirety:

> At that time a certain *paṇḍaka* was ordained among the monks. He approached a number of young monks and said: "Come, Venerable Ones, defile me" (*etha, maṃ āyasmanto dūsethā*). The monks reproached

> him: "Begone *paṇḍaka*, away with you! What have we to do with that?" Reproached by the monks he approached a number of large, stout novices. "Come, Venerable Ones, defile me." The novices reproached him: "Begone, *paṇḍaka*, away with you! What have we to do with that?" Reproached by the novices he approached the elephant keepers and the grooms and said: "Come, Sirs, defile me." The elephant keepers and the grooms defiled him. They grumbled, became angry and irritated: "These recluses, these followers of the Buddha are *paṇḍakas* and those who are not *paṇḍakas* defile *paṇḍakas*. Thus do they all lack discipline." Monks heard those elephant keepers and grooms who grumbled, were angry, and irritated and those monks told this matter to the Blessed One who said: "Monks, if a *paṇḍaka* is not ordained, let him not be ordained. If he is already ordained let him be expelled."[38]

A similar prohibition would appear to be extended to the sexually nonconformist woman as well. According to the *Cullavagga*,[39] among the individuals to be denied ordination are the *animittā* and the *itthipaṇḍaka*. The latter, by analogy with the male *paṇḍaka*, would seem to be no more than the female of the species and the equivalent of the *nārīṣaṇḍa*, or lesbian, of the medical literature.[40] However, in commenting on this passage Buddhaghosa takes *animittā* to mean "without sexual organs" (*nimittarahitā*) and then glosses *itthipaṇḍaka* as *animittā*![41] What this clearly shows, I believe, is the confusion centering upon the signification of the traditional sexual category of *paṇḍaka* by the Indian classical authors, and the utter inadequacy of rendering it by *eunuch* as is customary by modern authors.

Beyond the prohibition against ordination, Asaṅga, like Vasubandhu, goes so far as to refuse the *paṇḍaka* recognition as a layman on the grounds that such persons are unfit to associate with or serve the *saṃgha* although, as a concession and perhaps reflecting a broader Mahāyāna perspective, he does allow them to practice the path of a layman if they so desire,[42] presumably without receiving recognition as a layman. Interestingly enough, the proto-Mahāyāna text *Mahāvastu* recognizes that even such a highly advanced practitioner as a fourth stage bodhisattva may backslide owing to homosexual activity.[43]

Although no explicit references to homosexuality are found in the *Nikāyas*, the collection of the Buddha's discourses in the Pali tradition, in the *Puggalappasādasutta* of the *Anguttaranikāya*[44] there is what may be construed as a warning to monks against homoerotic feelings. The Buddha warns that a monk who is devoted (*abhippasanna*) to another, who thinks: "This person is dear and pleasing (*piyo manāpo*) to me," will be adversely affected if his friend is suspended or expelled by the order, leaves, becomes mentally unbalanced, or dies. And again, Buddhaghosa, in commenting on a passage in the *Cakkavattisutta* of the *Dīgha Nikāya*,[45] describing the progressive degeneration in the life span of human beings following upon their increasing corporeality and sinfulness, takes the expression "wrong conduct" (*micchādhamma*) as "the sexual desire of men for men and women for women."[46] In associating homosexuality with decline and decadence Buddhaghosa is undoubtedly reflecting a commonly held view of his time, a view also expressed in the great Indian epic, the *Mahābhārata*.[47]

In the *sūtra* literature of Sanskrit Buddhism, the *Saddharmasmṛtyupasthānasūtra* describes at length the hellish torments awaiting those men who indulge in sexual relations with other men.[48] Oddly enough, the punishment meted out to the boy lover in the same *sūtra* is described, it seems, not without a certain amount of sympathy, which is made more striking by the otherwise virtual silence on the subject of pederasty in pre-Muslim Indian literature.[49] "The one who commits misconduct with boys sees boys being swept away in the Acid River who cry out to him, and owing to the suffering and pain born of his deep affection for them, plunges in after them."[50]

Whereas Indian Buddhism cannot truthfully be characterized as a sex-positive religion in the sense that Islam, Judaism, or Hinduism are (at least where heterosexuality is concerned), when homosexual behavior is not ignored in Indian Buddhist writings it is derogated much to the same degree as comparable heterosexual acts. The bar to the ordination of *paṇḍakas*, who I propose to have been a socially stigmatized class of passive, probably transvestite, homosexuals, or the unwillingness to formally recognize them as members of the Buddhist community can be seen as a practical concession to prevailing conventions to prevent the charge of dissolute conduct from being leveled at the order as a whole.

Turning from homosexual behavior to homoerotic emotion, we find that the *Jatakas* repeatedly extol same sex love and friendship while disparaging marriage and heterosexual relations throughout. The *bodhisatta*, or Buddha-to-be, is often pictured as having a devoted male companion or attendant, usually Ānanda, in his quest for enlightenment. We should also recognize that in a certain way homosexuality, not to speak of homoerotic friendship, is not entirely incompatible with the monastic life, in that it presents no temptation for the parties involved to forsake the order to which they are committed, nor does it lead to the family encumbrances many must have joined the *saṃgha* to escape.[51] That a certain laxity toward homosexuality has existed at times among Buddhist monastics is confirmed by such phenomena as the *dob dob* of Tibet, a semimilitary monastic fraternity who openly engaged in pederasty,[52] as well as by the Mongolian monks reported by Owen Lattimore to have justified their homosexual relationships on "theological grounds."[53] Even farther afield, it is interesting to note the popular association of homosexuality with Buddhist monks, and the belief that these practices were introduced into Japan by Kōbō Daishi, founder of the Shingon sect of tantric Buddhism.[54]

The question of sexual ethics for laypeople is one that was little addressed by Indian Buddhist thinkers. With the exception of tantric esotericism, Buddhist texts take a consistently negative stance toward all expressions of sexuality as being impediments to spiritual progress. Nevertheless, the vast majority of lay followers were not, and are not, expected to be sexually abstinent. Although adultery and other forms of sexual misconduct are to be eschewed by the holders of the fourth precept, it traditionally has been the case that only exceptionally pious or aged laypersons are expected to keep all the precepts, apart from specific holy days or ritual occasions. No Buddhist societies require teetotaling, despite the fifth precept, and both the Tibetans and the Sinhalese, to take two disparate examples, are far more flexible and nonjudgmental on such matters as pre- and extramarital sexuality than are Hindus, or conservative Christians for that matter. Because the classical Buddhist definitions of sexual misconduct mirror the taboos and concerns of premodern Indian society, might they not be reformulated based on a relativistic and situational appraisal of contemporary sexual mores? The textual sources surveyed here are at least consonant with a contemporary view of homosexuality as a probably organically or genetically based orientation, with the same moral significance (or insignificance) of heterosexuality.

Notes

An earlier (and expurgated) version of this paper appeared in *Amalā Prajñā-Aspects of Buddhist Studies* (Prof. P. V. Bapat Felicitation Volume), ed. N. H. Samtani and H. S. Prasad (New Delhi: Sri Satgura Publications, 1989). All Pali texts are of the Nava Nalanda Edition unless other wise indicated.

1. This etymology was suggested to me by Stanley Insler of Yale University.

2. "Sexual Terminology Dealing with Sexual Variation and Dysfunction with Special Reference to Homosexuality," presented at the annual meeting of the American Oriental Society, Boston, March 16, 1981.

3. In the aforementioned paper, I concluded that the term *tṛtīyāprakṛti* as employed in the *Kāmasūtra, Nāṭyaśāstra,* and Vararuci's *Ubhayābhisārikā* referred specifically to a homosexual transvestite. I was gratified to find that the same conclusion had been arrived at by George T. Artola in "The Transvestite in Sanskrit Story and Drama," *Annals of Oriental Research*, University of Madras (1975): 56–68, which was unknown to me at the time my own paper was being written.

4. *Amarakośa*, (2.6.39); ed. Pt. H. Sastri (Varanasi: Chowkhamba, 1978), p. 199.

5. *Mahāvyutpatti* , ed. R. Sasaki, 8768–8773.

6. For example, *Suśruta* (*Śārira*.) (II.40–45); *Caraka* (*Śārira*.) (II.16–20); *Nāradasmṛti* (XIII.11–15).

7. *Samantapāsādikā* III, pp. 1068–1069.

8. *Yo pana Paṭisandhiyaṃyeva abhāvako uppanno, ayaṃ napuṃsakapaṇḍako.*

9. *Yassa paresaṃ ajjhācāraṃ passato usūyāya uppannāya pariḷāho vūpasammati, ayaṃ usūyapaṇḍako.*

10. *Ekacco pana akusalavipākānubhāvena, kalapakkhe paṇḍako hoti, juṇhapakkhe panassa pariḷāho vūpasammati, ayaṃ pakkhapaṇḍako.*

11. *Yassa paresam aṅgajatam mukhena gahetvā asucinā āssittassa pariḷāho vūpassati, ayaṃ āsittapaṇḍako.*

12. *Yassa upakkamena bījāni appanītāni, ayam opakkamikapaṇḍako.*

13. Yaśomitra on *Abhidharmakosa* (II, 1c); ed. Swami D. Sastri, 2d ed. (Varanasi: Bauddha Bharati, 1981), pp. 136–138.

14. Castration, whether severance of the penis or excision of the testes, is referred to at *Caraka* (Cikitsa.) (XXX.187) and, not unsurprisingly, is considered an incurable form of impotence. No form of homosexual behavior treated in the medical literature is associated with castration.

15. Vasubandhu at (II.1c) (and elsewhere in the *Abhidharmakośa*, see Note 13) draws a distinction between the *ṣaṇḍa* and the *paṇḍaka*, which Yaśomitra understands in the following way: *paṇḍakas* are those individuals who have lost their *indriya*, that is, the masculinity or femininity principle, through some means (*upakrama*), whereas *ṣaṇḍa* is taken to apply to category 1, the congenitally impotent. Categories 2–4 are considered by him to suffer from an impairment (*akarmanyatva*) of their *indriya*, yet, he goes on to say that even if their *indriya* is entirely functional they do not experience sexual pleasure and they do not generate offspring (*prasavajana*). This view is not shared by other authorities.

16. Arno Karlen, *Sexuality and Homosexuality* (New York: W. W. Norton, 1971), p. 478.

17. The *Vinaya* distinguishes among sexual acts where the object is human or nonhuman (for example, a god), male, female, animal, or *paṇḍaka*; see the lengthy discussion of *methunadhamma* at *Pārājika*, pp. 35ff.

18. *Samantapāsādikā* III, p. 1042.

19. *Abhidharmakośa* (IV.43), pp. 650–651.

20. *Abhidharmakośa* (IV.97a–c), pp. 722–723.

21. See Yaśomitra on *Abhidharmakośa* (IV.80b).

22. On the *hiñjras* see Serena Nanda, "The Hijras of India: Cultural and Individual Dimensions of an Institutionalized Third Gender Role," *Journal of Homosexuality* 11, nos. 3–4 (1986): 35–55; James M. Freeman, *Untouchable* (Stanford Calif.: Stanford University Press, 1979), pp. 294–315; G. Morris Carstairs, *The Twice Born* (London: Hogarth Press, 1961), pp. 59–60; also Appendix 2 to C. H. Tawney's translation of *The Ocean of Story* (Delhi: Motilal Banarsidass, 1968).

23. See, for example, *Manu* (III.165).

24. On male homosexuality, see, for example, *Caraka* (*Śārira*.) (II.18) and *Cakrapaṇidatta*, also Ḍalhana on *Suśruta* (*Śārira*.) (II.40, 44); on female homosexuality, see *Suśruta* (*Śārira*.) (II.45) and (*Uttara*.) (XXXVIII.8), and *Caraka* (*Cikitsa*.) (XXX.33–34).

25. See *Samantapāsādikā* III, pp. 1078–1079 and *Atthasalini* (Pali Text Society ed.) IV, pp. 61ff.

26. Cf *Abhidharmakośa* (II, 2c–d), pp. 136–139.

27. *Yadā itthiyā rāgacittaṃ uppajjati tadā ca purisabyañjaṇam pākaṭam hoti itthī lingabyañjanaṃ paṭicchannaṃ guyaṃ hoti.*

28. See, for example, Jonathan Katz, *Gay American History* (New York: Avon Books, 1976), pp. 65, 430, 42, 479–480.

29. See, for example *Pārājika*, pp. 36, 199–201; *Śikṣāsamuccaya*, ed. P. L. Vaidya (Darbhanga: Mithila Institute, 1961), pp. 45–46; *Abhidharmakośa* (IV. 74a–b), pp. 688–689; *Upāsakajanālaṃkāra* (Pali Text Society ed.), pp. 188–189.

30. *Abhidharmasamuccayabhāṣyam*, ed. Nathmal Tatia, p. 63; *Papañcasudanī* (Pali Text Society ed.), p. 199.

31. *Pārājika*, pp. 15ff.

32. Ibid., p. 166.

33. It is interesting to note that in Jaina monastic law homosexual contact between monks is a relatively insignificant offense on a par with sharpening a needle or keeping a garment beyond the permitted length of time, whereas

sexual offenses committed with a woman are considered serious breaches of discipline; see Nathmal Tatia, "The Interaction of Jainism and Buddhism," in *Studies in History of Buddhism* (Delhi: B. R. Publishing Corp., 1980), p. 355.

34. *Pācattiya*, p. 355.

35. Ibid., pp. 393–395.

36. *Te aññamaññaṃ dūsesum. Mahāvagga*, p. 82. I hesitate to suggest the nature of their offense. The root *dus* is common to both brahmanical and nonbrahmanical literature when discussing sexual offenses and does not refer to any specific act.

37. *Mahāvagga*, ibid.

38. In his remarks on this passage Buddhaghosa refers to a lost commentary that understood this prohibition as applying only to the fellator and voyeur but not to the other three: *āsittapaṇḍakassa ca usūyapaṇḍakassa ca pabbajā na vāritā, itaresaṃ tiṇṇam vāritā. . .kurundiyaṃ vuttaṃ; Samantapāsādikā* III, p. 1069. Phra Chao, who was leader of the Thai *Saṃgha* at the beginning of this century, understood this prohibition to apply to homosexuals; see Phra Chao, *The Entrance to the Vinaya* (Bangkok: *Mahamukutarajavidyalaya*, 1969), vol. 1, p. 57.

39. *Cullavagga*, p. 391.

40. See *Suśruta* (*Uttara*.) (XXXVIII,8), and *Caraka* (Cikitsa.) (XXX.33–34).

41. *Samantapāsādikā* II, p. 546.

42. *Teṣām [ṣaṇḍapaṇḍakānām] upāsakasamvaro na pratiṣidhyate / kevalam tesāṃ upāsakatvaṃ pratiṣidhyate / bhikṣubhikṣunīnam ubhayapravrajitānām saṃghasya pakṣasya saṃsevopāsanā 'yogyatvāt. Abhidharmasamuccaya*, ed. Pralhad Pradhan, p. 57; see its *Bhāṣya*, p. 68.

43. *Mahāvastu*, p. 82, 4–6. Specifically the "*defilers of males*" (*puruṣaduṣaka* and "*defilers of paṇḍakas*" (*paṇḍakaduṣaka*).

44. *Aṅguttara Nikāya* III, pp. 507–508.

45. *Dīghanikāya* IV, p. 56.

46. *Sumangalavilāsinī* III, p. 172.

47. *Mahābhārata* (Poona Ed.) 12.91.31ff.

48. *Puruṣasya puruṣeṇa saha maithunavipratipatteḥ aprameyāḥ kāraṇaviśesāḥ paṭhyante*; in the *Śikṣāsamuccaya*, Vaidya, ed., p. 45, lines 23–24. *Peking Tripitaka Reprint*, vol. 37, p. 152, plate 2, lines 2ff.

49. See, for example, the verse following *Kāma Sūtra* 2.9.31 in the *Jayamaṅgala* commentary of Yaśodhara.

50. *Śiśubhiḥ saha vipratipatteh kṣāranadyām uhyamānān dārakān paśyati / te taṃ vilapanti / sa tāṃ nadīm avagāhate teṣu bālakeṣu tīvrasnehapratibandhaśoka-duḥkhavegat*; in the *Śikṣāsamuccaya*, Vaidya ed., p. 45, lines 24–26.

51. See John Garrett Jones, *Tales and Teachings of the Buddha* (London: George Allen and Unwin, 1979), pp. 80, 113, 116.

52. Melvyn C. Goldstein, "Study of the Ldab-Ldob," *Central Asian Journal*, 9 (1964): 123–141.

53. Owen Lattimore, *Nomads and Commissars* (New York: Oxford University Press, 1962), p. 211.

54. Iwada Junichi, *Honcho Danshokuko*, p. 1.

10

Kūkai and the Tradition of Male Love in Japanese Buddhism

Paul Gordon Schalow

A popular legend in Japan stated that male homosexual love *(nanshoku)* was introduced to Japan from China in the ninth century by Kūkai (774–835), founder of the True Word *(Shingon)* sect of esoteric Buddhism.[1] This legend cannot be taken as fact, of course. The introduction of a uniquely "priestly" mode of male homosexual practice may have been accomplished in the eighth and ninth centuries during Kūkai's lifetime, but it is safe to conclude that Kūkai played no more role in its introduction than to serve as a focus for attribution of the phenomenon.[2] The legend's significance lies, rather, in the purpose it served in the lives of Buddhist believers and in how it was given new meaning for secular society in the seventeenth century. To clarify the scope of the legend, this chapter will look at three texts in which the legend appears: *Kōbō daishi ikkan no sho* (1598, *Kōbō Daishi's Book);*[3] *Iwatsutsuji* (1667, *Rock Azaleas*) by Kitamura Kigin;[4] and *Nanshoku ōkagami* (1687, *The Great Mirror of Male Love*) by Ihara Saikaku.[5] These texts will show that the Kūkai legend affirmed same-sex relations between men and boys in seventeenth century Japan, both in the spiritual world of temples and monasteries and in the secular world of samurai and merchants.

The Kūkai Legend

Kūkai transmitted the Buddhist esoteric tradition to Japan in 806 after his return from China, where he studied for almost two years under the Chinese master Hui-kuo (764–805). It was customary in True Word Buddhism for the mysteries of the faith to be transmitted orally from master to pupil, rather than in book form, and this meant that the relationship between master and disciple was of greatest importance. By the time Kūkai founded the True Word temple complex on Mt. Kōya in 816, his remarkable spiritual powers had already attracted a large number of disciples and made him the subject of legend even before his death there in 835.

During his lifetime, Kūkai made great contributions to the life and culture of Heian Japan through major civil engineering projects, his mastery and teaching of Chinese scholarship, and his original writings on Buddhist doctrine. In recognition of his contributions and the continued spiritual hold he exerted on Japanese believers, the imperial court conferred on him the posthumous title of Kōbō Daishi ("Great Teacher Transmitting the Dharma") in 921. In the centuries after Kūkai's death, the name Kōbō Daishi became associated with several important cultural, social, and historical developments that occurred during his lifetime and in which he may have played a role. In aggregate, the legends constituted a religious construct called Kōbō Daishi worship.[6] Among the legends in that religious invention was one that he introduced male homosexual love to Japan.[7] It is not known when this legend first developed, but a poem in Chinese by Ikkyū (1394–1481) is the first evidence we have of it. "Monju, the holy one, first opened this path; Kōbō of Kongō then revived it. Without male and female, its pleasures are like an endless circle; men shout with pleasure when they attain entrance."[8] Far from detracting from his reputation as the object of Kōbō Daishi worship, this legend, like others, enhanced Kūkai's stature and apparently was thought of as compatible with his other spiritual and secular accomplishments.

Kōbō Daishi's Book

One of the earliest surviving manuscripts—dated 1598—to state a connection between Kūkai and male love is *Kōbō Daishi's Book.* The use of Kūkai's posthumous name in the title indicates that the connection was already well established, and that *Kōbō Daishi* is used largely as a byword for male love. The preface of the brief work describes how a layman goes into seclusion to pray to Kōbō Daishi for instruction in "the mysteries of loving boys in Japan" *(nihon shudō no gokui).* On the seventeenth day of the man's austerities, Kōbō Daishi appears and agrees to present him with a one-volume book explaining the love of boys, the basics of which "even monkeys in the hills and fields can comprehend." The text speaks of the "mysteries" of loving boys, implying a connection with the esoteric mysteries of True Word Buddhism. The fact that the preface identifies the book as personally transmitted by Kōbō Daishi substantiates the primary importance of the relationship between master and pupil in True Word Buddhism and, in a sense, legitimizes the book's contents.

Kōbō Daishi's Book, divided into three sections, claims to reveal secret teachings regarding the love of boys. The first section describes hand positions used by young acolytes to communicate their feelings to priests; the second section advises priests on how to evaluate an acolyte's emotions by observing him closely; and the final section describes methods of anal intercourse. The categories—hand positions, observations and penetration—bear a close resemblance to the four classes of Indian *tantras* associated with looking, touching, embrace, and penetration.

Part One

Part One decodes ten hand signals. The concern with positions of the hands and their meaning mimics, and possibly parodies, the holy hand positions *(mudrā)* that were an integral part of True Word teaching and religious practice. Priests and acolytes communicated their sexual feelings in the esoteric idiom of hand positions.

1. If an acolyte clenches his fingers—from the index finger to the little finger[9]—it means "You are the only one I love."
2. If an acolyte clenches both hands completely except for one thumb,[10] it means "I acknowledge your love and will make myself yours to do with as you please."
3. If an acolyte touches the index and middle finger to his thumb,[11] it means he wants to see you.
4. If an acolyte flips the tassle of his fan, it is an invitation to visit.
5. If an acolyte forms a circle with the index finger and thumb on both hands, it means "Tonight." If he uses the middle finger, it means "Tomorrow night." And if he uses the ring finger, it means "Some other time."[12]
6. If an acolyte touches the middle finger and ring finger to his thumb on both hands, it is an invitation to come visit.
7. If an acolyte touches the ring finger and little finger to his thumb, it means he wants to tell you something but cannot because people are watching; he'll try again the next night.
8. If something will prevent his coming as promised, he will touch the ring finger to his thumb on both hands.[13]

9. If an acolyte touches the index and little fingers to his thumb, it means he will come again tomorrow night.
10. If an acolyte tugs at your sleeve, it means he definitely wants you to visit.

Part Two

Part Two instructs priests on seven ways to observe an acolyte so they can tell whether he is ready for lovemaking; and, if he is not, how to arouse him and make him ready. Several of the instructions are accompanied by twenty-one syllable Japanese poems *(waka)* that illustrate the lesson. The most important quality a priest looks for in an acolyte is *nasake,* an empathetic sensitivity to love. When a boy possesses this sensitivity, seduction is hardly necessary; without it, the task of seduction is difficult, at best.

1. After an acolyte has spoken, observe him carefully. The acolyte who speaks quietly is sensitive to love. To such a boy, show your sincerity by being somewhat shy. Make your interest in him clear by leaning against his lap. When you remove his robes, calm him by explaining exactly what you will be doing.

   White snow on a mountain peak
   turns to pure water on the rocks
   and finally flows down.

   As this poem illustrates, snow on even the highest mountain peak is destined to melt and flow downward. Likewise, no matter how lacking in sensitivity to the mysteries of love an acolyte may be, he can be made yours if you approach him right.
2. An acolyte may be very beautiful but insensitive to love. Such a boy must be dealt with aggressively. Stroke his penis, massage his chest, and then gradually move your hand to the area of his ass. By then he'll be ready for you to strip off his robe and seduce him without a word.

   I gaze up at the distant top of a cedar tree;
   the wind blows strong,
   and even the cedar bends.

   The poem illustrates that even a proud heart will yield if the effort is strong enough.

3. It is best to deal gently, not aggressively, with a gentle-hearted acolyte. Quietly put him at ease, and then penetrate him.

   I gaze up at the quiet moon at Isobé
   and my heart, too, grows calm.

4. If an acolyte practices martial arts, be sure to praise his swordsmanship. Then tell him some warrior tales. Things will proceed naturally from there.

   Before snow accumulates,
   it is shaken off the branches;
   in a windy pine, snow breaks no limbs.

   As this poem illustrates, if snow is shaken off a pine before it has a chance to build up, it will not accumulate to the breaking point. Likewise, an acolyte's resistance should not be allowed to accumulate but be met as it comes; this is the only way to success.
5. If an acolyte is known to like birds, talk about birds—even if you hate them—as if you shared his interest. To an acolyte who likes to study, talk about his studies. After he opens up, you can do what you will with him.
6. The greatest pleasure is to proceed without resistance with an acolyte who possesses a great sensitivity to love.
7. If an acolyte is too shy to show himself to you, delay by plucking the hairs of your nose and then try again.[14]

Part Three

Part Three concerns final consummation of the seduction in the form of anal intercourse with the acolyte. Seven positions are described in the idiom of tantric meditation postures; the sexual positions are given names evocative of those used in Buddhist texts to describe postures for meditation.

1. There is a method called *skylark rising.* The ass is raised in the air like a skylark rising in the sky. Insertion is painless.
2. Always keep "cut plums" on hand in case you want to attempt insertion without saliva.
3. There is a method call *turned-up soles.* Place the acolyte's legs on your shoulders and penetrate him from the front.
4. There is a method called *reverse drop.* Insertion is from above the turtle's tail, and should be accomplished gradually.

5. There is a method called *summer moat.* Press the boy's ass to the moat of your belly as you enter. The method is painless, even for a young acolyte.
6. There is a method called *dry insertion.* Moisten only slightly with saliva, then penetrate. The method causes severe pain.
7. The method for initiation is called *tearing the hole.* In this method, a man with a large penis penetrates in one thrust without lubrication. The method causes severe pain.

Conclusion

In the conclusion, the author attributes the teachings in *Kōbō Daishi's Book* to Kūkai himself, conveyed to him as a reward for his religious devotion. That attribution is the central legitimizing fact of the book. The postscript to the main manuscript consists of three popular beliefs about boy love that have parallels in beliefs about women: that women with small mouths were amorous, and that facial features gave clues to the shape of a woman's genitals.

> I received this book of secret teachings from the founder of boy love in Japan, Kōbō Daishi, under the condition that I not show it to anyone. Signed Mitsuo Sadatomo, a hermit in Satsuma Fief.
>
> 1. An acolyte with a tiny mouth is best. They say that those with large mouths do not have tight asses.
> 2. It is best if the ass is slightly reddish in color. A dull ass may contain feces.
> 3. One look at a boy's face will tell you what his ass looks like.
>
> I have taken the liberty of adding the above three lines. Submitted with humble respect by Mitsuo Sadatomo, in the third year of Keichō [1598], third month, a felicitous day.

Kōbō Daishi's Book bears the date 1598, well before the Genroku era (1688–1703) when books on sexuality were tinged with irony. Although not meant to be read ironically, the book nevertheless foreshadows the more modern Genroku approach to sex in the playfulness that comes through in certain passages. One such passage appears in the book's introduction: "The love of boys began in olden times when Kōbō Daishi made a vow of love with Wen Zhou. Sentient Being *(shujō)* refers to a man and boy who fall in love with each other, become fast friends, and make a vow of brotherly love; the phenomenon is recorded in many books. Because Kōbō Daishi began the practice of this way of love, it has been preserved all these years and continues to the present day in both Japan and abroad."

Sentient Beings *(shujō)* is a proper Buddhist term referring to all living things, but here it is defined as the love of boys *(shudō)*. The confusion of the two terms may have been meant to elicit a laugh from the book's readers. If that is the case, what necessitated this linguistic inventiveness? The use of religious language and symbols in *Kōbō Daishi's Book* may represent not just religious heterodoxy but a challenge directed at a society defined by Confucian ethical constructs that discouraged sexual activity as socially disruptive in all but its most conventional forms.

Rock Azaleas

Rock Azaleas was the first collection of homoerotic poetry and prose in Japan, compiled in 1667 by Kitamura Kigin (1624–1705), scholar and adviser to the ruling Tokugawa shoguns. Most of the poems in the collection are addressed by priests to their acolyte lovers. The title comes from the opening poem, thought to be the first homoerotic poem in Japan, which appeared originally as an anonymous love poem in the tenth-century imperial anthology, *Kokinshū*.[15]

> My stony silence
> recalls the rock azaleas
> of Mt. Tokiwa:
> you cannot know of my love—
> but how I long to meet you!

Kigin attributes this anonymous poem to Shinga Sōzu, one of Kūkai's ten major disciples who carried on the True Word tradition after Kūkai's death. Kigin's attribution is based on a fourteenth century commentary by Kitabatake Chikafusa (1293–1354), *Kokinshū-chū*, containing oral traditions about *Kokinshū* from the Nijō and Fujiwara court families and other sources. It is generally recognized that many anonymous poems in Japan's imperial anthologies were listed as such to conceal the identity of the poet. It therefore is a remote possibility that Kigin's attribution is based on knowledge of the true circumstances of the poem's composition. Far more likely, however, is the possibility that the poem's connection with Shinga Sōzu was a later invention.

Preface

Kigin's preface to *Rock Azaleas* is of great interest for the insight it provides into the way the connection between Buddhism and male love was conceptualized by at least one seventeenth century scholar.

> To take pleasure in a beautiful woman has been in the nature of men's hearts since the age of male and female gods, but for a man to take pleasure in the beauty of another man goes against nature. Nevertheless, as relations betweem the sexes were forbidden by the Buddha, priests of the law—being made of neither stone nor wood—had no recourse but to practice the love of boys as an outlet for their feelings. Just as the waters that plummet and flow below the pass at Tsukubané form the deep pools of the Mino River, so this form of love proved to be deeper than the love between men and women. It afflicts the heart of aristocrat and warrior alike. Even the mountain dwellers who cut brushwood have learned of its pleasures. This form of love is rarely celebrated in Japanese poetry, however. Perhaps the first poem to do so was the one in *Kokinshū* by Kūkai's disciple, Shinga. This poem made the nature of male love apparent to the world, like a tassle of pampas grass waving in the wind, so that even the uninitiated learned of its existence.

For our purposes, the most interesting point made in the preface is the connection between the supposed origins of male homosexuality in Japan and the Buddha's injunction forbidding priests to have sexual relations with women. It gives evidence of a generous view of human sexual need in the Japanese religious tradition, that "need"—in the unnatural situation where relations with the opposite sex are forbidden—supersedes the "natural" legitimacy of male and female relations. Whether physical necessity is enough to explain why priests became enamoured of boys is an issue that will be discussed in the following section, where Saikaku's stories suggest that more is involved in the love of boys rather than just deprivation. By the seventeenth century, men may have entered the Buddhist priesthood because they were predisposed to the love of boys, the complete reverse of Kigin's vision.

The Great Mirror of Male Love

Ihara Saikaku (1624–1693) was known for most of his life as a poet of comic linked verse *(haikai)*, but in the last ten years of his life he turned to prose and became Japan's first commercial writer. His works are now ranked among the classics of Japanese literature. In 1687, he published a book called *The Great Mirror of Male Love*, a collection of forty short stories idealizing romantic relations between men and boys in samurai and merchant class circles. The introductory chapter of the book recounts the history of male love in Japan. Because Saikaku's purpose was to entertain his readership, he was inventive in his account. At one point he makes reference to the Kūkai legend: "Kōbō Daishi did not preach the profound pleasures of this love outside the monasteries because he feared the extinction of humankind. No doubt he forsaw the popularity of boy love in these last days of the law."[16]

Saikaku took the legend of Kūkai and made it relevant outside the Buddhist tradition by claiming that Kūkai originally suppressed knowledge of male love except in Japan's monastaries and temples because the time was not yet ripe for universal dissemination of its secrets; he forsaw that male love would gain followers and be better suited to the "last days of the law" *(mappō)*, the period of degeneration and decline heralding the end of the world, when the impending extinction of humankind made sexual procreation a moot issue. What more fitting form of sexuality for a doomed age—Saikaku seems to suggest—than nonprocreative love between men and boys? Saikaku's readership must have enjoyed the bold humor of this claim.

The Great Mirror of Male Love contains several detailed depictions of Buddhist priests and monks involved in homosexual relations with boys. The second story in the collection, "The ABCs of Boy Love" (1.2), is the story of Daikichi and Shinnosuké, two boys who "were always side by side, inseparable as two trees grafted together or a pair of one-winged birds. When the boys later reached their peak of youthful beauty, men and women, clergy and layman alike were all smitten with the handsome youths. The two were the cause of a thousand sorrows, a hundred illnesses, and untold deaths from lovesickness."[17] The narrative continues with a brief but fascinating passage about the effect of their beauty on a certain Buddhist monk.

> At about this time, there lived in the far reaches of Shishigatani a Buddhist ascetic who was over eighty years old. They say that from the moment he chanced to see these two splendid boys, his concentration on future salvation failed him and the good deeds he had accumulated in previous incarnations went to naught. News of the priest's feelings reached the boys. Not sure which of them the old gentleman had his heart set on, both went to his crude abode for a visit. Predictably, he found it impossible to dispense with either cherry blossoms or fall foliage. Thus, he satisfied with both of them the love he had harbored from spring through autumn.
>
> The next day, both boys paid another visit to the priest, for there was something they had neglected to tell him, but he was nowhere to be found. They discovered only a poem, dated the previous day, tied to a forked branch of bamboo:

Here are travel weeds
Tear-stained like my faithless heart
Torn between the two;
I shall cut my earthly ties
And hide myself away in bamboo leaves.

Of what was this old priest ashamed? Long ago, the priest Shinga Sōjō wrote:

Memories of love revive,
Like rock azaleas bursting into bloom
On Mt. Tokiwa;
My stony silence only shows
How desperately I want you!

The boys took the bamboo branch and had a skilled artisan make it into a pair of flutes.[18]

The juxtaposition of these two poems and the implication of guilt suggests an interpretation of their meaning. The first poem represents the parting words of an old monk who consummated his love for the boys, whereas the second poem is by a priest who denied himself even the expression of his love in words. There is deliberate ambiguity in the line "torn between the two" in the first poem; does it refer to the choice between two boys, or the choice between earthly and spiritual concerns? The poem states that the conflict has caused the monk to vow to sever his ties with the world—a vow first made when he originally took the tonsure—and live in seclusion. It implies that he was ashamed by his failure to concentrate on spiritual concerns. But that failure ultimately led to the renewal of his vow and represents a triumph of sorts. The positive outcome is typical of the literary tradition of Acolyte Tales *(chigo monogatari)* dating from the Muromachi period (1392–1568).[19] The old ascetic's faithless heart in the first poem contrasts dramatically with the other priest's faithfulness to his vows in the second poem. Shinga's heart—if the poem is indeed by Shinga Sōjō—burns in silence, unconsummated but guiltless. Ironically, unspoken passion may be the greater sin of the two, for unresolved lust is among the most powerful earthly ties in Buddhism. By sinning, the old priest achieves a spiritual renewal that eludes the second poet. Perhaps that is why Saikaku asks, "Of what was this old priest ashamed?"

In "The Sword That Survived Love's Flames" (3.3), Saikaku's narrative tells the story of two traveling companions on their way to worship at Mt. Kōya, Kūkai's seat of spiritual power. Along the way, they observe the following:

> [A] priest who looked as if he might be in charge of one of Mt. Kōya's temples came by with a young cowherd from one of the temple-owned farm villages. He had obviously tried to disguise the boy as a temple acolyte, but dirt was plainly visible behind the boy's ears. His hair was properly bound up, but it looked reddish and dry. The sleeves of his plain, light-blue hemp robe were far too short; it seemed to be an adult's round-sleeved robe slit under the arms to make him look boyish. He sported a pair of long swords, no doubt consigned to the temple by a parishioner in mourning. The sword guards were too big for the small hilts. The boy slouched under their unaccustomed weight as he walked along in the priest's tow. The men watched them pass, impressed with the priest's ingenuity.[20]

The humor in this passage derives from the priest's not entirely successful attempt to disguise a farmboy as an acolyte so that he can smuggle the boy into his temple quarters. The majority of temple acolytes would have been of samurai or aristocratic birth, making it difficult for a farmboy to resemble them. His hair lacked the luster of a samurai boy's well-groomed and oiled hair; he was unaccustomed to the weight of a sword, something samurai always carried; and as he already was too old to wear the open-vented sleeves of an adolescent boy, slits had to be cut in the sleeves of his own adult robe so he would look like a younger man. Saikaku was writing primarily for an urban merchant-class audience, who would have enjoyed making fun of the Buddhist clergy. The humor is directed not at the priest's taste for boys, which Saikaku's readers shared, but at the duplicity involved in smuggling a young man into the temple for sexual purposes. Saikaku's concern is not to moralize, but to draw attention to the hypocrisy in much of human behavior, and he does so to great effect.

Saikaku reserves his most scathing depiction of hypocrisy in the clergy for the latter half of *The Great Mirror of Male Love,* where he deals with boy prostitution in the kabuki theater. Although merchant-class men can properly engage kabuki actors for prostitution without breaking any vows, priests who do so are branded as wayward for their failure to abandon sexual pleasures. In "A Huge Winecup Overflowing with Love" (6.1), Saikaku opens the narrative with biting sarcasm.

> They say that Buddhist priests are "scraps of wood" purged of all feeling, but there is no occupation more pleasant in the world. They can hold parties in their temples whenever they please, their only duties to intone the *sūtras* of their sects and don robes when meeting parishioners. Rather than waste the offerings of the faithful on things without meaning, they use the money to buy the love of young actors, entertainment well suited to the priest's lot.

> Even when entertaining boys in their rooms, they never once forget the gravity of their vows and adhere religiously to their vegetarian diet of stewed dumplings and mushrooms, chilled chestnuts with silvervine pickled in miso, and clear soup of sweet seaweed and salted plums. With these delicacies they extend their drinking bouts through the long nights. (How they can drink!) Such sincere devotion to their vows is highly commendable. Just because they do not suffer Buddha's immediate divine punishment does not mean chief priests can go ahead and enjoy the meat of fish and fowl. After all, if priests could indulge in fish and women to their hearts' content, it would be foolish for a man not to take the tonsure![21]

The preceding passage sets a humorous tone in a story about a boy actor, Itō Kodayū. Condemnation of priests for humorous effect is not uncommon in Saikaku's narratives. In an earlier narrative, Saikaku went so far as to blame priests of the wealthy Rinzai sect for inflating the price of boy prostitutes. "Tears in a Paper Shop" (5.1) begins with a brief history of boy prostitution in the kabuki theater, the major features of which are historically accurate, though his comments about priests are difficult to verify.

> [O]ne year wealthy priests assembled in the capital from all over the country to commemorate the 350th anniversary of the death of Zen Master Kanzan, first rector of Myōshin-ji. After the religious services were over, they went sightseeing at the pleasure quarter on the dry riverbed. They fell in love with the handsome youths there, the likes of which they had never seen in the countryside, and began buying them up indiscriminately without a thought for their priestly duties. Any boy with forelocks who had eyes and a nose on his face was guaranteed to be busy all day.
>
> Since that time, boy actors have continued to sell themselves in two shifts, daytime and nighttime. The fee for a boy who was appearing onstage rose to one piece of silver. The priests did not care about the cost, since they had only a short time to amuse themselves in the capital. But their extravagance continues to cause untold hardship for the pleasure-seekers of our day.[22]

Saikaku's narrator expresses resentment of the priests for making boy actors too expensive for local men to afford as prostitutes, a perspective that would have appealed to Saikaku's merchant-class readers. The Rinzai sect, of which Kanzan Egen (d.1359) was a major spiritual leader, was known as a wealthy one, so its priests could have afforded actor's fees more easily than most. Priests from less well-to-do sects often went to extreme lengths to pay for their nights of love. Saikaku records some of their methods in "Love's Flame Kindled by a Flint Seller" (5.3).

> At his appointments, Sennojō entertained with a slight flush of wine on his cheeks, pale red like maple leaves in autumn. One look could drive a man mad with desire. Wayward priests from Takao, Nanzen-ji, and Tōfuku-ji, not to mention myriad other temples, sometimes sold entire collections of calligraphy passed down for generations in their temples, whereas others cut down and sold whole forests of trees and bamboo under temple jurisdiction, all for the sake of acquiring the love of this boy. Afterwards they were invariably thrown out of their temples with nothing but an umbrella to hide their shame.[23]

If there were those, as the preceding passage suggests, who were driven from Buddhist orders for the sake of boy love, there also were those who joined Buddhist orders for the same reason. One such example appears in "Bamboo Clappers Strike the Hateful Number" (7.4). In the story , a group of young actors and their patrons are on an excursion to pick mushrooms in Fushimi, outside the capital of Kyoto. They come upon an isolated hut in the hills and look inside. It is the home of a recluse monk.

> Inside, the walls were papered at the base with letters from actors. Their signatures had been torn off and discarded. Curious, the boys looked more closely and discovered that each letter concerned matters of love. Each was written in a different hand, the parting messages of kabuki boy actors. The monk who lived there must once have been a man of some means, they thought. He apparently belonged to the Shingon sect, for when they opened the Buddhist altar they found a figure of Kōbō Daishi adorned with chrysanthemums and bush clover, and next to it a picture of a lovely young actor, the object no doubt of this monk's fervent devotion.
>
> When they questioned him, the monk told them about his past. As they suspected, he was devoted body and soul to the way of boy love.
>
> "I was unhappy with my strict father and decided to seclude myself in this mountain hermitage. More then two years have passed, but I have not been able to forget about boy love even in my dreams." The tears of grief he wept were enough to fade the black dye of his priestly robes. Those who heard it were filled with pity for him.[24]

This passage indicates the strong hold that the legend of Kūkai must have had on the imaginations of both Saikaku and his readers. It suggests that there was a strong positive association between Buddhist tradition, particularly in the True Word sect, and male love. The association of True Word Buddhism with male love stemmed in part from its condemnation of sexual relations with women, in part because of its emphasis on the personal transmission of secret teachings from master to pupil, something that apparently led to strong emotional bonds between priests and their acolytes. Finally, because of the strong Confucian orthodoxy that discouraged overly personal visions of self and society, it was perhaps natural that the esoteric religious tradition and its founder in Japan, Kūkai, be rediscovered and, in a sense, reinvented in the seventeenth century as a social heterodoxy legitimizing the sexuality of men in the urban merchant class. Only further study clarifying the complex blend of social, religious, and sexual issues at play in the Kūkai legend will allow us to answer why this component of the Japanese Buddhist tradition of male love had such an impact on secular life and literature in the seventeenth century.

Notes

1. This paper was originally presented on December 7, 1987, in a panel on "Buddhism and Gender" at the annual meeting of the American Academy of Religion. The author gratefully acknowledges input from fellow panelists and the audience in making his revisions. All translations from the Japanese are the author's, unless otherwise noted.

2. By the fifteenth century, orthodox Shingon Buddhism was plagued with numerous "heresies," of which this may be one. Speaking of the Tachikawa School, which preached sex between men and women as the only means of obtaining buddahood and gaining the Way, the Shingon priest Yūkai (1345–1416) said, "Many secret manuals and texts of this heretical school were in circulation, often called 'oral transmission of the secrets of esoteric doctrine.' To this day there are ignorant people who study such works and believe them to possess the loftiest thoughts. In truth they are neither exoteric nor esoteric, but merely so many stones wrapped in jade. . . .Many people studied these teachings, but they did not meet with divine favor, and for the most part both the teachings and the men have perished." R. Tsunoda, et. al., eds. *Sources of Japanese Tradition* (New York: Columbia University Press, 1958), p. 169.

3. Excerpts of *Kōbō Daishi's Book* were translated for this article from the unannotated printed version of *Kōbō Daishi ikkan no sho* in Okada Yasushi, ed., *Kinsei shomin bunka kenkyūkai,* no. 13, *Nanshoku bunken tokushū* (Tokyo: Oranda Shobo, 1952), pp. 14–23.

4. Excerpts of *Rock Azaleas* were translated for this article from the unannotated printed version of *Iwatsutsuji* in Asakura Haruhiko, ed., *Kanazōshi shūsei,* vol. 5 (Tokyo: Tokyodo Shuppan, 1984), pp. 351–369.

5. A complete translation of *Nanshoku ōkagami* by Ihara Saikaku appears in P. G. Schalow, trans., *The Great Mirror of Male Love* (Stanford, Calif.: Stanford University press, 1990).

6. Described in J. Kitagawa, "Master and Saviour" in *On Understanding Japanese Religion* (Princeton, N.J.: Princeton University Press, 1987), pp. 182–202.

7. The legend's appearance may have been related to another legend claiming that Kūkai was so holy he never lusted for a woman his entire life *(isshō fubon)*. In the popular mind, the fact that Kūkai felt no lust for women meant that he simply preferred boys.

8. The poem is quoted in *Inu-tsurezure* (1619; 1653) in Asakura Haruhiko, ed. *Kana-zōshi shūsei,* vol. 4 (Tokyo: Tokyodo Shuppan, 1983), p. 12. Monju *(Mañjuśrī)* generally is considered the diety of wisdom. His connection with boy love in Japan derives from the fact that the bodhisattva's name in Japanese, Monju shiri, contains a homophone for the word ass *(shiri)*. Kūkai is referred to as "Kōbō of Kongō" after the name of his main temple on Mt. Kōya, Kongōbu-ji.

9. This resembles the clenched fists of the *kongō ken-in mudrā*. "The right hand (Buddha) symbolizes Sentient Beings in whom intelligence of the Buddha exists in a perfect state, and the left hand (Beings) rings the bell in order to disperse illusion and error." E. D. Saunders, *Mudrā: A Study of Symbolic Gestures in Japanese Buddhist Sculpture* (Princeton, N.J.: Princeton University Press, 1960), p. 114.

10. This *mudrā* resembles the folded hands of the outer bonds fist, *gebaku ken-in,* and suggests a frankly sexual interpretation of its spiritual meaning: "*dai yoku* (great avidity), indicates the love of Vairocana for all Beings, a love, which, in man, is represented by the limited desire for affection: in Kongōsattva (Vajrasattva, the Bodhisattva who emanates from Vairocana), this love is translated by an Avidity *(yoku)* to love all Beings at the same time. Thus in Shingon ritual, the *gebaku ken-in,* emblematic of Great Avidity, symbolizes the Heart and the Compassion of the Buddha." Ibid., p. 120.

11. This *mudrā* is vaguely like the *tembōrin-in mudrā* of the turning wheel of the law. "In the Japanese Esoteric sects, making the mudrā, accompanied by the right ritual words, may for the celebrant take the place 'of all sermons, for no predication is more perfect than the Law.' " Ibid., p. 100.

12. These are three variations on the Amida *Mudrā,* a form of the *an-i-in mudrā* of appeasement. See Ibid., pp. 73–74. The remaining *mudrā* in 6–10 do not resemble any commonly known hand positions in Japanese Buddhism.

13. This *mudrā* resembles the circle formed by the ring finger and thumb in 5. The meanings seem to be similar.

14. The sense here is obscure.

15. Translated in H. C. McCullough, *Kokin Wakashū: The First Imperial Anthology of Japanese Poetry* (Stanford, Calif.: Stanford University Press, 1985), p. 115.

16. Schalow, *The Great Mirror of Male Love,* p. 56.

17. Ibid., p. 61.

18. Ibid.

19. For a discussion of Acolyte Tales, see M. H. Childs, "*Chigo Monogatari:* Love Stories or Buddhist Sermons?" *Monumenta Nipponica* 35, no. 2, (Summer 1980): 127–151.

20. Schalow, *The Great Mirror of Male Love,* p. 139.

21. Ibid., pp. 219–220.

22. Ibid., p. 190.

23. Ibid., p. 204.

24. Ibid., p. 268.

The Contributors

Tessa Bartholomeusz has a Ph.D. in Buddhist Studies from the University of Virginia and an M.A. in Religious Studies from Florida State University. She has been an instructor in Hindi in the Department of Oriental Languages at the University of Virginia since 1989. The recipient of Fulbright-Hays, American Institute of Indian Studies, and National Education Research Fellowships, her research in recent years has focused on the Buddhist nuns of Srī Laṅkā.

José Ignacio Cabezón has taught at Carleton and Trinity Colleges and at the Ohio State University. He is currently Assistant Professor of the Philosophy of Religion at the Iliff School of Theology. He received his doctorate in Buddhist Studies from the University of Wisconsin, Madison, in 1987. His translation of mKhas grub dGe legs dpal bzang's *sTong thun chen mo* was published by SUNY Press under the title *A Dose of Emptiness*.

Miriam L. Levering received her Ph.D. in the Comparative History of Religion from Harvard University in 1978. She has taught at Bates and Oberlin Colleges and is currently Associate Professor of Religious Studies at the University of Tennessee. Aside from many articles in the field of East Asian Studies, she is the editor of *Rethinking Scripture: Essays from a Comparative Perspective,* published by SUNY Press.

Barbara Reed is Associate Professor of Religion at St. Olaf College. She received her Ph.D. in Religion from the University of Iowa in 1982. She was contributor to *Women in World Religions* (SUNY Press) and is currently engaged in research on popular Chinese Buddhist literature in contemporary Taiwan.

Paula Richman received her Ph.D. in South Asian Languages and Civilizations from the University of Chicago in 1983. Presently she is Associate Professor of South Asian Religions at Oberlin College. Among her many publications are *Women, Branch Stories, and Religious Rhetoric in a Tamil Buddhist Text* (1988). She also is coeditor of *Gender and Religion: On the Complexity of Symbols* (1986) and editor of *Many Rāmāyaṇas: The Diversity of a Narrative Tradition in South Asia* (Berkeley: University of California Press, 1991).

Paul Gordon Schalow is Assistant Professor of Japanese Literature at Rutgers University. He received his doctorate in Japanese Literature from Harvard University (1985) and has taught at Brown University and the University of Massachusetts at Amherst. His translation of Ihara Saikaku's *The Great Mirror of Male Love* appeared from Stanford University Press in 1990.

Bardwell Smith is John W. Nason Professor of Asian Studies at Carleton College. He received his Ph.D. from Yale University in 1964. A distinguished scholar and educator and a prolific writer, he has authored or edited over a dozen books and monographs and countless articles. His research interests have focused on the relationship of Sinhalese and Japanese Buddhism to the social order. His most recent publication is *The City as a Sacred Center: Essays on Six Asian Contexts* (Leiden: E. J. Brill, 1987), coedited with Holly Baker Reynolds.

Alan Sponberg has recently accepted an associate professorship in the Humanities Program at the University of Montana after teaching for the last ten years at Princeton and Stanford. He completed graduate work in South Asian Buddhism at the University of Wisconsin and received his doctorate in Chinese Language and Literature from the University of British Columbia in 1979. His most recent publication is *Maitreya, the Future Buddha* (Cambridge University Press, 1988), a collection of essays for which he was senior editor and a major contributor.

Eleanor Zelliot has taught at Carleton College since 1969 and is now chair of the History Department. Her Ph.D. is from the University of Pennsylvania in South Asian Regional Studies. She has published extensively on Dr. B. R. Ambedkar and his movement, on the sixteenth century saint-poet Eknath, on Marathi-speaking intellectuals, and on the all-India *bhakti* movement. She also is coeditor of *The Experience of Hinduism.*

Leonard Zwilling holds the positions of Assistant Editor and Bibliographer with the Dictionary of American Regional English. His Ph.D. is from the University of Wisconsin, Madison (1976), where he also has taught. He has taught, as well, at Gustavus Adolphus College, Western Illinois University, Beloit College, and at the University of Wisconsin, Milwaukee. His publications are diverse, in fields ranging from Buddhist logic to the language of the comic strip. He is the author of *Mongolian Xylographs in the Department of Rare Books and Special Collections, University of Wisconsin—Madison Libraries.*

Index